D0487918

16 0358155 4 TELEPEN

Limited

Two week loan
Benthyciad pythefnos

Please return on or before the due date to avoid overdue charges
*A wnewch chi ddychwelyd ar neu cyn y dyddiad a nodir ar eich llyfr os
gwelwch yn dda, er mwyn osgoi taliadau*

WITHDRAWN

http://library.cardiff.ac.uk
http://llyfrgell.caerdydd.ac.uk

TITLES IN THE SERIES

'A' Level Law - Paper 1

'A' Level Law - Paper 2

Child Law

Civil Liberties

Commercial Law

Company Law

Constitutional & Administrative Law

Contract Law

Criminal Law

Criminology

Employment Law

English Legal System

Equity & Trusts

Evidence

Family Law

International Trade Law

Jurisprudence

Land Law

Law of Tort

Revenue Law

Cavendish
Publishing
Limited

CONTRACT LAW

Professor Richard Stone, LLB, LLM
Head of Department of Law
Nottingham Trent University

347.1 S

First published in Great Britain 1994 by Cavendish Publishing
Limited, The Glass House, Wharton Street, London WC1X 9PX
Telephone: 071-278 8000   Facsimile: 071-278 8080

© Stone, R 1994

All rights reserved. No part of this publication may be
reproduced, stored in a retrieval system, or transmitted in any
form or by any means, electronic, mechanical, photocopying,
recording or otherwise, without the prior permission of the
publisher and copyright owner.

The right of the author of this work has been asserted in
accordance with the Copyright, Designs and Patents Act 1988.

Any person who infringes the above in relation to this
publication may be liable to criminal prosecution and civil
claims for damages.

British Library Cataloguing in Publication Data

Stone, Richard
Contract Law - (Lecture Notes Series)
I Title II Series
244.2062

19 SEP 1994

ISBN 1-874241-69-4
Cover photograph by Jerome Yeats
Printed and bound in Great Britain

Preface

Although the Law of Contract is often studied early in the law student's career it is not in fact a simple subject. There are complexities in the analysis of the basis of contractual obligations, and in many of the areas which are regarded as fundamental, such as the doctrines of consideration and privity, which create difficulties of understanding for the novice. In addition, there are other areas, such as mistake, where the case law is confusing and inconsistent, or where the relationship between common law and equity (eg in relation to estoppel), or common law and statute (eg in relation to exclusion clauses), requires careful analysis. The temptation in writing a book such as this, which is intended as a straightforward readable guide to the English law of contract, is to gloss over these difficulties, or to simplify them out of existence. This is a trap which I hope that I have avoided. My object has been, based on my experience of 18 years of teaching contract law both to first year LLB students, and to non-law students, to explain the subject in a way which is easy to understand, but which nevertheless gives the student some idea that the 'orthodox' analysis is not necessarily the only possible one, and the subject has depths which (for those who have the opportunity to do so) will repay further study, beyond the demands of the first year examination.

The subject areas covered are those of the standard contract syllabus. A chapter on restitution is included. This is a subject of increasing importance, as recognised by its recent inclusion amongst the topics required to be studied for the purposes of professional exemption. The coverage of agency and sale of goods (in Chapters 15 and 16) is more detailed than will be required by many contract courses, but it is hoped that these will be of particular help to those studying contract as part of business studies, or accountancy, courses.

The order of treatment, and division between chapters, matches that of my *Contract Law Questions and Answers* (also published by Cavendish Publishing), to which this may be seen as a companion volume. A student who has mastered the material contained in this book will be in an excellent position to tackle the sample questions in the *Q&A* book. An additional study aid is provided by the summaries at the end of each chapter. These are intended to be usable as a framework for revision, and to that end the relevant pages are perforated so that the summaries can be removed and incorporated with the student's own file of notes.

The law has been stated, as far as possible, as it stood on 31 December 1993.

Richard Stone
Oadby
January 1994

Outline Table of Contents

Detailed Table of Contents

Table of Cases

Table of Statutes

Chapter 1

Introduction

This chapter deals with some preliminary issues which need discussion before embarking on a detailed consideration of the case law and statutes which make up the English law of contract. These issues are:

- the subject matter of contract law;

- different approaches to analysing contract; and

- the identification of agreements.

1.1 The subject matter of contract law

What is the law of contract about? This is a question to which, perhaps surprisingly, there is no clear, universally accepted answer. Some would argue that the law of contract is simply part of a wider law of 'obligations', which includes tort, and perhaps restitution, and that the boundaries between all three should not be treated as fixed. Others would argue that because there are now so many special rules applying to particular types of contract, such as sale of goods, hire purchase, employment etc, that to talk of a general 'law of contract' is unrealistic. At best one can discuss a law of 'contracts'.

1.1.2 Voluntary transactions

The approach of this book, however, is that there is still a sufficient area of generally applicable principles, which are in practice regarded by the courts as forming a distinct body of law, to justify the attempt to identify a 'law of contract'. Its subject matter is transactions under which people, more or less voluntarily, assume obligations towards each other, in connection with the transfer of property (including money), or the provision of services. The transactions are only 'more or less' voluntary since people have little real choice whether or not to enter into some contracts, for example, contracts to buy food or to obtain work. Even where there is a real choice in this sense, for example as regards a decision to buy a new CD player, there is likely be little choice about the terms on which the contract can be made. Large retail organisations are rarely prepared to enter into bargaining with a consumer. Nevertheless, it is only in very rare situations, for example the compulsory purchase of property by central or local government, that people are forced into a transaction which is clearly against their will. We may therefore use the definition at the beginning of this paragraph, in terms of voluntary transactions, as a broad indication of the situations with which we are concerned. The rules of contract law help to determine which transactions will be enforced by the courts and on what terms. They also provide a framework of remedies, when contracts are broken.

Before leaving this point, it is important to remember that, to the extent that there is a 'general law of contract' it applies to all transactions within its scope. That is, the same general rules will apply to the purchase of a packet of sweets from a local newsagent, as to a multi-million pound deal between large international corporations.

1.2 Different approaches to analysing contract

The approach in this book is, for the most part to analyse the law of contract within its own terms. In other words, the concentration will be on analysing the relevant cases and statutes, examining how contractual principles have developed through them, and critically appraising the end result. This does not mean that all issues of social and political context, or legal history should be ignored, but simply that the focus is on the law as it has emerged through decisions of the courts and legislation.

1.2.1 Economic analysis

Other approaches are, of course, possible. Since contract is intimately linked with the commercial world, it is not surprising that attempts have been made to analyse it in terms of economics. Much of this work has originated in the United States (see, for example, Kronman & Posner, *Economics of Contract Law* (1979)). The approach is generally to try to criticise the rules of contract law in terms of their economic efficiency and consequences. To take a simple example, as regards consumer contracts it may be thought desirable that producers of goods should be strictly liable for the quality of what they sell. If they are to be liable however, they may need either to introduce strict quality control procedures, or to take out insurance. The costs of either of these two measures will almost certainly be added to the price of the goods. In economic terms, therefore, the cost of greater consumer protection is higher prices. Economic analysis also looks at 'transaction costs' (which may lead to the conclusion that standard form contracts are more economically efficient than those that are individually negotiated), and 'adjudication costs' (which may suggest that it is more economically efficient to have fixed rules of law, rather than leave it to judges to resolve disputes 'on their merits'). To take an example from later in the book, the decision of the House of Lords in the case of *Photo Production v Securicor* (1980) (below, para 7.2.3), upholding a very widely based clause excluding one of the parties from virtually all liability for breach of contract, might be analysed in economic terms as follows. First, it might be said to be based on an assumption that as between two parties, freely negotiating, they will have allocated responsibilities and risks in the most efficient way, and so will have 'maximised wealth'. Secondly, the refusal of the court to interfere in a bargain of this kind may discourage others from litigating, and therefore have the overall beneficial economic effect of reducing transaction costs.

A further way of looking at the law of contract is from a socio-political standpoint. In fact, we all have some political assumptions in the background, even if we are looking at contract cases purely within their own terms. It is, for example, impossible to debate the merits of numerous contract principles without some notion of the value or otherwise of the idea of 'freedom of contract', which is, of course, a political concept. Some writers feel, however, that this political/ideological background, be it capitalist, Marxist, or whatever, should be made explicit. For example, Hugh Collins in *The Law of Contract* (1st ed, Weidenfeld & Nicolson, p 1) stated:

> 'This book identifies the purpose of the law of contract as the channelling and regulation of market transactions according to ideals of social justice.'

Another approach is to try to identify the ideologies which underpin the decision of the courts on contract issues. Adams and Brownsword in *Understanding Contract Law* (Fontana, 1987), identify three competing ideologies which may be found in the cases. These are:

- formalism;
- consumer-welfarism;
- market-individualism.

A court may be said to adopt a formalist approach if it feels obliged to follow rules established in earlier cases, even if it does not agree with them, or feels that they do not produce the most satisfactory result on the facts before the court. The case of *Foakes v Beer* (1884) (below, para 3.10) may be said to be an example of this type of approach, at least as far as some members of the House of Lords were concerned, in that they felt bound to follow what was regarded as an established rule that part payment of a debt could never discharge the debtor's liability for the balance, even if the creditor had promised to treat it as so doing.

1.2.2   Socio-political analysis

1.2.3   Formalism

1.2.4	Consumer-welfarism	'Consumer-welfarism' on the other hand, may operate where a court recognises that individuals may be in a weak position as regards dealings with large organisations, and that the rules of contract need, therefore, to be developed and applied so as to protect them. Examples of this type of approach would be *Carlill v Carbolic Smoke Ball Co* (1893) (below, para 2.2.4), where an advertiser was bound by a promise made to consumers who had relied on the advert; or the pre-1977 exclusion clause cases (below, para 7.2), where the courts devised rules to prevent large organisations from imposing wide clauses exempting them from liability to people who bought their products and services.
1.2.5	Market-individualism	A 'market-individualism' approach, on the other hand, gives freedom of contract the highest priority and leaves the parties to their bargain, even if it appears to operate harshly on one side. In this situation, the court adopts the role simply of 'referee', determining what obligations the parties must be taken to have agreed to, and then applying them to the situation. A case mentioned above in connection with the economic analysis, *Photo Productions v Securicor* (1980), is a good example of the court adopting this approach.
1.2.6	Empirical research	Finally, contract may be approached from the bottom rather than the top. In other words, instead of looking at decisions of the appellate courts, and the rules which they have developed, the focus could be on how contract law operates in people's day-to-day lives. Does the existence of a particular set of contractual rules affect the way in which people behave? Do businesses have contractual principles in mind when they enter into agreements? When things go wrong, to what extent does the law influence the way in which disputes are resolved? There has been surprisingly little research on these issues, but such as there is (eg the work of Beale & Dugdale ((1975) 2 Brit J Law & Soc 45), and Yates)Exclusion Clauses, 2nd ed, 1982, pp 16-33), in this country, and Macaulay ((1963) 28 Am Sociological Rev 45) in the United States) suggests that the law of contract is of much less importance to business people than lawyers would like to think. In particular, where parties to a long-standing business relationship find themselves in a dispute, the maintenance of their relationship is likely to be a much stronger influence over the way they resolve their differences, than are the strict legal rights between the parties, as determined by the law of contract.

As has been indicated above, the approach taken here is primarily based on looking at legal materials within their own terms. From time to time, however, aspects of one or more of the alternative approaches outlined above, may be referred to, in order to produce a fuller understanding of the way in which the law has developed, or is likely to develop in the future. For that reason it is worth spending a little time becoming familiar with the basic ideas lying behind them. Since the subject matter of this book is, as we have seen, transactions which are entered into voluntarily, we now need to turn to a preliminary consideration of the concept of 'agreement'.

1.3 The identification of agreements

It is easy to say that the law of contract is based on agreements between two parties. This simple assertion, however, masks a considerable problem in identifying precisely what is meant by an agreement. This may seem easy enough: it is simply a question of identifying a 'meeting of the minds' between the parties at a particular point in time. That, however, is easier said than done. By the time two parties to a contract have arrived in court, they are clearly no longer of one mind. They may dispute whether there was ever an agreement between them at all, or, while accepting that there was an agreement, they may disagree as to its terms. How are such disputes to be resolved? Clearly the courts cannot discover as a matter of fact what was actually going on in the minds of the parties at the time of the alleged agreement. Nor are they prepared to rely solely on what the parties now say was in their minds at that time (which would be a 'subjective' approach), even if they are very convincing. Instead, the courts adopt what is primarily an 'objective' approach to deciding whether there was an agreement, and if so what its terms were. This means that they look at what was said and done between the parties from the point of view of the 'reasonable person' and try to decide what they would have thought was going on.

1.3.1 Promisor, promisee and detached objectivity

As has been pointed out by Howarth, however, there are different types of objectivity ((1984) 100 LQR 265). There is 'promisor objectivity' where the court tries to decide what the reasonable promisor would have intended, 'promisee objectivity', where the focus is on what the reasonable person being made a promise would have thought was intended, and 'detached' objectivity which views what has happened through the eyes of an independent third party. In *Smith v Hughes* (1871), for example, where the dispute was over what type of oats the parties were contracting about, the test was said to be whether the party who wishes to deny the contract acted so that 'a reasonable man would believe that he was assenting to the terms proposed by the other party.' In other words, promisee objectivity. As we shall see, however, in subsequent chapters, the courts are not consistent as to which of these types of objectivity they use, changing between one and another as seems most appropriate in a particular case.

1.3.2   State of mind

The objective approach will not be applied, however, if there is clear evidence of a particular state of mind. *The Hannah Blumenthal* (1983), for example, was a case concerning the sale of a ship, where the point at issue was whether the parties had agreed to abandon their dispute. The behaviour of the buyers was such that it would have been reasonable for the sellers to have believed that the action had been dropped. In fact, the sellers had continued to act (by seeking witnesses, etc) in a way which indicated that they did not think the action had been dropped.This evidence of their actual state of mind overrode the conclusion which the court might well have reached by applying a purely objective test. (See also the similar case of *The Leonidas D* (1985).)

1.4   The external signs of agreement

The process by which the courts try to decide whether the parties had made an agreement has been described by Cheshire and Fifoot and Furmston as a search for 'The Phenomena of Agreement' (*Law of Contract*, 12th ed, Butterworths, 1991, Chapter 3). This means that the courts, as we have seen, are not necessarily looking for actual agreement but for the external signs, or 'phenomena' of agreement. They have also come to rely on a number of specific elements, which are regarded as both necessary and sufficient to identify an agreement which is intended to be legally binding. These are:

- offer;

- acceptance;

- consideration.

These three factors, together with an overarching requirement that the court is satisfied that there was an intention to create legal relations, form the basis for the identification of contracts in English law. The next two chapters explore these concepts in detail.

Introduction

It may be argued that there is no general law of contract, but that the rules relating to contract are simply part of a more general law of obligations, or are made up of a variable law of 'contracts'.

Insofar as there is a general law of contract, it is concerned with transactions under which people, more or less voluntarily, assume obligations towards each other, in connection with the transfer of property, or the provision of services.

The general law of contract applies the same rules to all transactions, no matter how large or small.

The subject matter of contact law

There are different approaches to analysing contract:

- Economic analysis - considers the rules of contract law in terms of their economic efficiency and consequences.

- Socio-political analysis - looks at the ideologies underlying contract, e.g. capitalist, marxist, etc.

  Adams & Brownsword identify formalism, consumer-welfarism, and market-individualism as three such ideologies used by English courts.

- Empirical research - looks at what actually happens when people make contracts.

Different approaches to analysing contract

English law uses an 'objective approach' - but note that there are different types of objectivity (eg promisor objectivity, promisee objectivity, or detached objectivity).

Evidence of a party's state of mind at a particular time may, however, override an objective approach (eg *The Hannah Blumenthal* (1983)).

The external signs, or 'phenomena', of agreement, are what the courts look for, in particular, 'offer and acceptance' and 'consideration'.

The identification of agreements

Chapter 2

Offer and Acceptance

As has been explained in Chapter 1, the English courts in trying to decide whether two parties have reached a legally binding agreement, look for certain external signs of such agreement. The first two, which inevitably have to be considered together, are 'offer' and 'acceptance'.

2.1 **Introduction**

It is important to note first that in most cases English law requires no particular formality in order for a contract to come into existence. In other words, the contract does not have to be put into writing, or signed, nor does any particular form of words have to be used. A purely verbal exchange can result in a binding contract. Many students, on first encountering this aspect of contract law, raise the question of how you establish the existence of an agreement, or what it contains, if nothing has been written down. Doesn't it simply become a question of one person's word against another? The answer is that yes it does, but that to get side-tracked into this issue is to forget that the primary function of a court in most cases of dispute is to decide what actually happened between the parties, even though there is no documentary evidence. This is true of the criminal law, where the determination of issues of fact in serious cases will be entrusted to the jury, and in tort cases, such as those arising out of road accidents, where a judge will have to decide who did what to whom, and whether they were acting negligently at the time. It is the same in contract. If there is a purely verbal agreement about which there is a dispute, the parties, and any witnesses, will have to give evidence as to their version of events, and the court will have to decide whom it believes. These issues are, however, more properly the province of the law of evidence and procedure, and do not involve substantive issues of contract law, which are our main concern.

2.2 **Lack of formality**

There are, however, some important types of contract where writing is required. Just two will be mentioned here. First, by virtue of the Law of Property (Miscellaneous Provisions) Act 1989, s 2(1), all contracts involving the sale, or other disposal, of an interest in land, must be in writing, and signed by the parties. This has long been the case in English law, and is justified by the fact that contracts involving land are likely to be both complicated and valuable. Many commercial contracts, however, are also complex and valuable, yet there is no

2.2.1 Written agreements

requirement of a written agreement (though in practice there is likely to be one). The second type of contract where there is a requirement of a certain degree of formality arises under the Consumer Credit Act 1974, which requires that contracts of hire purchase, and other credit transactions, should be in writing and signed. This is a protective provision, designed to make sure that the individual consumer has written evidence of the agreement, and has the opportunity to see all its terms.

These types of contract are exceptions, however. In most cases a verbal offer and acceptance will suffice.

2.3   Offer

An offer may be defined as an indication by one person that he or she is prepared to contract with one or more others, on certain terms, which are fixed, or capable of being fixed, at the time the offer is made. All that is required from the other person is a simple assent to the terms suggested, and a contract will be formed. As we shall see, the 'indication' referred to above may take a number of forms - for example, the spoken word, a letter, a fax message, a radio signal or a newspaper advertisement. As long as it communicates to the potential acceptor or acceptors the basis on which the offeror is prepared to contract, then that is enough. It is not necessary for the offer itself to set out all the terms of the contract. The parties may have been negotiating over a period of time, and the offer may simply refer to terms appearing in earlier communications. That is quite acceptable, provided that it is clear what the terms are.

2.3.1   Distinction from 'invitation to treat'

Distinction should be made between an offer and an 'invitation to treat'. Sometimes a person will wish simply to open negotiations, rather than make an offer which will lead immediately to a contract on acceptance. If I wish to sell my car, for example, I may enquire if you are interested in buying it. This is clearly not an offer. Even if I indicate a price at which I am willing to sell, this may simply be an attempt to discover your interest, rather than committing me to particular terms. The courts refer to such a preliminary communication as an 'invitation to treat' or, even more archaically, as an 'invitation to chaffer'. The distinction between an offer and an invitation to treat is an important one, but is not always easy to draw. Even where the parties appear to have reached agreement on the terms on which they are prepared to contract, the courts may decide that the language they have used is more appropriate to an invitation to treat than an offer.

This was the view taken in *Gibson v Manchester City Council* (1979). Mr Gibson was a tenant of a house owned by Manchester City Council. The Council, which was at the time under the control of Conservative Party members, decided that it wished to give its tenants the opportunity to purchase the houses which they were renting. Mr Gibson wished to take advantage of this opportunity, and started negotiations with the Council. He received a letter which indicated a price, and which stated 'The Corporation may be prepared to sell the house to you' at that price. It also instructed Mr Gibson, if he wished to make 'a formal application', to complete a form and return it. This Mr Gibson did. At this point local elections took place, and control of the Council changed from the Conservative Party to the Labour Party. The new Labour Council immediately reversed the policy of the sale of council houses, and refused to proceed with the sale to Mr Gibson. Despite the fact that all terms appeared to have been agreed between the parties, the House of Lords held that there was no contract. The language of the Council's letter to Mr Gibson was not sufficiently definite to amount to an offer. It was simply an invitation to treat. Mr Gibson had made an offer to buy, but that had not been accepted.

The narrowness of the distinction being drawn can be seen by comparing this case with *Storer v Manchester City Council* (1974), where on very similar facts a contract was held to exist, as Mr Storer had signed and returned a document entitled 'Agreement for Sale'. This document was deemed to be sufficiently definite to amount to an offer which Mr Storer had accepted. As regards the state of mind of the parties in the two cases, however, it is arguable that there was little difference. In both parties had indicated a willingness to enter into the transaction, and there was agreement on the price. The fact that the courts focus on the external signs, rather than the underlying agreement, however, led to the different result arrived at in the two cases.

Another area of difficulty arises in relation to the display of goods in a shop window, or on the shelves of a supermarket, or other shop where customers serve themselves. We commonly talk of such a situation as one in which the shop has the goods 'on offer'. This is especially true of attractive bargains which may be labelled 'special offer'. Are these 'offers' for the purpose of the law of contract? The issue has been addressed in a number of criminal cases where the offence in question was based on a 'sale' or an 'offer for sale'. These cases are taken to establish the position under the law of contract, even though they were decided in a criminal law context. The first to consider is *Pharmaceutical Society of Great Britain v Boots Cash Chemists* (1953).

Section 18(1) of the Pharmacy and Poisons Act 1933 made

2.3.2   Self-service displays

it an offence to sell certain medicines unless 'the sale is effected by, or under the supervision of, a registered pharmacist'. Boots introduced a system under which some of these medicines were made available to customers on a self-service basis. There was no supervision until the customer went to the cashier. At this point a registered pharmacist would supervise the transaction, and could intervene, if necessary. The Pharmaceutical Society claimed that this was an offence under s 18, because, it was argued, the sale was complete when the customer took an article from the shelves and put it into his or her basket. The Court of Appeal disagreed, and held that the sale was made at the cash desk, where the customer made an offer to buy, which could be accepted or rejected by the cashier. The reason for this decision was that it is clearly unacceptable to say that the contract is complete as soon as the goods are put into the basket, because the customer may want to change his or her mind, and it is undoubtedly the intention of all concerned that this should be possible. The display of goods is therefore an invitation to treat, and not an offer.

With respect to the Court of Appeal, the conclusion that was reached was not necessary to avoid the problem of the customer becoming committed too soon. It would have been quite possible to have said that the display of goods is an offer, but that the customer does not accept that offer until presenting the goods to the cashier. This analysis would, of course, also have meant that the sale took place at the cash desk and that no offence was committed under s 18. Strictly speaking, therefore, the details of the Court of Appeal's analysis in this case as to what constitutes the offer, and what is the acceptance, may be regarded as *obiter*. It has, however, generally been accepted subsequently that the display of goods within a shop is an invitation to treat and not an offer.

2.3.3 Shop-window displays

The slightly different issue of the shop-window display was dealt with in *Fisher v Bell* (1961). The defendant displayed in his shop window a 'flick-knife' with price attached. He was charged with an offence under s 1(1) of the Restriction of Offensive Weapons Act 1959, namely, 'offering for sale' a 'flick-knife'. It was held by the Divisional Court that no offence had been committed, because the display of the knife was an invitation to treat, not an offer.

A similar conclusion was reached in *Mella v Monahan* (1961) as regards a charge under the Obscene Publications Act 1959 of 'offering for sale' obscene articles, by displaying them in a shop window.

These cases lead to the conclusion that, as far the law of

contract is concerned, a shopkeeper is not bound by any price that is attached to goods displayed in the shop, or in the window. He or she is entitled to say to the customer seeking to buy the item '... that is a mistake. I am afraid the price is different.' Such action would, however, almost certainly constitute a criminal offence under the Trade Descriptions Act 1968, s 11. The shopkeeper's right to refuse to sell at all to a particular customer is not, however, affected by this legislation.

Where goods or services are advertised, does this constitute an offer or an invitation to treat? Generally speaking, an advertisement on a hoarding, a newspaper 'display', or a television commercial, will not be regarded as an offer. These are simply attempts to make the public aware of what is available, and will in any case generally not be specific enough to amount to an offer. Even where goods are clearly identified, and a price specified, however, there may still not be an offer. A good example of the problem is yet another criminal law case, *Partridge v Crittenden* (1968).

2.3.4   Advertisements

The defendant put an advertisement in the 'Classified' section of a periodical, advertising bramblefinches for sale at 25s each. He was charged under the Protection of Birds Act 1954 with 'offering for sale' a live wild bird, contrary to s 6(1) of that Act. It was held that he had committed no offence, because the advert was an invitation to treat and not an offer. The court relied heavily on *Fisher v Bell* (1961), and appeared to feel that this kind of advertisement should be treated in the same way as the display of goods with a price attached. Lord Parker, however, pointed out an additional, and very practical reason for not treating it as an offer. If it was an offer, this would mean that everyone who replied to the advertisement would be accepting it, and would therefore be entitled to a bramblefinch. Assuming that the advertiser did not have an unlimited supply of bramblefinches, this cannot be what he intended. This is an analysis based on 'promisor objectivity' (see Chapter 1 at para 1.3), looking at what the reasonable advertiser would be taken to have meant by the advert. As a result, the advertisement was properly to be categorised as an invitation to treat.

This does not mean, however, that all newspaper advertisements will be treated as invitations to treat. Provided that the wording is clear, and that there are no problems of limited supply, then there seems no reason why such an advertisement should be an offer. If, for example, the advertiser in *Partridge v Crittenden* had said, '100 bramblefinches for sale. The first 100 replies enclosing 25s will secure a bird', then in all probability this would be construed as an offer. An advertisement of a similar kind was held to be an offer in the American case of *Lefkowitz v Great Minneapolis Surplus Stores* (1957), where the defendants published an advertisement in a newspaper, stating:

> 'Saturday 9 am sharp; 3 Brand new fur coats, worth to $100. First come first served, $1 each.'

The plaintiff was one of the first three customers, but the firm refused to sell him a coat, because they said the offer was only open to women. The court held that the advertisement constituted an offer, which the plaintiff had accepted, and that he was therefore entitled to the coat.

2.3.5   *Carlill v Carbolic Smoke Ball Co*

In England the most famous case of an advertisement constituting an offer is *Carlill v Carbolic Smoke Ball Co* (1893). The manufacturers of a 'smoke ball' published an advertisement at the time of an influenza epidemic, proclaiming the virtues of their smoke ball for curing all kinds of ailments. In addition, they stated that anybody who bought one of their smoke balls, used it as directed, and then caught influenza, would be paid £100. Mrs Carlill, having bought and used a smoke ball, but nevertheless having caught influenza, claimed £100 from the company. They argued that the advertisement could not be taken to be an offer which could turn into a contract by acceptance. The court, however, took the view that the fact that the advertisement stated that the firm had deposited £1,000 in their bank in order to 'show their sincerity', meant that reasonable people would treat this as indicating that the promise to pay £100 was meant to be taken seriously, and to create a binding obligation in appropriate circumstances.

It should be noted that the offer in *Carlill*, in *Lefkowitz*, and the suggested reformulation of the offer in *Partridge v Crittenden* (above), are all offers of a particular kind, known in English law as an offer in a 'unilateral' (as opposed to a 'bilateral') contract. The difference between these two types of contract must now be examined.

2.4   Unilateral and bilateral contracts

The typical model of the bilateral contract arises where A promises to sell goods to B in return for B promising to pay the purchase price. In this situation the contract is bilateral, because as soon as these promises have been exchanged there is a contract to which both are bound. In relation to services, the same applies, so that an agreement between A and B that B will dig A's garden for £20 next Tuesday is a bilateral agreement. Suppose, however, that the arrangement is slightly different, and that A says to B 'If you dig my garden next Tuesday, I will pay you £20'. B makes no commitment, but says, 'I am not sure that I shall be able to, but if I do, I shall be happy to take £20.' This arrangement is not bilateral. A has committed himself to pay the £20 in certain circumstances, but B has made no commitment at all. He is totally free to decide whether or not he wants to dig A's garden or not, and if he wakes up on Tuesday morning and decides that he just does not feel like doing so, then there is nothing that A can do about it. If, however, B does decide to go and do the work, that will be regarded as an acceptance of A's offer of £20, and the contract will be formed. Because of its one-sided nature, therefore, this type of arrangement is known as a 'unilateral contract'. Another way of describing them is as 'if' contracts, in that it is always possible to formulate the offer as a statement beginning with the word 'if'. 'If you dig my garden I will pay you £20'. As has been noted above, the arrangements in *Carlill*, and *Lefkowitz*, were of this type: 'If you use our smoke-ball and catch influenza, we will pay you £100'; 'If you are the first person to offer to buy one of these coats, we will sell it to you for $1'.

The distinction between unilateral and bilateral contracts is important in relation to the areas of 'acceptance', and 'consideration', which are discussed further below.

Some confusion may arise as to what constitutes an offer when a person, or more probably, a company, decides to put work out to tender. This means that potential contractors are invited to submit quotations. The invitation may be issued to the world, or to specific parties. Generally speaking, such a request will amount simply to an invitation to treat, and the person making it will be free to accept or reject any of the responses: *Spencer v Harding* (1870). If, however, the invitation indicates that the lowest quotation will definitely be accepted, then it will be regarded as an offer in a unilateral contract. The recipients of the invitation will not be bound to reply, but if they do, the one who submits the lowest quotation will be entitled to insist that the contract is made with them. A similar situation arose in *Blackpool and Fylde Aero Club Ltd v Blackpool Borough Council* (1990). The council had invited tenders for the operation of pleasure flights from an air field. The plaintiffs put in a tender, which was submitted by the deadline, but was overlooked by the council. It was held that this was a breach of a unilateral contract, under which the council was obliged to give consideration to all tenders received by the deadline. This obligation had not been undertaken explicitly, but was implicit in the form of the invitation to tender, and the surrounding circumstances.

2.5   Tenders

2.6	**Auctions**	The Sale of Goods Act 1979 makes it clear that in relation to a sale of goods by auction the bids constitute offers which are accepted by the fall of the hammer (s 57). The same is also the case in relation to any other type of sale by auction. The normal position will be that the auctioneer will be entitled to reject any of the bids made, and will not be obliged to sell to the highest bidder. If, however, the auction sale is advertised as being 'without reserve', this will be taken as implying an obligation to sell to the highest bidder: *Warlow v Harrison* (1859). Similarly in *Harvela Investments v Royal Trust of Canada* (1987), an invitation to two firms to submit sealed bids for a block of shares, together with a commitment to accept the highest offer, was treated as the equivalent of an auction sale. There was an obligation to sell to the highest bidder. This case was complicated, however, by the fact that one of the bids was what was described as a 'referential bid'. That is, it was in the form 'C\$2,100,000 or C\$101,000 in excess of any other offer'. The House of Lords held that this bid was invalid and that the owner of the shares was obliged to sell to the other party, who had offered C\$2,175,000.
2.7	**Acceptance**	As has been explained above, an offer must be in a form whereby a simple assent to it is sufficient to lead to a contract being formed. It is in many cases, therefore, enough for an acceptance to take the form of the person to whom the offer has been made simply saying 'yes, I agree'. In some situations, however, particularly where there is a course of negotiations between the parties, it may become more difficult to determine precisely the point when the parties have exchanged a matching offer and acceptance. Unless they do match exactly there can be no contract. An 'offer' and an 'acceptance' must fit together like two pieces of a jigsaw puzzle. If they are not the same, they will not slot together, and the picture will be incomplete. If they do match, however, it is as if they had been previously treated with 'superglue', for once in position it will be very hard, if not impossible to pull them apart.
2.7.1	Distinction from counter-offer	Where parties are in negotiation, the response to an offer may be for the offeree to suggest slightly (or even substantially) different terms. Such a response will not, of course, be an acceptance, since it does not match the offer, but will be a 'counter-offer'. During lengthy negotiations, many such offers and counter-offers may be put on the table. Do they all remain there, available for acceptance at any stage? Or is only the last offer, or counter-offer, the one that can be accepted? This issue was addressed in *Hyde v Wrench* (1840). D offered to sell a

farm to P for £1,000. P offered £900, which was rejected. P then purported to accept the offer to sell at £1,000. D refused to go through with the transaction, and P brought an action for specific performance. The court held that a rejection of an offer in effect destroyed it. It could not later be accepted. Moreover, a counter-offer operated in the same way as a rejection. P's counter-offer of £900, therefore, had the effect of rejecting, and destroying, D's original offer to sell at £1,000. P could not accept it. In effect, P's final communication had to be treated, not as an acceptance, but as a further offer buy at £1,000, which D was free to accept or reject.

The answer to the question posed above, therefore, is that only the last offer submitted survives and is available for acceptance. All earlier offers are destroyed by rejection or counter-offer.

In some situations, however, it may be more difficult to determine whether a particular communication is a counter-offer or not. If, for example, a person offers to sell a television to another for £100, the potential buyer may ask whether cash is required, or whether a cheque is acceptable. Such an inquiry is not a counter-offer. It is not suggesting alternative terms for the contract, but attempting to clarify the way in which the contract will be performed, and in particular, whether a specific type of performance will be acceptable. The effect of an inquiry of this type was considered in *Stevenson, Jaques & Co v McLean* (1880). D wrote to P, offering to sell some iron at a particular price, and saying that the offer would be kept open until the following Monday. On the Monday morning P replied by telegram, saying 'Please wire whether you would accept 40 for delivery over two months, or if not, longest limit you could give.' D did not reply, but sold the iron elsewhere. In the meantime, P sent a telegram accepting D's offer. P sued for breach of contract. D argued that P's first telegram was a counter-offer, and that therefore the second telegram could not operate as an acceptance of D's offer. The court held that it was necessary to look at both the circumstances in which P's telegram was sent, and the form which it took. As to the first aspect, the market in iron was very uncertain, and it was not unreasonable for the P to wish to clarify the position as to delivery. Moreover, as regards the form of the telegram, it did not say 'I offer 40 for delivery over two months', but was put as an inquiry. If it had been in the form of an offer, then *Hyde v Wrench* would have been applied, but since it was clearly only an inquiry, D's original offer still survived, and P was entitled to accept it.

2.7.2   Request for information

2.7.3	Battle of the forms

One situation where it may become vital to decide whether a particular communication is a counter-offer or not, is where there is, what is frequently referred to as a 'battle of the forms'. This arises where two companies are in negotiation, and as part of their exchanges they send each other standard contract forms. If the two sets of forms are incompatible, as is likely to be the case, what is the result? There are three possibilities:

- the contract is made on the terms of the party whose form was put forward first;

- the contract is made on the terms of the party whose form was put forward last - the 'last shot' approach;

- there is no contract at all, because the parties are not in agreement, and there is no matching offer and acceptance.

Application of the principles outlined above as regards offers, counter-offers, etc, suggests that the third of the possibilities is the right answer. There is, however, a reluctance to apply it, because it will often be the case that the parties are willing, or indeed keen, to have a contract, and will often have carried on their business as if such a contract had been validly made. If they are then told by the court that they have no contract at all, it may become very difficult to unscramble their respective rights and liabilities. (This sort of situation may be dealt with by the law of 'quasi-contract' or 'restitution' - for which see Chapter 14 below).

2.7.4	The traditional view

An example of the way in which the courts have generally tackled the problem is to be found in *Butler Machine Tool Co Ltd v Ex-Cell-O Corporation (England) Ltd* (1979). The buyers wished to purchase a machine for their business. On 23 May the sellers offered to sell them one for £75,535, with delivery in 10 months. The offer incorporated the sellers' standard terms, which were said to prevail over any terms in the buyers' order. It also contained a price variation clause, allowing the sellers to increase the price in certain situations. The buyers responded with an order on 27 May. This order incorporated the buyers' terms, which did not include a price variation clause. It also included a tear-off acknowledgment slip, stating: 'We accept your order on the Terms and Conditions stated therein.' The sellers signed and returned this acknowledgment, together with a covering letter, referring back to their terms as set out in their offer of 23 May. There were no further relevant communications. When the sellers delivered the machine, they tried to enforce the price variation clause, but the buyers insisted that they were only obliged to pay £75,535. The trial judge upheld the sellers' claim, but the Court of Appeal reversed this decision. Lord Denning would have liked to do so on the basis that the overall negotiations between the parties indicated that there was a contract, even if it was not possible to identify a clear, matching, offer and acceptance. He had previously argued along these lines in the Court of Appeal in *Manchester City Council v Gibson*. He recognised, however, that the rejection of such an approach by the House of Lords' in *Gibson* precluded his use of it, and so he fell back on the traditional 'offer/counter-offer' analysis. This was the line taken by the other members of the Court of Appeal. On this basis the Court was unanimous in holding that the buyers' terms should prevail. The sellers' original offer of 23 May was met with a counter-offer from the buyers, which, on the basis of *Hyde v Wrench* destroyed the sellers' original offer. By completing and returning the acknowledgment slip the sellers were accepting this counter-offer, and their covering letter was thought not to be sufficiently specific so as to revive the detailed terms of the offer of the 23 May.

Butler Machine Tool v Ex-Cell-O confirmed the courts' adherence to the traditional analysis in terms of looking for what objectively appears to be a matching offer and acceptance. It did little to resolve a true 'battle of the forms' such as might have arisen had there been no acknowledgment slip, but simply an exchange of incompatible terms, followed by the manufacture and delivery of the machinery. In such a situation a court which followed the traditional line would probably be forced to say that there was no contract. Other possibilities might be to argue that delivery, or taking delivery, of the machinery amounted to acceptance by conduct, or that the failure to respond to the last offer sent amounted to acceptance by silence. These two concepts are considered below. A further attempt has recently been made by the Court of Appeal, however, to adopt an approach similar to that advocated by Lord Denning, and this needs to be discussed first.

In *Trentham Ltd v Archital Luxfer* (1993) the plaintiffs, were the main contractors on a building contract. They entered into negotiations with the defendants, for sub-contracts to supply and instal doors, windows, etc. The work was done, and paid for, but when the plaintiffs tried to recover a contribution from the defendants towards a penalty which the plaintiffs had had to pay under the main contract, the defendants denied that a binding contract had ever been formed. There had been exchanges of letters, and various telephone conversation s, but there was no matching offer and acceptance. In particular there was a dispute as to whose standard terms should govern the contract. The trial judge held that there was a contract, in that

2.7.5   New developments

the defendants, in carrying out the work, had accepted T's offer - in other words, acceptance by conduct (as in *Brogden v Metropolitan Rly* (1877), which is discussed further below). The defendants appealed. The only full judgment was delivered by Steyn LJ, with whom the other two members of the Court agreed. Steyn LJ agreed that there was a contract here. In reaching this conclusion he started by stating four basic points which he considered relevant to the case:

- The approach to the issue of contract formation is 'objective', and so does not take account of the 'subjective expectations and unexpressed mental reservations of the parties'. In this case the relevant yardstick was 'the reasonable expectations of sensible businessmen'.

- In the vast majority of cases the coincidence of offer and acceptance represents the mechanism of contract formation, but 'it is not necessarily so in the case of a contract alleged to have come into existence during and as a result of performance' (for this proposition he cited *Brogden v Metropolitan Rly*; *New Zealand Shipping Co Ltd v Satterthwaite* (1975); and *Gibson v Manchester City Council* (1979), none of which provide clear authority for it).

- The fact that a contract is executed (ie performance has taken place, as in this case) rather than executory, is of considerable importance - it will almost certainly preclude, for example, an argument that there was no intention to create legal relations, or that the contract is void for vagueness or uncertainty.

- If a contract only comes into existence during and as a result of performance of the transaction it will frequently be possible to hold that the contract impliedly and retrospectively covers pre-contractual performance (for this proposition he cited *Trollope & Colls v Atomic Power Construction Ltd* (1963)).

2.7.6   Application of the new approach

Applying these points to the case before him, Steyn LJ concluded that the judge had sufficient evidence before him to conclude that there was a binding contract. The parties had clearly intended to enter into a legal relationship. The contemporary exchanges, and the carrying out of what was agreed in those exchanges, support the view that there was a course of dealing which on Trentham's side created a right to performance of the work by Archital, and on Archital's side it created a right to be paid on an agreed basis. Thus, although the trial judge had found that there was offer and acceptance, Steyn J was of the view that, in any event:

'... in this fully executed transaction a contract came into existence during performance even if it cannot be precisely analysed in terms of offer and acceptance.'

Moreover, even if the contract came into existence after part of the work had been carried out and paid for, it impliedly governed pre-contractual performance.

This case is of potentially great significance. The two main points that it raises are, first, the potential retrospective effect of a contract. This is of considerable importance in relation to major contracts, in particular construction contracts, where it is common for at least some work to take place before any formal agreement has been reached. This decision clearly recognises that such work will generally be governed by any later agreement that is entered into. The need to use restitutionary remedies (which are discussed in Chapter 14) will therefore be reduced. The second issue, which is of more importance to the subject matter of this chapter, is the finding that contracts do not necessarily have to be formed by means of a matching offer and acceptance. This unanimous finding by the Court of Appeal is difficult to reconcile, however, with the rejection by the House of Lords in *Gibson* of Lord Denning's similar attempt to weaken the dominance of 'offer and acceptance'. It is true that Steyn LJ emphasises that he is concerned with the particular circumstances of a wholly executed transaction, but nevertheless the case opens the door for broader arguments that the straitjacket of offer and acceptance does not accord with commercial reality, and for that reason should be loosened in appropriate cases. It will be interesting to see whether the House of Lords, when it next has the opportunity to consider the issue, will take any different line from that which it took in *Gibson*.

We now turn to look in more detail at the issues of acceptance by conduct, or by silence.

2.8 Methods of acceptance

2.8.1 Acceptance by conduct

In unilateral contracts, the acceptance will always be by conduct - using the smoke-ball, digging the garden, etc - though there are some problems as to just what conduct amounts to acceptance, which will be considered further later. Can the same apply in bilateral contracts, so that they too can be accepted by conduct? In some everyday situations, this would seem to be the case. In a shop transaction, for example, there may be no exchange of words between the customer and cashier. The customer may simply present the goods selected together with payment, constituting an offer to buy, which will be accepted by the cashier taking the money and, generally, giving a receipt. Can there be acceptance by conduct in more complicated, commercial, transactions? This issue was considered in *Brogden v Metropolitan Railway* (1877). The plaintiffs sent the defendants a draft agreement for the supply of a certain quantity of coal per week from 1 January 1872, at £1 per ton. The defendants completed the draft by adding the name of an arbitrator, signed it, and returned it to the plaintiffs. The plaintiffs' manager simply put the signed agreement into a drawer. Coal was ordered and delivered on the terms specified in the contract for a period of time, until there was a dispute between the parties. The defendants then argued that there was no contract, because the plaintiffs had never accepted their offer, as contained in the signed agreement. The House of Lords confirmed that it was not enough that the plaintiffs should have decided to accept: there had to be some external manifestation of acceptance. In this case, however, that was supplied by the fact that the plaintiffs had placed orders on the basis of the agreement. The defendants should therefore be taken to be bound by its terms.

This decision confirms that a bilateral contract may be accepted by conduct, and there is no need for a verbal or written indication of acceptance. It does not deal, however, with the question as to whether the fact of acceptance must be communicated to the other party, and it is to that issue that we now turn.

| 2.8.2 | Acceptance by silence |

In *Brogden v Metropolitan Railway*, as we have just seen, it was held that you cannot accept a contract simply by deciding that you are going to do so. There must be some external evidence which would lead a reasonable person to believe that your intention was to accept. Does that external evidence have to come to the attention of the third party? Or is it enough that there was agreement, even if one side was in ignorance of it?

In some cases, the issue will be determined by the form of the offer. In unilateral contracts, for example, it has been recognised since *Carlill v Carbolic Smoke Ball Co* (1893), that the offeree may waive the need for communication of acceptance. The court thought that it clearly could not have been intended that everyone who bought a smoke ball in reliance on the Company's advertisement should be expected to tell the Company of this. It would be perfectly possible, of course, for an offeror to require such notice, but where an offer is made to the world, as in *Carlill's* case, or where a reward is offered for the return of property or the provision of information, the intention to waive such a requirement will easily be found.

In relation to bilateral contracts the position is different. The leading authority is *Felthouse v Bindley* (1863). An uncle was negotiating to buy a horse from his nephew. The uncle wrote to his nephew offering a particular sum and saying 'If I hear no more about him, I consider the horse mine.' The nephew did not respond, but told an auctioneer to remove this horse from a forthcoming auction. The auctioneer omitted to do so, and the horse was sold to a third party. The uncle sued the auctioneer, and the question arose as to whether the uncle had made a binding contract for the purchase of the horse. It was held that he had not done so, because the nephew had never communicated his intention to accept his uncle's offer. It is true that he had taken an action which objectively could be taken to have indicated his intention to accept, but because his uncle knew nothing of this at the time, it was not effective to complete the contract.

This case has long been taken to be authority for the proposition that silence cannot amount to acceptance, at least in bilateral contracts. It is by no means clear that the court intended to go this far. It is uncertain, for example, what the court's attitude would have been had it been the nephew, rather than the uncle, who was trying to enforce the contract. Nevertheless, later courts have taken the principle to be well-established. In *The Leonidas D* (1985), for example, Robert Goff J commented:

> 'We have all been brought up to believe it to be axiomatic that acceptance of an offer cannot be inferred from silence, save in the most exceptional circumstances.'

No court has challenged the correctness of the general principle said to be established by *Felthouse v Bindley*, though many commentators have doubted it.

The policy which may be said to lie behind the principle is that one potential contracting party should not be able to impose a contract on another by requiring the other to take some action in order not to be bound. It was felt that someone in the position of the nephew in *Felthouse v Bindley* should not be obliged to tell his uncle if he did not want to accept the offer. He should be entitled to do nothing, and not incur contractual obligations simply by inaction.

During the 1960s a related problem arose out of the growing practice of what came to be known as 'inertia selling'. The seller in these transactions would send a person who was thought to be a potential buyer, a copy of a book, for example, with a covering letter stating that unless the book was returned within a certain time limit, the recipient would be

2.8.3　　Bilateral contracts

2.8.4　　Inertia selling

assumed to want to keep it, and would be obliged to pay the purchase price. As we have seen, on the basis of *Felthouse v Bindley*, no binding contract could arise in this way. But, of course, many people were ignorant of their rights under contract law, and were led in this way to pay for items which they did not really want. In order to remedy this the Unsolicited Goods and Services Act 1971 was passed, which allows the recipient of unsolicited goods, in circumstances such as those outlined above, to treat them as an unconditional gift, with all rights of the sender being extinguished.

The basic rule, therefore, as derived from *Felthouse v Bindley*, and reinforced by the Unsolicited Goods and Services Act 1971, is that acceptance, whether by words or action, must be communicated to the the offeror. It is only in relation to certain types of unilateral contract that the offeror may waive the need for communication.

2.8.5   Acceptance by post

The requirement of communication does not, however, answer all problems. In the modern world communication can take many forms: face to face conversations, by telephone, letters, faxes, or e-mail. In some of these there will be a delay between the sending of an acceptance and its coming to the attention of the offeror. The law of contract has to have rules, therefore, to make clear what is meant by 'communication'. The simplest rule would be to say that no communication is effective until it is received and understood by the person to whom it is addressed. This is in effect the rule that applies to offers, though as we shall see below (acceptance in ignorance of the offer) there are some cases which suggest that it may be possible to accept an offer of which you are unaware. These cases are of dubious authority, however, and can only possibly apply in very restricted circumstances. In any case they simply suggest that in some situations communication of an offer may not be necessary. Where communication of the offer is required, which is the case in virtually all situations, it is safe to say that communication means that the person to whom the offer is addressed is aware of it. Why should the position be any different as regards acceptances?

The problem first arose in relation to the post, where the delay is likely to be longest. Generally speaking there will be a delay of at least 12 to 18 hours between the sending of an acceptance by post, and its receipt by the addressee. Does the sender of the acceptance have to wait until it is certain that the letter has arrived before being sure that a contract has been made? The issue was considered in *Adams v Lindsell* (1818).

The defendants sent a letter to the plaintiffs offering wool for sale, and asking for a reply 'in course of post'. The letter was misdirected by the defendants, and arrived later than would normally have been the case. The plaintiffs replied at once accepting, but the defendants, having decided that because of the delay the plaintiffs were not going to accept, had already sold the wool elsewhere. The plaintiffs sued for breach of contract. The court decided that to require a posted acceptance to arrive at its destination before it could be effective would be impractical, and inefficient. The acceptor would not be able to take any action on the contract until it had been confirmed that the acceptance had arrived. The court felt that this might result in each side waiting for confirmation of receipt of the last communication *ad infitum*. This would not promote business efficacy. It would be much better if, as soon as the letter was posted, the acceptor could proceed on the basis that a contract had been made, and taken action accordingly.

The rule that comes from *Adams v Lindsell* is thus that a posted acceptance is complete on posting. The offeror is therefore bound to a contract without being aware that this has happened. The same rule was applied to telegrams, where a similar, though shorter, delay in communication would occur. Because the rule is a rather unusual one, however, its limitations must be noted. First, it only applies to acceptances, and not to any other type of communication which may pass between potential contracting parties. Offers, counter-offers, revocations of offers, etc must all be properly communicated, even if sent through the post, or by telegram: *Byrne v van Tienhoven* (1880). Secondly, it only applies where it was reasonable for the acceptance to be sent by post: *Henthorn v Fraser* (1892). Clearly, where the offer was made by post, then, in the absence of any indication from the offeror to the contrary, it will certainly be reasonable to reply in the same form, and the postal rule will operate. Wherever the parties are communicating over a distance, it is likely to be reasonable to use the post, even if the offer has been made in some other way. As Lord Herschell put it in *Henthorn v Fraser* (1892):

> 'Where the circumstances are such that it must have been within the contemplation of the parties that, according to the ordinary usages of mankind, the post might be used as a means of communicating the acceptance of an offer, the acceptance is complete as soon as it is posted.'

In this case, the fact that the parties were based in towns some distance apart was held to make the use of the post reasonable, despite the fact that the offer had been hand delivered.

The final limitation that must be noted is that the rule can always be displaced by the offeror. The offer itself may

2.8.6   Limitations on the postal rule

expressly, or possibly impliedly, require the acceptance to take a particular form. In *Quenerduaine v Cole* (1883), for example, it was held that an offer that was made by telegram impliedly required an equally speedy reply. A reply by post would not, therefore, take effect on posting. This implication, of course, has to be looked at alongside the more general rule as to what is reasonable to expect, as set out in *Henthorn v Fraser*. If the offeror wants to be sure that the postal rule will not operate, this should be made explicit in the offer. In *Holwell Securities Ltd v Hughes* (1974) the offer required the acceptance (in fact the exercise of an option) to be given by 'notice in writing' to the offeror. It was held that this formulation meant that the acceptance would only take effect when actually received by the offeror. The insertion of this phrase is all that is required, therefore, to displace the postal rule. Other language may, of course, be used, provided the intention is clear.

If, however, the postal rule is to operate, the fact that the acceptance is complete on posting has been taken to its logical limit. It does not matter that the letter is delayed in the post, the offeror is still bound. And in *Household Fire and Carriage Accident Insurance Co v Grant* (1879) it was held that an acceptance that was entirely lost in the post, and never arrived at its destination, was still effective to create a contract.

2.8.7 Acceptance by private courier

The cases that have been discussed in the previous section were all concerned with the service provided by the Post Office. Recently there has been a growth in the availability of various kinds of private courier service, which might also be used to deliver communications creating a contract. Does the postal rule apply to acceptances sent by such means? There is no authority on this point. There are two possible lines which the law might take. First, it might be argued that the reasons for applying the postal rule in *Adams v Lindsell* apply equally to communications via a private courier. The acceptor gives the letter to a private courier, and thereby puts the acceptance out of his or her control. It would not be conducive to business efficiency to require the acceptor to wait for notification that the acceptance had been received before being able to take any action on the contract. Provided that it was reasonable for the acceptor to use the courier service, the acceptance should take effect as soon as it is given to the courier.

The second line of argument might resist the notion of extending the postal rule beyond its current application. It might well be said that communications have developed dramatically since 1818, when *Adams v Lindsell* was decided. Nowadays, if an acceptor wants to proceed quickly on the basis of a contract, where the acceptance has been given to a private courier, there is no need to wait a long time to receive confirmation that the acceptance has arrived. A telephone call to the offeror will enable the acceptor to find out very quickly whether this has happened or not. If the need for speed is even greater, then the acceptance could be sent by fax, with a request for confirmation by phone, or return fax, as soon as it has arrived.

It is difficult to predict which line of argument the courts would find more attractive. As will appear from the following section, however, there has been no move by the courts in recent years to extend the postal rule to other media, and this may be an indication of an acceptance that in the modern context the *Adams v Lindsell* approach has much less to recommend it than it did at the time it was decided. While there have been no moves to overrule that decision, or the case law flowing from it, it may be that the tendency will be to limit its scope, and confine it strictly to the area of communications via the Post Office, by letter or telegram.

In the modern world contracts may well be made by much more sophisticated means of communication than the post. Telexes, faxes and e-mail are all widely used, in addition to letters and the telephone, as means of transmitting offers, counter-offers, acceptances and rejections. If one of these methods is used for an acceptance, when is it effective?

2.8.8   Acceptance by electronic communication

The starting point for the law in this area is the case of *Entores v Miles Far East Corpn* (1955). This was concerned with communications by telex machine. The primary issue before the court was the question of where the acceptance took effect, if it was sent from a telex machine in one country, and received on a telex machine in another country. The answer to this would affect the position as to which country's law governed the contract.

2.8.9   The *Entores* approach

The leading judgment in the Court of Appeal was given by Lord Denning. His approach was to take as his starting point a very simple form of communication over a distance (albeit a rather unlikely one in factual terms), that is, two people making a contract by shouting across a river. In this situation, he argued, there would be no contract unless and until the acceptance was heard by the offeror. If, for example, an aeroplane flew overhead just as the acceptor was shouting his or her agreement, so that the offeror could not hear what was being said, there would be no contract. The acceptor would be expected to repeat the acceptance once the noise from the aeroplane had diminished. Taking this as his starting point, he argued by analogy, that the same approach should apply to all contracts made by means of commununication which are instantaneous or virtually instantaneous (as opposed to post or telegram, where there is a delay). On this basis, regarding telex as falling into the 'instantaneous' category, he held that the acceptance by telex took place where it was received, rather than where it was sent.

The same answer must be presumed to apply to all other forms of more sophisticated electronic communication which can be said to be instantaneous in their effect. They will all take effect at the place where they are received.

2.8.10   Time of acceptance

Note, however, that *Entores* was concerned with the *place* of communication, and not the *time* of communication. It provides no direct authority on the issue of the time when a telexed acceptance takes effect. Clearly, the postal rule cannot apply, since that is based on the acceptance taking effect as soon as it is out of the hands of the acceptor, whereas *Entores* requires it to have arrived at the offeror's address. Several other possibilities are possible. It could take effect only when it is actually read by the person to whom it addressed; or when it is read by someone other than the addressee; or when it is received on the addressee's telex machine, although not read by anyone; or when the acceptor would reasonably expect it to have been read.

Two cases subsequent to *Entores* have considered this issue in relation to telexes. In *The Brimnes* (1974) the communication was a not an acceptance, but a notice of the withdrawal of a ship from a charterparty. It was held to be effective when it was 'received' on the charterers' telex machine during office hours, although it was not actually read until the following morning. In *Brinkibon Ltd v Stahag Stahl* (1982) the House of Lords was dealing with a situation virtually identical to that under consideration in *Entores*, and approved the approach taken there. The House refused to indicate whether the same rule should apply in all circumstances, for example where the message is sent out of office hours, or at night, in the expectation that it will be read at a later time, or where there is some fault with the recipient's machine of which the sender is unaware. As Lord Wilberforce put it:

> 'No universal rule can cover all such cases: they must be resolved by reference to the intentions of the parties, by sound business practice and in some cases by a judgment where the risks should lie.'

This is not particularly helpful, but insofar as any general principle can be read into it, it would seem to be the last of those suggested above, that is that the communication should take effect at the time when the acceptor could reasonably have expected it to be read. This may suggest variations according to the type of communication system being used. There does not seem to be any reason for treating faxes differently from telex, but electronic mail, sent to an electronic 'post-box' which will only be checked once or twice a day, might well be be said only to be communicated once the expected time for checking has passed. A similar appproach might need to be used in relation to messages left on a telephone answering system. That is, the message should only be regardeds as communicated once a reasonable time has elapsed to allow it to be heard by the offeror.

If this line is to be taken, it is clearly to the advantage of the acceptor, in that it allows an acceptance to be treated as effective although the offeror may be unaware of it (as is the case under the postal rule). As with *Adams v Lindsell* the counter-argument to those who say that this give the acceptor too much of an advantage would be that the courts have always made it clear that the offeror can specify and insist on a particular mode of acceptance. If actual communication is required, this should be spelt out in the offer. If this is not done, the acceptor must be allowed to proceed on the basis that the acceptance will be read at a time which could reasonably be expected in the normal course of events.

Particular difficulties arise in connection with acceptances in unilateral contracts. We have already seen that one of the characteristics of the unilateral contract is that the acceptance occurs through the performance of an act, rather than the expression of agreement. It has also been noted that in certain cases the offeror in a unilateral contract may be taken to have waived the need for communication of the fact of acceptance eg *Carlill v Carbolic Smoke Ball Company* (1893).

2.8.11   Acceptance in unilateral contracts

A further problem arises as to when acceptance is complete. Is it when the acceptor starts to perform? Or when performance is complete? If I offer a prize of £100 for the first person to walk from the Town Hall in Leicester to Trafalgar Square in London during the month of February, do you accept this offer when you take your first step away from Leicester, or only when you arrive at Trafalgar Square? An acceptor in a unilateral contract is generally regarded as incurring no obligations until the specified act is completed, so that if you decide to give up half way to London, I will have no claim against you for breach of contract. This would suggest that acceptance only occurs with complete performance. There are problems with this, however, in relation to the offeror's power to withdraw the offer. As will be seen below, the offeror is generally free to withdraw an offer at any point before it has been accepted. If, in a unilateral contract, acceptance means complete performance, then this means that the offeror would be able to back out at any point before this had occurred. So, to use the example given above, if you have started out to walk from Leicester to London, and have managed two-thirds of the distance, I would be entitled to come up to you and say: 'I'm sorry, I have changed my mind. My offer of £100 is withdrawn.' You would have no redress, despite the fact that you might be perfectly willing to continue the walk, because we would not at that stage have a contract (*Great Northern Rly v Witham* (1873)).

2.8.12 **Prevention of withdrawal by the offeror**

This result has been regarded by many as unfair, and there have therefore been attempts to argue that partial performance may in some circumstances amount to a sufficient indication of acceptance so as to prevent withdrawal by the offeror. In *Errington v Errington* (1952) a father had promised to his son and daughter-in-law, that if they paid off the mortgage on a house owned by the father, he would transfer it to them. The young couple started to make the required payments, but made no promise that they would continue. This appeared to be, therefore, a unilateral contract. The father died, and his representatives denied that there was any binding agreement in relation to the house. They argued that his offer could be withdrawn, because there had not been full acceptance. The Court of Appeal refused to allow this conclusion. Lord Denning recognised that this was a unilateral contract, but nevertheless held that the offer could not be withdrawn:

> 'The father's promise was a unilateral contract - a promise of the house in return for their act of paying the instalments. It could not be revoked by him once the couple entered on performance of the act, but it would cease to bind him if they left it incomplete and unperformed.'

The reasons behind this conclusion are not made clear, other than that this was a fair result where the young couple had acted in reliance on the father's promise. This approach has clear links with the idea of estoppel, of which as we shall see (below, para 3.8) Lord Denning has made inventive use in other areas, but this concept was not raised directly in this case.

The approach taken by Lord Denning in *Errington* received support from a differently constituted Court of Appeal in *Daulia v Four Millbank Nominees Ltd* (1978). The unilateral contract here was that the defendants promised the plaintiffs that if they produced a signed contract plus a banker's draft by 10 am the next morning, the defendants would go ahead with the sale of some properties to the defendants. The plaintiffs did what was requested, but the defendants refused to go through with the contract. In the course of his judgment Goff LJ considered the question of when the offeror in a unilateral contract is entitled to withdraw that offer. He started by confirming that in general the offeror cannot be bound to a unilateral contract until the acceptor has provided full performance of the condition imposed. That general rule is, however, subject to an important qualification, namely:

> '... that there must be an implied obligation on the part of the offeror not to prevent the condition becoming satisfied, which obligation it seems to me must arise as soon as the offeree starts to perform. Until then the offeror can revoke the whole thing, but once the offeree has embarked on performance it is too late for the offeror to revoke his offer.'

Goff LJ provided no authority for this proposition, but it received the support of Buckley LJ. It was not, however, part of the ratio of the case, since the court decided against the plaintiffs on other grounds. It seems likely, nevertheless, that the approach taken by Denning and Goff in these two cases would be followed in similar circumstances.

It may be significant, however, that in both *Errington* and *Daulia* the offeror was aware that the other person had embarked upon performance. It is not clear that in a case, such as the offer of a reward or prize, where the offer is made to the world, that precisely the same approach should apply. In the case, for example, of the offer of £100 for the return of a lost dog, it seems right that where a person is seen at the opposite end of the street, bringing the dog home, the offeror should not be able to shout out a withdrawal of the reward. But suppose the offeror has run into financial problems since offering the reward, and cannot now afford to pay it. Must the offeror remain committed to keeping the offer open as regards anyone who has started looking for the dog, even if the offeror is unaware of this? It would seem more reasonable that the offeror should be allowed, by giving notice in a reasonable manner (perhaps in the same way as which the offer was made), to withdraw the offer. It is an issue on which there is no English authority, so it is not possible to say with any certainty what the approach of the courts would be, but it is submitted that the fairest rule to all parties would be to hold that the *Errnington/Daulia* approach should only apply where the offeror is aware that the other person is trying to perform the condition.

2.8.13   Position in 'reward' contracts

2.8.14	Acceptance in ignorance of an offer

It would seem logical that there can be no acceptance of an offer of which the person accepting was ignorant. Some problems have arisen, however, in relation in particular to unilateral contracts. Suppose a reward is offered for the return of a stolen bicycle, belonging to A, and posters are displayed advertising this fact. B, who has not seen any of the posters, finds the bicycle, and recognising it, returns it to A, its rightful owner. Can B claim the reward from A? There is one authority which suggests that he might be able to. That is *Gibbons v Proctor* (1891), where a police officer gave information for which a reward had been offered. At the time that he gave the information the officer was unaware of the reward, though he had learnt of it by the time the information reached the person who had offered the reward. It was held that the officer was entitled to claim the reward. This decision has not been followed in any later case, however, and must be regarded as being of doubtful authority. The better view seems to be that knowledge is necessary for an effective acceptance. This was accepted as being the case, though without any authority being cited, in the ciminal law case of *Taylor v Allon* (1965).

A slightly different issue arises where the person performing the act has previously known of the offer, but is acting from different motives. In the Australian case of *R v Clarke* (1927) it was held that a person who had known of the offer, but was at the time acting purely out of consideration of his own danger, should be treated as acting in ignorance of the offer. On the other hand, in *Williams v Carwardine* (1833), it was held that acting for mixed motives, that is to ease one's conscience, while at the same time having the reward in mind, did not preclude a valid acceptance of the offer.

2.8.15	Cross-offers

The above cases have all been concerned with unilateral contracts. The parallel situation in a bilateral contract is where there are 'cross-offers'. Suppose, for example, that two parties send each other a letter offering respectively to buy and to sell certain goods at a certain price. Suppose, also, that the two offers match precisely. Does this create a contract? If what the courts were concerned with was a 'meeting of the minds' the answer might well be 'yes'. In *Tinn v Hoffman* (1873), however, it was held that such an exchange does not result in a contract. The case is not conclusive on the general issue, because on the facts there were differences between the two offers. It seems likely, however, that given the general enthusiasm of the courts for looking for an 'exchange' of offer and acceptance, rather than simply general agreement, that *Tinn v Hoffman* would be followed, and that cross-offers would not be regarded as forming a contract.

The general rule is that an offer can be revoked at any point before it is accepted (*Payne v Cave* (1789)), though as we have seen that requires some modification in relation to unilateral contracts. In this section the focus will be entirely on bilateral contracts.

The general rule will apply despite the fact that the offeror may have promised to keep the offer open for a specified time: *Routledge v Grant* (1828). The reason for this is that before there is an acceptance, there is no contract, and if there is no contract, then the offeror cannot be bound to a promise. If the offeree has paid for the time allowance in some way (that is, has given consideration for the promise), as may well be the case with the exercise of an option, then it will be upheld. In the absence of this, however, there can be no complaint if the offer is withdrawn.

Revocation of an offer must be communicated to be effective. This was implicit in the decision in *Byrne v van Tienhoven* (1880) where the withdrawal of an offer, which was sent by telegram, was held not to take effect until it was received. The *Adams v Lindsell* postal rule does not apply to revocations of offers, but there may still be difficulties as to what exactly amounts to communication, and when a revocation takes effect. The issues are much the same as those dealt with in the section on acceptance by electronic communication, above, and are not discussed again here.

It is clear, however, that communication of revocation need not come directly from the offeror. Provided that the offeree is fully aware at the time of a purported acceptance that the offeror has decided not to proceed with the contract, then the offer will be regarded as having been revoked, and no acceptance will be possible. This was the position in *Dickinson v Dodds* (1876), where the plaintiff was told by a third party that the defendant was negotiating with someone else for the sale of properties which he had previously offered to the plaintiff. The defendant had also indicated to the plaintiff that the offer would be kept open for a specified period.

The plaintiff tried to accept the offer within the time limit. The Court of Appeal decided that acceptance was not possible, because the plaintiff knew that the defendant was no longer minded to sell the property to him 'as plainly and clearly as if [the defendant] had told him so in so many words.' The reasoning of at least some of the judges in this case was clearly influenced by the idea of their needing to be a 'meeting of the minds' in order for their to be a contract. Despite the fact that this approach to identifying agreements no longer has any support, *Dickinson v Dodds* is still regarded as good authority

2.9   Acceptance and the termination of an offer

2.9.1   Need for communication

for the more general proposition that an offeree cannot accept an offer where he or she has learnt from a reliable source that the offer has been withdrawn, even where that source was acting without the knowledge of the offeror.

2.9.2   Effect of lapse of time

An offer may also become incapable of acceptance because of lapse of time. If the offeror has specified a time within which acceptance must be received, any acceptance received outside that time limit cannot create a contract. At best it will be a fresh offer, which may be accepted or rejected. If no time is specified, then the offer will remain open for a reasonable time, which will be a matter of fact in each case. In *Ramsgate Victoria Hotel Co v Montefiore* (1866) it was held that a delay of five months meant that an attempt to accept an offer to buy shares was ineffective.

2.10   Retraction of acceptance

As soon as an acceptance takes effect, then a contract is made, and both parties are bound. It would seem, then, that in the normal course of events, retraction, or revocation, of an acceptance will be impossible. The issue arises, however, in relation to situations where the law deems acceptance to take effect at a point in time before that at which it actually comes to the attention of the offeror. The most obvious example of this is the *Adams v Lindsell* postal rule. It may also apply, however, in relation to, for example, acceptances by telex which are received during office hours, but not read until some time later, or messages left on a telephone answering machine. As we have seen the law as yet provides no clear answer to the question of when acceptance takes effect in such cases, but if it is decided that the relevant time is when the acceptance is received on the offeror's machine, rather than when it is read, there is again a delay between acceptance and actual communication, which may lead to the possibility of a retraction. The rest of this section will discuss the issue in relation to posted acceptances, but the principles should surely apply in the same way to any acceptance where there is a delay between the point in time when the law says that the acceptance takes effect (for example, on posting) and when it is read by the offeror.

2.10.1   Formalist approach

If a 'formalist' approach is taken to this issue (see Chapter 1, at para 1.2.1), then the answer must be that no retraction of an acceptance is possible. The general rule of the contract being complete on acceptance should be applied. So even if the acceptor is able, for example, by telephoning the offeror, to indicate that an acceptance which is in the post is to be ignored, the offeror should be entitled to say 'Too bad! Your acceptance took effect on posting, and we have a contract. If you fail to go through with it, you will be in breach.'

This is not the only possible approach, however. It might also be argued that the purpose of the postal rule is to provide a benefit to the acceptor. As we have seen, the main reason for the decision in *Adams v Lindsell* was that such a rule allowed the acceptor to proceed on the basis that a contract had been made, and that this promoted business efficiency. If that is the case, it might be argued that it is a little odd to then apply the rule in a way which is to the acceptor's disadvantage. Moreover, if, as must be the case for there to be any possibility of retraction, we are considering a point in time at which the offeror is as yet unaware of the acceptance, how can there be any harm in allowing the acceptor to withdraw? The offeror cannot in any way have acted on the acceptance, and so can suffer no harm from its retraction. There seems little point in forcing people to go through with a contract, when one party no longer wishes to proceed, and the other party is unaware of the fact that there is a contract at all.

This argument is said by some to be too favourable to the acceptor. The example is given of an acceptance of an offer to buy shares, or goods which have a greatly fluctuating market price. If retraction of acceptance is allowed, then it is said that this gives the acceptor the best of both worlds. The offer can be accepted by posting a letter, which will bind the offeror. Then, if before the acceptance is read, the market price falls below the contract price, the acceptor can avoid what has now become a bad bargain, by telephoning a withdrawal. This is regarded as unfair. In an argument which is the converse of the one put forward in the last paragraph, it is said that the postal rule exists for the benefit of the acceptor. It is tipping the scales too far in the acceptor's favour, however, to allow the possibility of retraction as well: a possibility which is not available in any other situation.

Attempts to argue the case from first principles, then, may lead to different conclusions. Three possibilities have been outlined above, one in favour of allowing retraction, the other two against. This writer's preferred view is the pragmatic one of allowing retraction, but it is by no means widely accepted. Unfortunately, there is little help from case law, either.

The only British case to deal with the issue at all is *Countess of Dunmore v Alexander* (1830). This is a Scottish case, which on one reading appears to support the view that a posted acceptance can be retracted by speedier means. The case is not a strong authority, however, since it is not absolutely clear that the court considered that the communication which was withdrawn was an acceptance, rather than an offer. Two cases from other common law jurisdictions suggest the opposite. In *Wenckheim v*

2.10.2	Purposive approach
2.10.3	Unfairness to offeror
2.10.4	Guidance from authority

Arndt (1873) (New Zealand) and *A to Z Bazaars (Pty) Ltd v Minister of Agriculture* (1974) (South Africa) it was held that the attempt to withdraw the acceptance was not effective.

An English court faced with this issue would be free to decide it without any clear guidance from authority. The answer that is given will depend on which of the various possibilities outlined above is the more attractive. It is not unlikely that the court's decision in a particular case will be influenced by what the court sees as the best way to achieve justice between the parties, rather than on any preference based on general principle.

2.11   Certainty in offer and acceptance

Even though the parties may have appeared to make an agreement by exchange of a matching offer and acceptance, the courts may refuse to enforce it if there appears to be uncertainty about what has been agreed, or if some important aspect of the agreement is left open to be decided later. In *Scammell v Ouston* (1941), for example, the parties had agreed to the supply of a lorry on 'hire-purchase terms'. The House of Lords held that in the absence of any other evidence of the details of the hire-purchase agreement (duration, number of instalments, etc) this was too vague to be enforceable, and there was therefore no contract.

This does not necessarily mean that all details of a contract must be finally settled in advance. It is not uncommon, for example, in relation to contracts for the supply of services, for the precise amount to be paid to be left unspecified at the time of the agreement. If a car is left at a garage for repair, it may not be possible to determine at that stage exactly what the repair will cost, because this may depend on what the mechanic finds once work has started. The car owner may well say something along the lines of 'Do the work, but if it looks as though it will cost more than £150, please contact me before going ahead.' It cannot be doubted that there is a contract for repairs up to the value of £150. The courts view of this situation is that there is in effect an agreement that the customer will pay a 'reasonable price', for the work that is done. What is a reasonable price is a question of fact, which can, if necessary, be determined by the courts. This approach now has statutory force by virtue of s 15 of the Supply of Goods and Services Act 1982. The same rule also operates in relation to goods by virtue of s 8(2) of the Sale of Goods Act 1979.

The possibility of the courts giving specific content to an apparently vague phrase can apply in other areas apart from the price to be paid for goods or services. In *Hillas v Arcos* (1932), for example, there was a contract to supply timber 'of fair specification'. It was held that in the context of the agreement, which was between parties who knew each other and the timber trade well, and taking account of the fact that there had been part performance, the phrase 'fair specification' must be capable of being given a meaning. The contract was therefore enforceable.

The decision in *Scammell v Ouston*, above, might be thought to open the door to an unscrupulous party to include some meaningless phrase in an agreement, which would then allow them to escape from the contract if they wished on the basis of uncertainty. To have such an effect, however, the phrase must relate to some significant aspect of the contract. If it can be deleted and still leave a perfectly workable agreement, then the courts will ignore it. This was the position in *Nicolene v Simmonds* (1953), where the contractual documentation contained the statement 'we are in agreement that the usual conditions of acceptance apply'. Since there were no 'usual conditions', it was held that this was simply a meaningless phrase, which could be ignored. There was nothing left open which needed to be determined.

2.11.1   Meaningless phrases

If an agreement leaves undecided, and undeterminable, some important aspect of the contract, then the courts will not enforce it. This can arise where perfectly clear words are used, about the meaning of which there is no dispute, but which do not settle some significant part of the contractual terms. In *May and Butcher v R* (1934), for example, the agreement provided that the price, and the date of payment, under a contract of sale, was to be 'agreed upon from time to time'. The House of Lords held that there was no contract. The parties had not left the price open - when, as we have seen a 'reasonable price' would have been payable - they had specifically stated that they would agree in the future. The contract contained an arbitration clause, but the House considered that this was only meant to be used in the event of disputes, and could not be the means of determining basic obligations. This refusal to give effect to an 'agreement to agree' was followed in *Courtney and Fairbairn Ltd v Tolaini Brothers (Hotels) Ltd* (1975), and confirmed in *Walford v Miles* (1992)

2.11.2   Incomplete agreements

The contract will not be regarded as incomplete if it provides a machinery for resolving an aspect which has been left uncertain. As we have seen, in relation to the price, the courts will often be prepared to assume that a 'reasonable price' was intended. They will also be prepared to give effect to an agreement where property is to be valued by an independent valuer, or where the price is to be determined by reference to the prevailing market price. In such situations, the contract provides a mechanism by which the uncertainty can be resolved.

2.11.3   Obligations distinguished from 'machinery'

In some recent cases, however, the courts have been prepared to stretch this principle rather further than might have been expected. In *Sudbrook Trading Estate v Eggleton* (1982) the price for exercise of an option to purchase was to be determined by two valuers, one to be nominated by each party. One party refused to appoint a valuer, and claimed that the agreement was therefore void for uncertainty. The House of Lords disagreed. The contract was not uncertain in that it provided a clear machinery by which the price was to be determined. This machinery was not, however, itself an essential term of the contract. It was simply a way of establishing a 'fair' price. If the machinery failed, then the court could substitute its own means of determining what was a fair price. This approach was relied on by the Court of Appeal in *Didymi Corporation v Atlantic Lines and Navigation Co Inc* (1987). The agreement contained a provision under which the hire under a charter of a ship could in some circumstances be increased 'equitably', by an amount 'to be mutually agreed between the parties'. At first sight this looks like an 'agreement to agree' which would be unenforceable. The Court, however, following the lead given by *Sudbrook Trading Estate v Eggleton*, ruled that the reference to 'mutual agreement' was simply part of the 'inessential machinery' by which the hire was to be determined. The agreement was that the hire should be 'equitable', which meant 'fair and reasonable'. There was therefore no reason why the court should not determine this, as a question of fact.

An incomplete agreement may nevertheless give rise to some legal obligations between the parties, under the doctrine of 'restitution'. This is discussed further below in Chapter 14.

Summary of Chapter 2

Offer and Acceptance

Contracts do not generally need to be in writing, or to use any particular form of words. A verbal offer and acceptance is sufficient.

Lack of need for formality

Exceptions to this exist in relation to contracts concerning land, and consumer credit agreements.

An offer is an indication by one person that he or she is prepared to contract with one or more others, on certain terms, which are fixed, or capable of being fixed, at the time the offer is made.

Offer

An offer can be distinguished from 'invitation to treat': preliminary negotiations, or expressions of interest will be regarded as invitations to treat, rather than offers. Note *Gibson v Manchester City Council* (1979).

Distinction from 'invitation to treat'

Displays of goods in shops, or shop windows, will generally be regarded as invitations to treat, not offers: *Pharmaceutical Society of Great Britain v Boots* (1953); *Fisher v Bell* (1961).

Displays of goods

Advertisements may be either invitations to treat (*Partridge v Crittenden* (1968)); or offers (*Carlill v Carbolic Smoke Ball Co* (1893)); *Lefkowitz v Great Minneapolis Surplus Stores* (1957) (American case), depending on the precise terms of the advert.

Advertisements

Advertisements which are offers, will normally involve 'unilateral', or 'if' contracts, under which the offeree incurs no obligation prior to performing an act requested by the offeror.

An invitation to tender for work will normally constitute an invitation to treat, with the responses being offers: *Spencer v Harding* (1870). There may, however, be a unilateral contract obliging the person inviting the tenders to comply with any procedures set out in the invitation: *Blackpool and Fylde Aero Club Ltd v Blackpool Borough Council* (1990).

Invitation to tender for work

Auctions: the bids are offers, which are accepted by the fall of the hammer. An auction advertised as being 'without reserve', however, implies an obligation to sell to the highest bidder: *Warlow v Harrison* (1859). (Note also *Harvela Investments v Royal Trust of Canada* (1987).)

Auctions

Acceptance

Definition of acceptance: an unconditional assent to an definite offer.

Distinction from counter-offer

Distinction from counter-offer: a response to an offer which introduces new terms or conditions is a 'counter-offer' not an acceptance. A counter-offer prevents later acceptance of the original offer: *Hyde v Wrench* (1840). A request for information which is not a counter-offer does not have this effect: *Stevenson, Jaques & Co v McLean* (1880).

Battle of the forms

'Battle of the forms': exchange of incompatible terms between businesses may make it difficult to identify an agreement. Courts have generally used traditional 'offer and acceptance' analysis: *Butler Machine Tool Co Ltd v Ex-Cell-O Corporation* (1979). Note recent broader approach in *Trentham v Archital Luxfer* (1993).

Methods of acceptance

Acceptance may be achieved by various means:

- Acceptance by conduct

  This is possible, as in *Brogden v Metropolitan Rly* (1877), provided the offeror is aware of the acceptance.

- Acceptance by silence

  This is not generally possible (*Felthouse v Bindley* (1863)).

- Acceptance by post

  Acceptance will take effect on posting (*Adams v Lindsell* (1818)) unless:

  (i) use of the post is unreasonable (*Henthorn v Fraser* (1892)); or

  (ii) the offeror has required actual communication (*Holwell Securities v Hughes* (1974)).

- Acceptance by private courier

  There is no authority on this. It is not clear whether the *Adams v Lindsell* rule would apply.

- Acceptance by electronic communication

  'Instantaneous' communications, such as telex, take effect at the point of receipt (*Entores v Miles Far East Corporation* (1955)). The time at which they take effect is not settled - note *The Brimnes* (1975) and *Brinkibon Ltd v Stahag Stahal* (1983).

- Acceptance in unilateral contracts

  If acceptance equals completion of performance, can the offer be withdrawn before performance is complete (as suggested in *Great Northern Rly v Witham* (1873)). Note

Errington v Errington (1952) and *Daulia v Four Millbank Nominees* (1978) which suggest that, at least where the offeror is aware of the attempt to perform, withdrawal of the offer will not be allowed.

• Acceptance in ignorance of the offer

The general view (despite *Gibbons v Proctor* (1891)) is that the person accepting must be aware of the offer, though this need not be the sole motive for acting (*Williams v Cawardine* (1833)). *Tinn v Hoffman* (1873) suggests that cross-offers do not make a contract.

• Acceptance and the termination of an offer

The general rule is that an offer can be revoked at any time before acceptance (*Payne v Cave* (1789)), even if there has been a promise to keep it open (*Routledge v Grant* (1828)). Withdrawal of the offer must be communicated (*Byrne v van Tienhoven* (1880), though this may be done via a third party (*Dickinson v Dodds* (1876)). An offer may also lapse after the expiry of a specified, or reasonable, time (*Ramsgate Victoria Hotel v Montefiore* (1866)).

Revocation of acceptance is not normally possible. The only exception may exist in relation to postal acceptances while they are still in transmission. There is no English authority on this - compare *Dunmore v Alexander* (1830) (Scottish case, revocation possible), with *Wenckeim v Arndt* (1873) (New Zealand) and *A to Z Bazaars (Pty) Ltd v Minister of Agriculture* (1974) (South Africa) (both of which suggest revocation is not permissible).

Revocation of acceptance

If an agreement is uncertain on some important issue, or leaves it open to be decided, the courts will hold that there is no contract (*Scammell v Ouston* (1941)). This does not prevent contracts to pay a 'reasonable price' for goods or services (Sale of Goods Act 1979, s 8(2); Supply of Goods and Services Act 1982, s 15).

Certainty in offer and acceptance

A meaningless phrase which can be excised without affecting the agreement will not prevent a contract (*Nicolene v Simmonds* (1953)).

Meaningless phrases

An 'agreement to agree' will not be enforced (*Courtney and Fairbairn Ltd v Tolaini Brothers* (1975), unless the contract itself contains a method for determining the matter left open (*Sudbrook Trading Estate v Eggleton* (1982)).

Incomplete agreements

Chapter 3

Consideration and Intention

This chapter is concerned with the remaining two elements which the courts look for in deciding whether a binding contract exists. As well as seeking a matching offer and acceptance, they will also look for 'consideration', and, in some situations, a clear 'intention to create legal relations'.

The doctrine of consideration is one of the characteristics of English contract law. No matter how much the parties to an agreement may wish it to be legally enforceable, it will not be so unless it contains 'consideration'. What does the word mean in this context? It is important to note that it does *not* have its ordinary, every day, meaning. It is used in a technical sense. Essentially it refers to what one party to an agreement is giving, or promising, in exchange for what is being given or promised from the other side. So, for example, in a contract where A is selling B 10 bags of grain for £100, what is the consideration? A is transferring the ownership of the grain to B. In consideration of this, B is paying £100. Or, to look at it the other way round: B is paying A £100. In consideration for this, A is transferring to B the ownership of the grain. From this example it will be seen that there is consideration on both sides of the agreement. It is this mutuality which makes the agreement enforceable. If B simply agreed to pay A £100, or A agreed to give B the grain, there would be no contract.

3.1 The nature and role of consideration

It is sometimes said that consideration requires benefit and detriment. In other words, what is provided by way of consideration should be a benefit to the person receiving it, and a detriment to the person giving it. In the example given above, B is suffering a detriment by paying the £100, and A is gaining a benefit. B is gaining a benefit in receiving the grain, A is suffering a detriment by losing it. In many cases, there will be both benefit and detriment involved, but it is not necessary that this should be the case. Benefit to one party, or detriment to the other, will be enough. Suppose that A agrees to transfer the grain, if B pays £100 to charity. In this case B's consideration in paying the £100 is a detriment to B, but not a benefit to A. Nevertheless, B's act is good consideration, and there is a contract. In theory it is enough that the recipient of the consideration receives a benefit, without the giver suffering a detriment. It is difficult, however, to think of practical examples of a situation of this kind.

3.2 Benefit and detriment

3.3	**Mutual promises**	The discussion so far has been in terms of acts constituting consideration. It is quite clear, however, that a promise to act can in itself be consideration. Suppose, continuing the example used above, that on Monday, A promises that he will deliver, and transfer the ownership of the grain to B on the following Friday; and B promises, again on Monday, that when it is delivered she will pay £100. There is no doubt that there is a contract as soon as these promises have been exchanged, so that if on Tuesday B decides that she does not want the grain, she will be in breach. But where is the consideration? On each side, the giving of the promise is the consideration. A's promise to transfer the grain is consideration for B's promise to pay for it, and vice versa. The problem is that this does not fit easily with the idea of benefit and detriment. A's promise is only a benefit to B, and a detriment to A, if it is enforceable. But it will only be enforceable if it is a benefit or a detriment. The argument is circular, and cannot therefore explain why promises are accepted as good consideration. There is no easy answer to this paradox, but the undoubted acceptance by the courts of promises as good consideration casts some doubt on whether benefit and detriment can truly be said to be essential parts of the definition of consideration. It may be that the concept simply requires the performance, or the promise to perform, some action which the other party would like to be done. This approach ignores the actual or potential detriment. Alternatively, if it is thought that the idea of benefit and detriment is too well established to be discarded, the test must surely be restated so that consideration is provided where a person performs an act which will be a detriment to him or a benefit to the other party, or promises to perform such an act. On this analysis benefit and detriment are not so much essential elements of consideration, as necessary consequences of its performance.
3.4	**Consideration need not be 'adequate' but must be 'sufficient'**	The view that the element of 'mutuality' is the most important aspect of the doctrine of consideration is perhaps supported by the fact that the courts will not inquire into the 'adequacy' of consideration. By 'adequacy' is meant the question of whether what is provided by way of consideration corresponds in value to what it is being given for. Thus, if I own a car valued at £20,000, and I agree to sell it to you for £1, the courts will treat this a binding contract. Your agreement to pay £1 provides sufficient consideration for my transfer of ownership of the car, even though it is totally 'inadequate' in terms of its relationship to the value of the car. This aspect of consideration was confirmed in *Thomas v Thomas* (1842). The testator, Mr Thomas, before his death, expressed a wish that his wife

should have for the rest of her life the house in which they had lived. After his death, his executors made an agreement with Mrs Thomas to this effect, expressed to be 'in consideration of' the testator's wishes. There was also an obligation on Mrs Thomas to pay £1 per year, and to keep the house in repair. It was argued that there was no contract here, because Mrs Thomas had provided no sufficient consideration. The court took the view that the statement that the agreement was 'in consideration' of the testator's wishes, was not using 'consideration' in its technical contractual sense, but expressing the motive for making the agreement. The actual 'consideration' was the payment of £1 and the agreement to keep the house in repair. Either of these was clearly recognised as good consideration, even though the payment of £1 could in no way be regarded as anything approaching a commercial rent for the property.

In coming to this conclusion, the court pointed out that consideration must be 'something which is of some value in the eye of the law'. This has generally been interpreted to mean that it must have some economic value. Thus, the moral obligation which the executors might have felt, or been under, to comply with the testator's wishes would not have been sufficient. An example of the application this principle may perhaps be found in the case of *White v Bluett* (1853). A father promised not to enforce a promissory note (that is, a document acknowledging a debt) against his son, provided that the son stopped complaining about the distribution of his father's property. It was held that this was not an enforceable agreement, because the son had not provided any consideration. As Pollock CB explained:

3.4.1   Economic value

> 'The son had no right to complain, for the father might make what distribution of his property he liked; and the son's abstaining from what he had no right to do can be no consideration.'

The courts have not been consistent in this approach, however. In the American case of *Hamer v Sidway* (1891) a promise not to drink alcohol, smoke tobacco, or swear, was held to be good consideration, and in *Ward v Byham* (1956) it was suggested that a promise to ensure that a child was happy could be good consideration.

Even in cases which have a more obvious commercial context, the requirement of economic value does not seem to have been applied very strictly. See, for example, *Chappell v Nestlé* (1960). This case arose out of a 'special offer' of a familiar kind, from Nestlés, under which a person who sent in three wrappers from bars of their chocolate could buy a record at a special price. For the purpose of the law of copyright it was important to decide whether the chocolate wrappers were part of the consideration in the contract to buy the record. The House of Lords decided that they were, despite the fact that it was established that they were thrown away by Nestlés, and were thus of no direct value to them.

The only economic value in the wrappers that it is at all possible to discern is that they represented sales of chocolate bars, which was obviously the point of Nestlés promotion. This is, however, very indirect. Another example of the lengths to which the courts will sometimes go to identify consideration is *De La Bere v Pearson* (1908). The plaintiff had written to a newspaper which invited readers to write in for financial advice. Some of the readers' letters, together with the newspaper's financial editor's advice was published. The plaintiff received and followed negligently given advice which caused him loss. Since the tort of negligent misstatement was at the time unrecognised, the plaintiff had to frame his action in contract. But where was the consideration for the defendants' apparently gratuitous advice? The purchase of the newspaper was one possibility, but there was no evidence that this was done in order to receive advice. The only other possibility, which was favoured by the court, was that the plaintiff, by submitting a letter, had provided free copy which could be published. This was thought to be sufficient consideration for the provision of the advice, which it would be implied should be given with due care.

As these cases illustrate, the requirement of 'economic value' is not particularly strict. Indeed, in the overall pattern of decisions in this area, it is the case of *White v Bluett* which looks increasingly out of line.

The issue of the 'sufficiency' of consideration looks to the type, or characteristics, of the thing which has been done or promised, rather than to its value. In addition to the requirement of economic value, which as we have seen is applied flexibly, there are two other issues which must be considered here. The first is the question of so-called 'past consideration'. The second is whether the performance of, or promise to perform, an existing duty can ever amount to consideration.

3.5	**Past consideration is no consideration**

Consideration must be given at the time of the contract or at some point after the contract is made. It is not generally possible to use as consideration some act or forebearance which has taken place prior to the contract. Suppose that I take pity on my poverty-stricken niece, and give her my old car. If the following week she wins £10,000 on the football pools, and says she will now give me £500 out of her winnings as payment for the car, is that promise enforceable? English law says no, because I have provided no consideration for it. My transfer of the car was undertaken and completed without any thought of payment, and before my niece made her promise. This is 'past consideration' and so cannot be used to enforce an agreement. A case which applies this basic principle is *Roscorla v Thomas* (1842). The plaintiff had bought a horse from the defendant. The defendant then promised that the horse was 'sound and free from vice', which turned out to be untrue. The plaintiff was unable to sue on this promise, however, since he had provided no consideration for it. The sale was already complete before the promise was made.

A more recent example of the same approach is *Re McArdle* (1951). William McArdle left a house to his sons and daughter. One of the sons was living in the house, and carried out various improvements to it. He then got each of his siblings to sign a document agreeing to contribute to the costs of the work. It was held that these agreements were unenforceable. The work had been completed before there was any suggestion of payment. It was, therefore, 'past consideration', and ineffective.

3.5.1 The exception

The doctrine of past consideration is not an absolute one, however. The courts have always recognised certain situations where a promise made subsequent to the performance of an act may nevertheless be enforceable. The rules derived from various cases have now been re-stated as a three-fold test by the Privy Council in *Pao On v Lau Yiu Long* (1979). Lord Scarman, delivering the opinion of the Privy Council, recognised that:

> '... an act done before the giving of a promise to make a payment or to confer some other benefit can sometimes be consideration for the promise.'

For the exception to apply, the following must be true:

- The act must have been done at the promisor's request. This derives from the case of *Lampleigh v Braithwait* (1615), where the defendant had asked the plaintiff to seek a pardon for him, in relation to a criminal offence which he had committed. After the plaintiff had made considerable efforts to do this, the defendant promised him £100 for his trouble. It was held that the promise was enforceable.

- The parties must have understood that the act was to be rewarded either by a payment or the conferment of some other benefit. In *Re Casey's Patents* (1892) the plaintiff had managed certain patents on behalf of the plaintiffs. They then promised him a one-third share in consideration of the work which he had done. It was held that the plaintiff must always have assumed that his work was to be paid for in some way. The defendants' promise was simply a crystallisation of this reasonable expectation and was therefore enforceable.

• The payment, or conferment of other benefit, must have been legally enforceable had it been promised in advance. There is little that needs to be said about this. It simply means that the usual requirements for a binding agreement must apply.

The effect of these tests is that consideration will be valid to support a later promise, provided that all along there was an expectation of reward. It is very similar to the situation where goods or services are provided without the exact price being specified. As we have seen, the courts will enforce the payment of a reasonable sum for what has been provided. That is, in effect, also what they are doing in situations falling within the three tests outlined above.

3.6   Performance of existing duties

Can the performance of, or the promise to perform, an act which the promisor is already under a legal obligation to carry out, ever amount to consideration? Three possible types of existing obligation may exist, and they need to be considered separately.

3.6.1   Existing duty imposed by law: public policy

Where the promisee is doing something which is a duty imposed by some public obligation, there is a reluctance to allow this to be used as the basis of a contract. It would clearly be contrary to public policy if, for example, an official with the duty to issue licences to market traders was allowed to make enforceable agreements under which the official received personal payment for issuing such a licence. The possibilities for corruption are obvious. It would be equally unacceptable for the householder whose house is on fire to be bound by a promise to a member of the fire brigade of payment for putting out the fire. The difficulty is in discerning whether the refusal to enforce such a contract is on the basis that it is vitiated as being contrary to public policy (which is discussed further in Chapter 10), or because the consideration which has been provided is not valid. The case law provides no clear answer. The starting point is *Collins v Godefroy* (1831). In this case a promise had been made to pay a witness, who was under an order to attend the court, six guineas for his trouble. It was held that this promise was unenforceable, because there was no consideration for it. This seems to have been on the basis that the duty to attend was 'a duty imposed by law'.

In cases where the possibilities for extortion are less obvious, there has been a greater willingness to regard performance of a existing non-contractual legal duty as being good consideration, though it must be said that the clearest statements to that effect have come from one judge, that is, Lord Denning. In *Ward v Byham* (1956) the duty was that of a mother to look after her illegitimate child. The father promised to make payments, provided that the child was well looked after, and happy, and was allowed to decide with whom she should live. Only the looking after the child could involve the provision of things of 'economic value' sufficient to amount to consideration. But the mother was already obliged to do this. Lord Denning had no doubt that this could, nevertheless, be good consideration:

> 'I have always thought that a promise to perform an existing duty, or the performance of it, should be regarded as good consideration, because it is a benefit to the person to whom it is given.'

The other two members of the Court of Appeal were not as explicit as Lord Denning, and seem to have regarded the whole package of what the father asked for as amounting to good consideration. This clearly went beyond the mother's exisiting obligation, but, as has been pointed out, did not involve anything of economic value. So, on either basis, the decision raises difficulties as regards consideration. Lord Denning returned to the same point in *Williams v Williams* (1957), which concerned a promise by a husband to make regular payments to his wife, who had deserted him, in return for her promise to maintain herself 'out of the said weekly sum or otherwise'. The question arose as to whether this provided any consideration for the husband's promise, since a wife in desertion had no claim on her husband for maintenance, and was in any case bound to support herself. Once again, Lord Denning commented:

> '[A] promise to perform an existing duty is, I think, sufficient consideration to support a promise, so long as there is nothing in the transaction which is contrary to the public interest.'

Once again, the other members of the Court of Appeal managed to find in the wife's favour without such an explicit statement. What this quote from Lord Denning makes clear, however, is that he regards the rule against using an existing non-contractual duty as consideration as being based on the requirements of the public interest, which would arise in the examples using government officials of one kind or another. Where this element is not present, however, he is saying that an existing duty of this kind can provide good consideration.

3.6.2   Existing duty imposed by law: other factors

The law on this issue remains uncertain, but in view of the recent developments in relation to contractual duties, in the case of *Williams v Roffey* (1990) which is discussed below (at para 3.6.9), it seems likely that Lord Denning's approach would be followed.

| 3.6.3 | Public duty: exceeding the duty |

Whatever the correct answer, it is clear that if what is promised or done goes beyond the existing duty imposed by law, then it can be regarded as good consideration. This applies whatever the nature of the duty, so that even as regards public officials, consideration may be provided by exceeding their statutory or other legal obligations. The point was confirmed in *Glasbrook Bros v Glamorgan CC* (1925). In the course of a strike at a coal mine, the owners of the mine were concerned that certain workers who had the obligation of keeping the mines safe and in good repair should not be prevented from carrying out their duties. They sought the assistance of the police in this. The police suggested the provision of a mobile group, but the owners insisted that the officers should be billeted on the premises. For this the owners promised to pay. Subsequently, however, they tried to deny any obligation to pay, claiming that the police were doing no more than fulfilling their legal obligation to keep the peace. It was held by the House of Lords that the provision of the force billeted on the premises went beyond what the police were obliged to do. Viscount Cave LC, accepted that if the police were simply taking the steps which they considered necessary to keep the peace etc, members of the public, who already pay for these police services through taxation, could not be made to pay again. Nevertheless, if at the request of a member of the public, the police provided services which went beyond what they (the police) reasonably considered necessary, this could provide good consideration for a promise of payment.

This rule is now generally accepted. In relation to the police the position is now dealt with largely by statute, but the approach taken in *Glasbrook* was confirmed in *Harris v Sheffield Utd FC* (1987), which concerned the provision of policing for football matches. The football club was held liable to pay for the services provided.

| 3.6.4 | Existing contractual duty owed to third party |

If a person is already bound to perform a particular act under a contract, can the performance of, or promise to perform, this act amount to good consideration for a contract with someone else? Suppose that A is contractually bound to deliver 5,000 widgets to B by 1 June. B is to use these widgets in producing items which he has contracted to supply to C. C therefore has an interest in A performing the contract for delivery to B on time, and promises A £5,000 if the goods are delivered by 1 June. Can A enforce this payment by C if the goods are delivered to B on the date required? Perhaps somewhat surprisingly, the courts have given a clear positive answer to this question. In other words, they have been quite happy to accept that doing something which forms part, or indeed the whole, of the consideration in one contract can perfectly well also be consideration in another contract. The starting point is the case of *Shadwell v Shadwell* (1860). An uncle promised his nephew, who was about to get married, the sum of £150 a year until the nephew's annual income as a barrister reached 600 guineas. The uncle paid 12 instalments on this basis, but then stopped. The nephew sued the uncle's estate for the outstanding instalments, to which the defence was raised that the nephew had provided no consideration. The nephew put forward his going through with the marriage as consideration. At the time, a promise to marry was as between the parties a legally enforceable contract. Nevertheless, the majority of the court had no doubt that performance of this contract could be used as consideration for the uncle's promise, on the basis that that promise was in effect an inducement to the nephew to go through with the marriage. Erle CJ recognised that there was some delicacy involved in categorising the nephew's marriage to the woman of his choice as a 'detriment' to him, but nevertheless considered that in financial terms it might well be.

This decision has been accepted as establishing the general principle that the performance of a contract with a third party can be good consideration. It was subsequently applied in a commercial context in *Scotson v Pegg* (1861), and was more recently accepted as good law in *The Eurymedon* (1974). Goods were being carried on a ship. The carriers contracted with a firm of stevedores to unload the ship. The consignees of the goods were taken to have promised the stevedores the benefit of an exclusion clause contained in the contract of carriage, if the stevedores unloaded the goods. The House of Lords viewed the stevedores performance of their unloading contract as being good consideration for this promise. As Lord Reid said:

3.6.5   Duty to third party: commercial application

> 'An agreement to do an act which the promisor is under an existing obligation to a third party to do, may quite well amount to consideration and does so in the present case: the promise obtains the benefit of a direct obligation which he can enforce.'

In all three cases so far considered it has been *performance* of the existing obligation which has constituted the consideration. Can a *promise* to perform an existing obligation also amount to consideration? To take the example used at the

3.6.6   Performance or promise?

start of this section, if A promises C that he will deliver on 1 June is there a contract, so that if A fails to deliver, C, as well as B, may sue for damages? This question was addressed by the Privy Council in *Pao On v Lau Yiu Long* (1979), where it was held that such a promise could be good consideration. Citing *The Eurymedon*, Lord Scarman simply stated (emphasis added):

> 'Their Lordships do not doubt that a *promise to perform*, or the performance of, a pre-existing contractual obligation to a third party can be valid consideration.'

Given the general approach to consideration, under which promises themselves can be good consideration, this decision is entirely consistent. The law on this point is, therefore, straightforward and simple. The fact that what is promised or performed is something which the promisor is already committed to do under a contract with someone else is irrelevant. Provided it has the other characteristics of valid consideration, it will be sufficient to make the new agreement enforceable.

3.6.7	Existing duty to the same promisor

The issue of whether an existing duty to the same promisor can be good consideration is the most difficult one of the three. If there is a contract between A and B, and A then promises B additional money for the performance of the same contract, is this promise binding? It would seem that the general answer should be 'no'. It is normally considered that once a contract is made, its terms are fixed. Any variation, to be binding, must be mutual, in the sense of both sides offering something additional. If the promise is simply to carry out exactly the same performance for extra money, it is totally one-sided. It would amount to a re-writing of the contract, and so should be unenforceable.

This approach was, until recently, taken to represent English law on this point. The authority was said to be the case of *Stilk v Myrick* (1809). The dispute arose out a contract between the crew of a ship and its owners. The crew had been employed to sail the ship from London to the Baltic and back. Part way through the voyage some of the crew deserted. The captain promised that if the rest of the crew sailed the ship back without the missing crew, the wages of the deserters would be divided among those who remained. When the ship returned to London, the owners refused to honour this promise. It was held that the sailors could not recover. There was some suggestion that this decision was based on public policy, in that there was a risk in this type of situation of the crew 'blackmailing' the captain into promising extra wages to avoid being stranded. Lord Ellenborough, however, seemed to base the decision on the lack of consideration. The remaining crew were only promising to do what they were already obliged to do under their existing contract, and this could not be good consideration.

It would have been different, of course, if the crew could have been said to be going beyond their existing duty. If, for example, so many of the crew had deserted that it was positively dangerous to proceed, then as in *Hartley v Ponsonby* (1857), an agreement to do so could amount to good consideration. The performance, or promise to perform, actions which were inside the existing duty could not, however, amount to consideration.

3.6.8   Going beyond the existing duty

The decision in *Stilk v Myrick* was accepted and applied, almost without question, in many cases (eg *North Ocean Shipping Co Ltd v Hyundai Construction Co* (1979), *Atlas Express v Kafco* (1989)), until 1990, when a decision of the Court of Appeal cast some doubt on its scope, and continued validity. This was in *Williams v Roffey* (1990). This case was concerned with a contract to refurbish a block of flats. The defendants were the main contractors for this work, and had engaged the plaintiffs as subcontractors to carry out carpentry work. The agreed price for this was £20,000. Part way through the contract, the plaintiffs got into financial difficulties, at least in part because the contract price for the carpentry work was too low. The defendants were worried that the plaintiffs would not complete the work on time, or would stop work altogether. There was a penalty clause in the main contract under which the defendants would have been liable in the event of late completion. The defendants therefore promised to pay the plaintiffs a further £10,300, at a rate of £575 for each flat completed. On this basis the plaintiffs continued to work on the flats, and completed a further eight. Because at this stage it seemed that the defendants were going to default on their promise of additional payments, the plaintiffs then ceased work, and subsequently sued for the additional sums in relation to the eight completed flats. The county court judge found for the plaintiffs, and the defendants appealed. The main issue before the Court of Appeal was whether there was any consideration for the promise to make the additional payments.

3.6.9   A re-consideration: *Williams v Roffey*

The defendants argued that since the plaintiffs in completing, or promising to complete, the work on the flats, were only doing something they were already bound to do under the existing contract with the defendants, they provided no new consideration. Glidewell LJ first outlined the benefits (as identified by counsel for the defendants) that accrued to the defendants from the plaintiffs' continuation with the contract. These were:

'(i) seeking to ensure that the plaintiff continued work and did not stop in breach of the sub-contract, (ii) avoiding the penalty for delay and (iii) avoiding the trouble and expense of engaging other people to complete the carpentry work.'

In the view of Glidewell LJ and the rest of the Court of Appeal, this was enough to support the defendant's promise to make the additional payments. In reaching this conclusion, all members of the court were at pains to stress that they were not suggesting that the principle in *Stilk v Myrick* was wrong, but that the present case could be distinguished from it.

3.6.10   *Williams v Roffey*: effect on *Stilk v Myrick*

The basis for this is not wholly clear from the judgments. Similar benefits to those identified could be said to have been present in *Stilk v Myrick*. For example, as a result of his promise, the captain did not have to seek replacement crew, avoided delays, and made sure the existing crew continued to work. The main reason for distinguishing *Stilk v Myrick* seems in fact to have beeen related to the alternative, public policy, basis for the decision mentioned above. In other words, the Court regarded it as significant that there was in *Williams v Roffey* no question of improper pressure having been put on the defendants. Indeed, it was they who suggested the increased payments.

The result is that the position as regards duties owed to the promisor is closely assimilated to the position in relation to duties owed to third parties. Thus Glidewell LJ summarised the current state of the law as follows:

'(i) if A has entered into a contract with B to do work for, or to supply goods or services to, B in return for payment by B and (ii) at some stage before A has completely performed his obligations under the contract B has reason to doubt whether A will, or will be able to, complete his side of the bargain and (iii) B thereupon promises A an additional payment in return for A's promise to perform his contractual obligations on time and (iv) as a result of giving his promise B obtains in practice a benefit, or obviates a disbenefit, then (vi) the benefit to B is capable of being consideration for B's promise, so that the promise will be legally binding.'

Williams v Roffey is clearly very significant as regards defining the limits of valid consideration, and undoubtedly has the effect of widening those limits. Promises to perform existing obligations can now amount to consideration, even between contracting parties. Nevertheless, within these wider limits, consideration must still be found, as Russell LJ makes clear:

'Consideration there must..be but in my judgment the courts nowadays should be more ready to find its existence so as to reflect the intention of the parties to the contract where the bargaining powers are not unequal and where the finding of consideration reflects the true intention of the parties.'

We now turn to consider the way in which the doctrine of consideration affects the freedom of parties to vary the obligations under a contract which they have entered into.

3.7   Consideration and the variation of contracts

We have already referred to the general principle that for a contract to be altered there must be consideration. To use the language of the courts, 'accord and satisfaction' must be present: 'accord' meaning agreement, and 'satisfaction' essentially consideration. The approach taken in *Stilk v Myrick*, as redefined in *Williams v Roffey* fits into this general principle. The same approach applies where a contract is brought to an end by mutual agreement. As long as there are outstanding obligations on both sides of the contract, the agreement to terminate will be binding.

3.7.1   Need for accord and satisfaction

Over the years, however, this approach, though still applied where appropriate, has often been found in practice too restrictive. Various concepts have been used to allow more flexibility, and to give some force to agreed variations, even where these are not supported by consideration. One such is the concept of 'waiver'. Under this principle a person who 'waives' (that is, promises not to enforce) certain rights under a contract for a period of time, may be stopped from later insisting on performance in accordance with the letter of the contract. So in *Hartley v Hymans* (1920) a seller requested to be allowed to make late delivery, and the buyer agreed to this. When the seller delivered, the buyer refused to accept. It was held that the seller was entitled to recover damages, despite the fact that delivery was outside the terms of the contract, and that the buyer's promise to accept late delivery was unsupported by consideration. The buyer had waived the right to insist on delivery at a particular time, and could not go back on that.

3.7.2   The concept of 'waiver'

Waiver was used by the common law courts, but was taken over by the chancery courts, and is now almost exclusively an equitable concept. It is important to note that waiver may not be permanent in its effect. The person waiving their rights may do so for a fixed period of time, or may be able to revive their original right by giving notice. The latter was the case in *Charles Rickards Ltd v Oppenheim* (1950). In a contract for the sale of a car, delivery was specified for a particular date. The buyer, however, did not sue for breach of contract as soon as the date had passed, but continued to seek delivery. This was regarded as the buyer's having waived the right to delivery at a particular time. Eventually, however, the buyer's patience ran out, and he specified a further date on which delivery must be made. This allowed the seller a reasonable time to deliver, and it was held that as soon as this date was passed the buyer was entitled to sue for breach. The waiver had been withdrawn.

Looked at in this way the concept of equitable waiver has clear links with the common law concept of estoppel. This is the rule, whereby if A, a party to an action has made a statement of fact on which the other party, B, has relied, A will not be allowed to deny that the original statement was untrue. This rule only applies to *statements of exisiting fact*, however. In *Jorden v Money* (1854) an attempt was made to apply it to a promise not to enforce a debt. It was held that this was not possible, since the doctrine of estoppel in the strict sense had no application to promises. Nevertheless, it has become common in recent years, following certain developments which will be looked at in more detail below, to refer to equitable waiver as 'promissory estoppel'.

3.8 **The doctrine of promissory estoppel**	The modern law on this topic, which gives rise to situations in which a contract can in effect be varied without there being consideration, derives from *Central London Property Trust Ltd v High Trees House Ltd* (1947). The plaintiffs were the owners of a block of flats in London, which they rented to the defendants at a rent of £2,500 pa. Following the outbreak of the Second World War in 1939, the defendants were unable to find sufficient tenants to take the flats, because of the large numbers of people leaving London. As a result the plaintiffs agreed that 'for the duration' (which was taken to mean the duration of the war), the rent could be reduced by half, to £1,250 pa. This arrangement continued until after the war ended in 1945. The plaintiffs then sought to return to the original terms of the agreement, and also queried whether they might not be entitled to claim the other half of the rent for the war years, since the promised to accept less was not supported by any consideration. Denning J, as he then was, confirmed that the plaintiffs were entitled to recover the full rent from the end of the war. Their promise to take less had clearly only been intended to last until that point. On the more general issue, however, on which his views were strictly *obiter*, he considered that the plaintiffs would not be able to recover the balance for the war years. The reason for this was that he thought that there was a general equitable principle whereby:

'A promise intended to be binding, intended to be acted upon, and in fact acted on, is binding so far as its terms properly apply.'

His main authority for this view was the 'equitable waiver' case of *Hughes v Metropolitan Rly* (1877). The defendant held a lease of certain houses from the plaintiff. The lease contained a covenant of repair within six months of being given notice. The plaintiff gave such notice. The defendant then suggested that a sale might be arranged, and said that they would defer carrying out any repairs until this had been discussed. Some negotiations took place, but they did not result in an agreement for the sale. The plaintiff then served notice to quit, on the basis of the defendant's failure to comply with the original notice to repair. It was held that the plaintiff was not entitled to do this. The effect of the notice had been suspended while the negotiations on the sale were taking place, and time did not start to run again until these had broken down. Lord Cairns stated the general principle in the following famous passage:

'[I]t is the first principle on which all Courts of Equity proceed, that if parties who have entered in to definite and distinct terms involving certain legal results - certain penalties or legal forfeiture - afterwards by their own act or with their own consent enter upon a course of negotiation which has the effect of leading one of the parties to suppose that the strict rights arising under the contract will not be enforced, or will be kept in suspense, or held in abeyance, the person who otherwise might have enforced those rights will not be allowed to enforce them where it would be inequitable having regard to the dealings which have thus taken place between the parties.'

Denning in *High Trees* asserted that this general principle supported his view of the relationship between the parties in the case before him. His own statement of the general principle (noted above), however, raised considerable controversy. First, taken at face value, it seemed to destroy the doctrine of consideration altogether. Secondly, the application of the 'equitable waiver' approach to the facts of the case, that is the non-payment of rent, appeared to run counter to the House of Lords decision in *Foakes v Beer* (1884) which stated that part payment of a debt can never be good satisfaction for the whole. Both of these objections, and their treatment in subsequent case law, must now be considered.

3.8.1 Implications of *High Trees*

The first point to consider is whether the doctrine of promissory estoppel as restated and developed by Lord Denning, does strike at the heart of the doctrine of consideration. The answer to this is that the broad statement of Denning in *High Trees* has

3.9 Promissory estoppel and consideration

been limited by subsequent decisions. There are five suggested limitations, of which four certainly apply: the status of the fifth is less clear.

3.9.1	There must be an existing legal relationship	Promissory estoppel cannot exist in a vacuum. There must be an existing legal relationship between the parties which is being altered by the promissory estoppel. This will generally, though not necessarily, be a contract (*Durham Fancy Goods Ltd v Michael Jackson (Fancy Goods) Ltd* (1968)). As Lord Denning said in *Combe v Combe* (1951), consideration remains 'a cardinal necessity of the formation of a contract, but not of its modification or discharge.'
3.9.2	There must have been (detrimental) reliance	Under the normal rules for the creation of a contract, obligations may arise as soon as promises have been exchanged. There is no need for either side to have relied on the other's promise in order to be able to enforce it. In relation to promissory estoppel, however, the party trying to enforce the promise must have taken some action on it. This simply means taking some action as a result of it, for example, paying the lower rent, as in *High Trees*. In some cases, it has been suggested that the promisee must have suffered a detriment from such reliance, but Lord Denning has consistently denied that this is necessary (for example, *WJ Alan &Co v El Nasr Export & Import Co* (1972)). The general view now is that reliance is enough, without detriment needing to be shown.
3.9.3	The doctrine can only be used as a 'shield not a sword'	This limitation derives from *Combe v Combe* (1951). In this case a husband and wife were getting divorced. Between the decree nisi and absolute, the husband agreed to pay his wife £100 per annum net of tax. The husband never paid any money, and after seven years his former wife sued on the basis of his promise. Byrne J held that, while there was no consideration for the husband's promise, the wife could recover on the basis of the *High Trees* decision. The Court of Appeal, including Lord Denning, thought that this was a inappropriate use of the doctrine. It could not form the basis of a cause of action, and would generally only be available as a defence - 'as a shield, not a sword.' As Lord Denning pointed out, it was only in relation to the variation or discharge of contractual obligations that the need for consideration was reduced by the doctrine of promissory estoppel. In relation to the creation of such obligations consideration remains an essential element.
3.9.4	It must be inequitable for the promisor to go back on the promise	Promissory estoppel is, as we have seen, derived from the concept of equitable waiver. Thus, as an equitable doctrine, its use is in the discretion of the courts, and even if the other elements for the applicability of it exist, it may still not be

applied because it would be inequitable in the circumstances to do so. A clear example of the kind of situation where this would apply is the case of *D & C Builders v Rees* (1966). The plaintiff builders had done work for the defendants, and were owed nearly £500. After pressing for payment for some time, the plaintiff agreed to take £300 in satisfaction of the account. Mrs Rees, who knew that the plaintiffs were in financial difficulties, had told them that that was all they were likely to get. Despite their promise to accept the £300 (a promise for which there was no consideration), the builders then sought to recover the balance of the debt. Lord Denning (again!) in the Court of Appeal, held that although there was clearly a promise here of a type which might raise promissory estoppel, the element of intimidation in the defendant's behaviour, knowingly taking advantage of the plaintiff's circumstance, meant that it was not inequitable to allow the plaintiffs to go back on their promise. (The other members of the Court of Appeal did not think it was even necessary to discuss the doctrine.)

The inequity in *D & C Builders* was fairly obvious. The concept of 'equitability' does not necessarily imply impropriety on the part of the promisee, however. In *The Post Chaser* (1982) the promise was made and withdrawn within a few days. Although the other side had relied on the promise, their position had not in fact been prejudiced by such reliance. It was not, therefore, inequitable to allow the promisor to withdraw the promise.

This is the limitation on promissory estoppel about which there is most uncertainty. There is no doubt that in some circumstances a promissory estoppel will have a purely suspensory effect. In *Hughes v Metropolitan Rly*, for example, the notice of obligation to repair was simply put in abeyance while the negotiations over a possible sale continued. It is also clear that in relation to some sorts of contract, the effect can be to both extinguish some rights and suspend others. This is what happened in *High Trees* itself. Because the promise was interpreted as having only been intended to be applicable during the war ('for the duration'), once that was over, the original terms of the lease automatically revived. Even if the promise is expressed to last indefinitely, however, in some circumstances it may be withdrawn by giving appropriate notice. In *Tool Metal Manufacturing Co v Tungsten Electric Company* (1955) for example, there was a promise to accept a reduced royalty in relation to the operation of some patents. It was held that the promisor could withdraw the promise by giving reasonable notice, from which point the original terms of the agreement would come back into operation. The House

3.9.5   The doctrine is only suspensory in its effect

of Lords in fact held that the initiation of a previous, unsuccessful, action to escape from the promise constituted notice of withdrawal. It is in relation to this type of continuing contract, therefore, that promissory estoppel operates to both extinguish and suspend contractual rights. The obligations to make the higher payments during the period of the operation promise in both *High Trees*, and *TMMC v TEC*, were destroyed. The promisor was unable to recover the additional amounts for that period. The original terms were not in themselves extinguished, however, and could be reinstated for the future.

What is not clear is whether the doctrine of promissory estoppel could be used to extinguish, rather than suspend, an obligation which is not a continuing obligation. If, for example, the issue of inequitability had not arisen in *D & C Builders v Rees*, would promissory estoppel have wiped out, or simply postponed, the payment of the balance? It seems clear that if the doctrine is to have any place at all in relation to this type of obligation, it must have the effect of extinguishing the right altogether. It would make no sense to say that the Rees's could rely on D & C Builders' promise to remit the balance of the debt, but that at any time the obligation to pay it could be revived by the giving of notice. It should be remembered, however, that it was only Lord Denning who seriously considered applying promissory estoppel in this situation, and that there has been no other reported case in which the doctrine has been applied to this kind of obligation.

The conclusion must be, then, that the precise effect of promissory estoppel, in terms of whether it suspends or extinguishes rights, will depend on the nature of the promise, and the type of contract to which it applies. It is not true to say, however, that promissory estoppel *only* operates in a suspensory way.

3.10   Promissory estoppel and the part payment of debts

The common law position on the part payment of debts is to be found in *Pinnel's* case (1602), as confirmed by the House of Lords in *Foakes v Beer* (1884). The rule is that part payment of a debt on the date that it is due can never be satisfaction for the full amount owed. The creditor will still be able to recover the balance of the debt, unless the debtor can show that some consideration was supplied in return for the creditor's agreement to take the lesser sum. Thus if payment is made early, or on the day, but at a different place from that specified in the contract, the debt may be discharged. Equally, if the debtor provides goods, or services, instead of cash, this , if accepted by the creditor, will discharge the debt fully, even if the value of what was supplied is less than the total amount owed: 'the gift of a horse, a hawk, or a robe, in satisfaction is good'. Thus the payment of £5 on the due date could never discharge a debt of £100; but if the debtor offered and the creditor accepted a book worth £5 in satisfaction, the creditor could not then claim the balance of £95. The justification for this rather odd rule is that the book must have been regarded by the creditor as more beneficial than money, otherwise it would not have been accepted, and the court will not inquire further into the creditor's motives.

The rule in *Pinnel's* case was strictly *obiter*, in that the debtor had paid early, and had therefore provided sufficient consideration to discharge the whole debt, but it was confirmed by the House of Lords in *Foakes v Beer*. Dr Foakes owed Mrs Beer a sum of money in relation to a judgment debt. Mrs Beer agreed that Dr Foakes could pay this off in instalments. When he had done so, Mrs Beer sued to recover the interest on the debt, in relation to the delay in the completion of payment resulting from the payment by instalments. The House of Lords held that, even if Mrs Beer had promised to forgo the interest (which was by no means certain), it was an unenforceable promise, because Dr Foakes had provided no consideration for it.

3.10.1   The decision in
          Foakes v Beer

It is important to note that *Foakes v Beer* was decided in 1884, that is, seven years after *Hughes v Metropolitan Rly*. *Hughes* was not even cited in the later case. Given that several members of the House of Lords in *Foakes v Beer* expressed some unhappiness about the outcome to which they felt that the common law bound them, so that they would gladly have accepted an escape route via the equitable doctrine of waiver, if that had been available, it must be assumed that the approach taken in *Hughes* was considered to have no relevance to the situation of part payment of debts. This, then, was a further way in which Lord Denning's decision in *Central London Property Trust v High Trees House* broke new ground. The case was concerned, in effect, with the partial payment of a debt (that is, half the rent for the war years). Nevertheless, Denning felt able to apply to it the *Hughes* principle of 'equitable waiver', and it seems now to be generally accepted that this doctrine, in its new guise of 'promissory estoppel', can mitigate the harshness of the rule in *Foakes v Beer*, in appropriate cases. This is not to say that *Foakes v Beer* would definitely be decided differently if it came before the House of Lords again today. That would depend on what exactly Mrs Beer was found to have promised, and also on whether promissory estoppel can ever be applied to extinguish a 'one-off' debt as opposed to payment obligations under a continuing contract. This issue has been discussed in the previous section, in considering whether promissory estoppel is only suspensory in its effect.

3.11 Other types of estoppel

Before leaving this area, we should also note two other types of estoppel which can have an effect on the operation of a contract. First there is *estoppel by convention*. This arises where the parties to an agreement have acted on the basis that some provision in the contract has a particular meaning. This type of estoppel will operate to prevent one of the parties later trying to argue that the provision means something different. An example of its use is *Amalgamated Investment and Property Co Ltd* (AIP) *v Texas Commerce International Bank Ltd* (TCIB) (1981). In this case a contract of guarantee between AIP and TCIB contained a promise by AIP to repay money 'owed to you' (that is, TCIB) by a subsidiary of AIP (ANPP). In fact, ANPP had been lent the money not by TCIB direct, but by a specially created subsidiary of TCIB named 'Portsoken'. When AIP got into financial difficulties, the liquidator sought a declaration that the guarantee was not binding, because there was no money owed to TCIB. It was held, however, that all parties had acted on the basis that the wording of the guarantee referred to the money lent by Portsoken to ANPP, and on that basis an estoppel by convention operated to prevent AIP arguing for a different meaning.

The second type of estoppel which needs to be noted is *proprietary estoppel*. This operates in relation to rights in land only. It also differs from promissory estoppel (though both are sometimes confusingly referred to as 'equitable estoppel') in that it may be used to found a cause of action. In other words it can be used as a sword rather than a shield. An example of its use is *Crabb v Arun District Council* (1975). Mr Crabb owned a plot of land adjacent to a road. He decided to sell one half of the plot to the Arun District Council (ADC). The ADC built a road along one edge of the piece of land which they had bought. Mr Crabb was allowed access to this road from a particular point on the land which he had retained. Mr Crabb then decided to sell another portion of this land. On the basis of a promise from the council that he would be allowed another access point on to their road, he sold the piece of land containing the first access point. The ADC, despite the fact that they had initially left a gap in their fencing at an appropriate point, then refused to allow the second access. The result was that the piece of land which Mr Crabb had retained was completely blocked in, without any access from either the original road, or the road built by the ADC. Mr Crabb brought an action to compel the ADC to grant him the second access point which had been promised. Although there was no consideration for this promise, Mr Crabb succeeded in his action. The words and actions of the ADC had led Mr Crabb to believe that he would have the second access point, and he had relied on this to his detriment in selling the piece of land containing the first access point. The Court of Appeal therefore allowed him to succeed on the basis of a proprietary estoppel.

Before we leave the topic of consideration, we should note briefly the views of Professor Atiyah on this issue, as set out, *inter alia*, in 'Consideration: A Re-Statement', reproduced as Chapter 8 of his *Essays on Contract*.

3.12   Atiyah's view of consideration

Atiyah's view is that 'consideration' originated simply as an indication of the need for a 'reason' for enforcing a promise or obligation, such as the fact that the promisee had given something to the promisor in expectation that the promise would be fulfilled. It became formalised, however, into a rigid set of rules, such as that there must be benefit and detriment; that past consideration is no consideration; that consideration must be of economic value; and that gratuitous promises will not generally be enforced.

In examining how these rules actually operate, however, Atiyah argues that they are not actually followed rigidly by the courts. For example, as regards the need for benefit/detriment, he cites *Chappell v Nestlé* (para 3.4.1) and *Hamer v Sidway* (above) as indicating that this is not necessary for a contract. Nor is it sufficient, in that contracts in which there is clearly benefit or detriment may still not be enforced, as we shall see in later chapters, because of considerations of illegality, duress, or undue influence. In relation to the need for economic value, *Ward v Byham* (above para 3.4.1) may be seen as an exception.

Moreover, the unenforceability of gratuitous promises is not applied where promissory estoppel operates. Atiyah argues that promissory estoppel, as expounded in *High Trees*, was a step in the right direction, following a wrong turning taken as a result of the misinterpretation of *Jorden v Money* as an authority for the proposition that a statement of intention cannot give rise to an estoppel. That case was actually decided as it was, according to Atiyah, because of the requirements of the Statute of Frauds, which at the time required that a promise given in consideration of marriage (which was the situation in *Jorden v Money*) had to be proved by writing. Because there was no writing, the case could not be pleaded in contract and was therefore pleaded as estoppel, but the court refused to allow this to be used as a means of circumventing the requirements of the Statute of Frauds. *High Trees*, which recognised the enforceability of a statement of intention which had been relied on, should have shown the way forward, but was thrown off course by *Combe v Combe* (above para 3.9.3: the 'shield not a sword' case). The real reason for the decision in that case, Atiyah says, was not the fact that the wife was trying to use promissory estoppel as a cause of action, but that justice was not on her side, because she was earning more than her ex-husband. This was a reason (or consideration?) for not enforcing the husband's promise. But in general, where there has been reasonable reliance on a promise, even if the promisee has not provided what we should recognise as 'consideration' in the technical sense, Atiyah is of the view that the promise should be enforceable. This concept of reliance would, he argues, be a more satisfactory way of determining the existence of contractual obligations, as opposed to the formalistic requirement of consideration, with all its technical limitations.

Atityah is not trying to substitute his own rigid doctrine of consideration for the current orthodoxy. What he is saying is that we should recognise the original idea of 'consideration' as meaning a reason for enforcing a promise, or acknowledging an obligation. This would be a much more flexible doctrine. The disadvantage, however, is that it would also be rather uncertain and unpredictable, and might depend too much on what the individual judge thinks amounts to a sufficient reason for enforcing a promise on a particular set of facts.

One possible basis on which this might be done is by giving a greater status to the requirement of 'intention to create legal relations'. We shall now return to more orthodox waters, and consider the role which this concept currently plays in determining the existence of contractual obligations.

| 3.13 | **Intention to create legal relations** | In many ways the requirements of offer, acceptance and consideration, may be regarded in themselves as indications of an intention to enter into a legally binding contract. Indeed, some have argued that there is no need for a separate heading of intention. The generally accepted view, however, is that there are some agreements which may have all the other characteristics of a contract, but which are nevertheless not to be regarded as legally binding. If for example, there is an agreement between a man and a woman that he will cook a meal for them both, in return for her providing the wine to go with it, this may involve an offer, acceptance, and consideration, but no-one would expect it to be regarded as legally binding. Equally, if the parties to an apparently binding commercial agreement specifically state that it is not |

to have legal consequences, should not the courts pay attention to this? In fact, English law operates on the basis of 'presumptions' as to intention, which differ according to whether the agreement is to be regarded as 'domestic' or 'commercial'. These two categories of agreement must therefore be looked at separately.

The leading case with regard to domestic agreements is *Balfour v Balfour* (1919). This involved an agreement between husband and wife, resulting from her inability (due to illness), to return with him to his place of work, in Ceylon. He agreed to pay her £30 per month while they were apart. Later the marriage broke down and the wife sued the husband for his failure to make the promised payments. The Court of Appeal held that her action must fail. Two members of the court centred their decision on the lack of any consideration supplied by the wife. Atkin LJ, however, stressed that even if there were consideration, domestic arrangements of this kind are clearly not intended by the parties to be legally binding. This judgment is the one which has been relied on in subsequent case law, and has been taken as establishing the position that in relation to domestic agreements there is a presumption that they are not intended to be legally binding.

There are two points to be noted here. First, the notion of the 'domestic' agreement relates more to the subject-matter than the relationship between the parties. If, for example, a woman agrees to sell her brother her car for £1,500, there seems little reason to deny this agreement the status of a contract. On the other hand, social arrangements between friends who are not related, or household agreements between a couple living together, but not married, will come in to the category of 'domestic', and will be presumed not to be binding.

Secondly, the rule is simply based on a presumption, and it will be possible for that to be rebutted. In *Merritt v Merritt* (1970), for example, an arrangement between husband and wife similar to that agreed in *Balfour v Balfour*, but here made in the context of the break up of the marriage, was held to be legally binding. In *Simpkins v Pays* (1955) an agreement to share in the winnings of a competition jointly entered by people living in the same house was enforced. And in *Parker v Clark* (1960), in relation to an arrangement whereby a young couple agreed to live with older relatives, the presumption was held to be rebutted. The young couple, by taking the serious step of selling their own property, had indicated that the arrangement was intended to be legally binding.

3.13.2	Commercial agreements	If the agreement is not a 'domestic' one, then it will be regarded as 'commercial'. This will mean that the presumption is that the agreement is intended to be legally binding. In *Edwards v Skyways* (1964) Megaw J emphasised that there will be a heavy onus on a party to such an agreement who wishes to argue that the presumption has been rebutted. In that case the plaintiff was a pilot who had been made redundant. As part of the arrangements for this he was offered and accepted a payment which was stated to be *ex gratia*. The company then found that the terms which had been offered would be more expensive for it than it had realised, and denied that there was any legal obligation to make the payment. The judge held that *ex gratia* did not mean 'not legally binding', but simply recognised that prior to the offer being made there had been no obligation to make such a payment. However, once it had been made and accepted as part of the redundancy arrangement, it was capable of being legally binding, and there was no evidence to overturn the presumption that this should be the case.

A similar reluctance to overturn the presumption is shown by the House of Lords decision in *Esso Petroleum Ltd v Commissioners of Customs and Excise* (1976). This concerned a 'special offer' of a common type, under which garage owners offered a free 'World Cup Coin' to every purchaser of four gallons of petrol. The coins could be collected to make a set, but had mininal intrinsic value. Nevertheless, the majority of the House held that there was a unilateral contract under which the garage proprietor was saying 'If you will buy four gallons of my petrol, I will give you one of these coins,' and that this was intended to be legally binding.

It is possible, however, by using sufficiently explicit wording, to rebut the presumption even in relation to a clearly commercial agreement. *Rose & Frank Co v Crompton Bros* (1925) was concerned with a continuing agency arrangement between two companies. The agreement specifically stated that it was not entered into as 'a formal or legal agreement', but was 'only a definite expression and record of the purpose and intention' of the parties. The House of Lords held that this was not a legally binding agreement and could therefore be terminated without notice.

3.13.3	Letters of comfort	Finally, the status of 'letters of comfort' should be noted. Such 'letters' are often used as a means of encouraging a creditor to lend money to a subsidiary or related company of the issuer of letter. The effect of a letter of this kind was considered in *Kleinwort Benson v Malaysian Mining Corporation* (1989). The relevant letter had been given by the defendants to the plaintiff

bank as part of a loan to a subsidiary of the defendants, MMC
Metals Ltd. It stated that 'It is our policy to ensure that the
business of MMC Metals Ltd is at all times in the position to
meet its liabilities to you.' When the subsidiary went into
liquidation, and the bank tried to recover from the defendants,
they argued that the letter had never been intended to create a
legal relationship. The trial judge disagreed, and held them
liable. The Court of Appeal, however, construed the letter as
simply stating the defendants' present intentions at the time
the letter was issued, and not representing a promise as to
future conduct. On that basis the plaintiff's action failed. But
there is nothing in the judgment of the Court of Appeal to
suggest that an appropriately worded letter of comfort, stating,
perhaps, 'it will at all times be our policy to ensure ...', would
not be regarded as intended to create legal relations.

Summary of Chapter 3

Consideration and Intention

Consideration may be defined as what one party to an agreement is giving, or promising, in exchange for what is being given or promised from the other side. It provides the mutuality which makes an agreement enforceable.

Consideration involves a detriment to the party providing it, or a benefit to the party receiving it.

Mutual promises are sufficient to constitute consideration.

Consideration need not be 'adequate'. The value of what is provided by way of consideration does not have to match what it being given in exchange: *Thomas v Thomas* (1842).

Consideration must be 'sufficient'. It must be of economic value (*White v Bluett* (1853)), but this requirement is not applied very strictly: *Chappell v Nestlé* (1960); *De La Bere v Pearson* (1908).

Past consideration is no consideration: *Re McArdle* (1951). But note the exceptions as set out in *Pao On v Lay Yiu Long* (1980), where there is (i) a prior request; (ii) an expectation of payment; and (iii) the payment would have been legally enforceable if promised in advance.

The performance of existing duties:

- Imposed by law

    This may well not amount to consideration (*Collins v Godefroy* (1831)) unless something additional is provided (*Glasbrook v Glamorgan CC* (1925)). But note Lord Denning's opposing view (eg *Williams v Williams* (1957)).

- Owed to a third party under another contract

    This will be good consideration: *Shadwell v Shadwell* (1860); *The Eurymedon* (1975); *Pao On v Lau Yiu Long* (1980).

- Owed to same promisor under a contract

    The position is uncertain. *Stilk v Myrick* (1809) states that this is not good consideration, unless something additional is provided (*Hartley v Ponsonby* (1857)); *Williams v Roffey* (1990), however, has established a potentially broad exception to this.

Consideration

Performance of existing duties

Consideration and the variation of contracts	An agreed variation which is supported by consideration will be fully enforceable.

An agreed variation which is supported by consideration will be fully enforceable.

- The concept of waiver

  A party may waive rights under a contract for a fixed period, or until notice is given to terminate the waiver: *Charles Rickards v Oppenheim* (1950). (This was a common law doctrine, now taken over by equity.) Note the link with estoppel, which operates in a similar way in relation to statements of existing fact only: *Jorden v Money* (1854).

- The doctrine of 'promissory estoppel'

  Invented by Denning in *Central London Property Trust v High Trees House* (1947) (relying on *Hughes v Metropolitan Rly* (1877)) - 'a promise intended to be binding intended to be acted upon, and in fact acted on, is binding in so far as its terms properly apply.'

Promissory estoppel and consideration

Promissory estoppel does not destroy the doctrine of consideration, because:

- it only applies where there is an existing legal relationship: *Durham Fancy Goods Ltd v Michael Jackson (Fancy Goods) Ltd* (1968);

- the promisee must have relied on the promise - though not necessarily to the promisee's detriment: *WJ Alan & Co v El Nasr Export & Import Co* (1972);

- the doctrine can only be used as a shield not a sword: *Combe v Combe* (1951);

- it must be inequitable for the promisor to go back on the promise: *D & C Builders v Rees* (1966); *The Post Chaser* (1982);

- the doctrine is, at least in some circumstances, only suspensory in its effect: *Tool Metal Manufacturing Co v Tungsten Electric Company* (1955). Note that is not clear to what extent this can or should apply outside the context of 'continuing' contracts (such as leases, or agreements for royalty payments).

Promissory estoppel and the part payment of debts

The doctrine of promissory estoppel and the part payment of debts may be taken to limit the common law rule as laid down in *Pinnel's* case (1602) and *Foakes v Beer* (1884) (that is, that payment of less than is owed on the due date can never satisfy the full debt, though payment early, or at a different place, or with something other than money, may do so).

Note 'estoppel by convention' (*Amalgamated Investment and Property Co Ltd v Texas Commerce International Bank Ltd* (1981); and also 'proprietary estoppel' (*Crabb v Arun District Council* (1975)).

Other types of estoppel

Atiyah argues that 'consideration' originally meant a 'reason for enforcing an agreement'. Problems have arisen from a misunderstanding of the case of *Jorden v Money*, and the development of a rather rigid doctrine of consideration. It would be more satisfactory to return to a concept of 'reasonable reliance' as the basis for enforcing agreements, as opposed to the current very formalistic approach, as exemplified by *Foakes v Beer*.

Atiyah's view of consideration

The identification of an intention to create legal relations depends on presumptions:

Intention to create legal relations

- Domestic agreements

  Presumed not to be intended to be legally binding: *Balfour v Balfour* (1919). Presumption can be rebutted, for example, where agreement is made in connection with the break-up of a marriage (*Merritt v Merritt* (1970)), or one party has undertaken a major commitment indicating an intention to be legally bound (*Parker v Clark* (1960)).

- Commercial agreements

  Will be presumed to be binding, and this presumption will be difficult to rebut: *Edwards v Skyways* (1964). Very clear words will be needed in order to do so: *Rose & Frank Co v Crompton Bros* (1925). Note also the effect of 'comfort letters' as discussed in *Kleinwort Benson v Malaysian Mining Corporation* (1989).

Chapter 4

Privity

The doctrine of privity is regarded as one of the fundamental characteristics of the English law of contract, although as will be seen later in this chapter, the courts have recognised a number of exceptions to it and sanctioned a variety of devices for avoiding its effect. Its essence is the idea that only those who are parties to a contract can have rights or liabilities under it. It is closely linked to the rule that consideration must move from the promisee, but can be shown to be distinct from it. Suppose, for example, that Aadvark Ltd agrees to buy shares from Bison Plc, provided that Cheetah Ltd (which is a subsidiary of Bison) makes a loan to Aadvark. If Cheetah makes the loan, but Aadvark breaks its promise to Bison, who can sue? Not Bison, who has supplied no consideration. But neither can Cheetah, although it has supplied consideration, because it is not a party to the agreement between Aadvark and Bison.

What is the reason for the doctrine? It is clearly justifiable as a general rule that the burden of a contract should not be placed on a third party. It is less clear that the same applies to a benefit. Suppose that Alison promises Bernard that she will pay £100 to Oxfam if Bernard gives up smoking for a year. This is a contract which (subject to the question of intention to create legal relations) is clearly enforceable by Bernard. But the charity which is to benefit will not be allowed to enforce, because it is not a party to the agreement. Treitel argues that once again, the answer lies with the doctrine of consideration (*Law of Contract*, 8th ed, pp 528):

> 'A system of law which does not give a gratuitous promisee a right to enforce a promise is not likely to give this right to a gratuitous beneficiary who is not even a promisee.'

This aspect of the privity doctrine has, however, attracted much criticism, and the Law Commission has put forward proposals for its reform, which are discussed later in this chapter. For the moment, this will be accepted as the basic rule, and we turn to look at the development of the doctrine.

There were some decisions dating from the 17th Century which allowed a third party beneficiary to enforce a promise, but these pre-dated the strict formulation of the doctrine of consideration. The modern law is generally taken to derive from the case of *Tweddle v Atkinson* (1861). This concerned an

4.1 The doctrine of privity

4.2 Development of the doctrine

agreement reached between the fathers of a couple who were about to get married, under which the father of the bride was to pay £200 and the father of the groom £100, to the bridegroom, William Tweddle, the plaintiff. William sought to enforce his father-in-law's promise, but it was held that he could not. The main justification appears to have been that it was necessary for there to be mutuality of obligations as between those enforcing a contract and having it enforced against them. As Crompton J put it:

> 'It would be a monstrous proposition to say that a person was a party to the contract for the purpose of suing upon it for his own advantage, and not a party to it for the purpose of being sued.'

It will be noted that it would have been quite possible for the Court to have found that William Tweddle had provided consideration for the promise. The agreement was clearly made in consideration of William's marriage, and, as we saw in the last chapter, in *Shadwell v Shadwell* (1860), decided just a year before *Tweddle v Atkinson*, going through with a marriage ceremony can be good consideration. This again indicates that the doctrine of privity is properly regarded as separate from, though closely linked to, the doctrine of consideration.

4.2.1   Affirmation by the House of Lords

Tweddle v Atkinson was a decision of the court of Queen's Bench, but the principle it stated was re-affirmed by the House of Lords in a commercial context in *Dunlop Pneumatic Tyre Co Ltd v Selfridge & Co Ltd* (1915). This concerned an attempt by Dunlop to control the price at which their tyres were sold to the public. They had a contract with Dew & Co, who were wholesalers in motor accessories, that in selling the tyres to retailers they would require the retailer to undertake to observe Dunlop's list price. Sefridge & Co entered into such an agreement with Dew & Co. Dunlop subsequently sought an injunction and damages in relation to alleged breaches of this agreement. The House of Lords held that they could not succeed. The following passage from the speech of Viscount Haldane LC, indicates the approach taken:

> 'My Lords, in the law of England certain principles are fundamental. One is that only a person who is a party to a contract can sue on it. Our law knows nothing a *jus quaesitum tertio* arising by way of contract. Such a right may be conferred by way of property, as, for example, under a trust, but it cannot be conferred on a stranger to a contract as a right to enforce the contract *in personam*. A second principle is that if a person with whom a contract not under seal has been made is to be able to enforce it consideration must have been given by him to the promisor or to some other person at the promisor's request.'

On both grounds Dunlop were doomed to failure. They were not parties to the agreement between Dew and Selfridge, and moreover, had provided no consideration for Selfridge's promise not to sell below the list price. Note also that, although this was not raised as an issue in the case, Dunlop could not, of course, rely on the terms of their contract with Dew, because Selfridge were not a party to this contract.

The doctrine is not one for which the courts have shown any great affection, but it was again re-affirmed by the House of Lords in 1968 in the case of *Beswick v Beswick*. A nephew had bought his uncle's coal merchant's business, and had promised as part of the deal, to pay his uncle £6.50 a week, and then, when his uncle died, to pay his aunt (if she survived) £5 a week. After his uncle's death, the nephew refused to make the payments to his aunt, and she sued. In the Court of Appeal Lord Denning tried to open up a broad exception to the doctrine of privity by relying on s 56(1) of the Law of Property Act 1925, which states that:

'A person may take an immediate or other interest in land or other property, or the benefit of any condition, right of entry, covenant or agreement over or respecting land or other property, although he may not be named as a party to the conveyance or other instrument.'

Lord Denning's view (with which Danckwerts LJ agreed) was that this in effect abolished the doctrine of privity in relation to written contracts, and therefore allowed Mrs Beswick to sue her nephew on the promise made to her husband for her benefit. The House of Lords rejected this, deciding that the history and context of s 56 meant that it should be interpreted as not intended to apply to a straightforward contractual situation such as that in *Beswick v Beswick*, although the exact scope of the section remains uncertain. Mrs Beswick was therefore prevented by the doctrine of privity from suing in her personal capacity. The House of Lords agreed, however, that as the administratrix of her husband's estate, she could take his place as a party to the contract with the nephew, and thus obtain an order for specific performance of the obligations obtained in it. Thus, while affirming the doctrine of privity, the House of Lords found a way to achieve what was clearly a just result.

There is one situation which does not fit neatly within the doctrine of privity, and which should be noted before moving on to consider the more general attempts which have been made to avoid the effects of the doctrine. This is the situation of the 'multi-party' contract.

4.2.2   A special case: multi-party contracts

We normally take as our typical model of a contract a two-party relationship. Nevertheless there are situations which are clearly governed by contract but which do not fall into this pattern. Where a group of people each contract with one body, for example on joining a sports club, and agree to abide the body's rules, can one member enforce those rules against another? Or is the only contract between each member and the club itself? The issue was considered in *Clarke v Dunraven* (1897). The case concerned the participants in a race organised by a yacht club. All who entered agreed to abide by the rules of the club. There was a collision during the race, as a result of which the plaintiff's yacht sank. The plaintiff sued the defendant, claiming damages based on provisions in the club rules. The defendant denied that there was any contractual relationship between him and the plaintiff. The House of Lords held that there was a contract between all the competitors, which they had each entered into when they entered the race. Thus, in the example given above, each member of the sports club is in a contractual relationship, based on the rules of the club, with every other member. This analysis avoids any problems of privity, but creates difficulties as regards offer and acceptance. Who exactly is making the offer and acceptance as between the first and last individuals to join? Any attempt to find a way around this, such as making the club the agent for the receipt of both offer and acceptance, is bound to look very artificial.

| 4.3 | **Evading the doctrine** |

The current position as regards the doctrine of privity is that, its status having been confirmed by *Beswick v Beswick*, there has not in recent years been any direct challenge to either aspect of the doctrine (that is, the conferring of benefits, or the imposition of obligations). There have, however, been various attempts to evade the effects of the doctrine, some of which have been more successful than others. In relation to the taking of benefits there have been attempts to allow one person to claim damages on behalf of another, to use the concept of the trust, and to construct collateral contracts. In addition, a range of statutory exceptions has been created. As regards the imposition of burdens, the main devices used have been the modification of the land law concept of the restrictive covenant. Each of these will now be considered in turn. (Note also that some aspects of the rules relating to agency, in particular the concept of the 'undisclosed principal', can be regarded as exceptions to privity: these are considered further in Chapter 15.)

It has been argued in some cases that where a contract is made by one person for the benefit of another, the contracting party should, in the event of breach, be able to recover damages to compensate the potential beneficiary's loss. This was the approach taken by Lord Denning in *Jackson v Horizon Holidays* (1975). Mr Jackson had booked a holiday for himself and his family, which turned out to be a disaster. The hotel for which the booking was made was not completed when the Jacksons arrived, and the alternative offered was of a very poor standard. The facilities did not match what had been promised, and the family found the food distasteful. There was no doubt that the defendants were in breach of contract. The trial judge, however, awarded £1,100 damages, and the defendants appealed against this as being excessive. The Court of Appeal, however, upheld the award, with Lord Denning holding that Mr Jackson was entitled to recover damages on behalf of the rest of his family. This would have had the potential of opening up a large hole in the doctrine of privity, since all that a third party beneficiary would need to do would be to persuade the contracting party to sue in order to obtain the promised benefit, or appropriate compensation. In *Woodar Investment Development Ltd v Wimpey Construction (UK) Ltd* (1980), the House of Lords rejected the idea that it was possible generally to circumvent the doctrine of privity in this way. The decision in *Jackson* was accepted as being right, either (according to Lord Wilberforce) because it related to a special situation of a kind which calls for special treatment (other examples being ordering a meal in a restaurant, or hiring a taxi for a group), or, more generally, because Mr Jackson's damages could justifiably be increased to take account of the fact that the discomfort of the rest of the family was part of his loss, in that it contributed to his own bad experience. This did not constitute, however, any significant exception to the doctrine of privity, and the more general basis on which Lord Denning had upheld the award of damages was specifically rejected. Lord Denning was held to have used out of context a quotation from *Lloyd's v Harper* (1880), which was properly to be limited to the relationship of principal and agent.

The chancery courts developed the concept of the 'trust' to deal with the situation where property was given to one person (the 'trustee') to look after and deal with for the benefit of another (the 'beneficiary'). Whereas the common law regarded the trustee as the legal owner of the property, and therefore as having a free hand to deal with it, in equity it was held that the trustee had to take account of the claims of the beneficiary, and, moreover, the beneficiary could take action to

4.4   Damages on behalf of another

4.5   The trust of a promise

compel the trustee to act in the beneficiary's interest. This tripartite trust arrangement has obvious possibilities for the development of a way round the doctrine of privity, and this was what was successfully attempted in *Les Affreteurs Reunis SA v Leopold Walford (London) Ltd* (1919). A contract for the hire of a ship (a 'time charterparty') included a clause promising a commission to the broker (Walford) who had arranged the contract. Walford was not a party to the contract, but was held by the House of Lords to be able to sue to recover the commission, on the basis that the charterers, to whom the promise had been made, were trustees of this promise. The House of Lords was thus ruling that the trust concept could apply to a promise to pay money, as well as to a situation where property was transferred into the hands of the trustee. This opened up a potentially substantial exception to the doctrine of privity. Later case law has, however, made the finding of the existence of a trust subject to some fairly strict requirements which have limited the usefulness of the device. There must have been a definite intention to create a trust and in looking for this, the court will expect to find a clear intention to benefit the third party, which is intended to be irrevocable.

4.5.1   Intention to create
a trust

The intention to create a trust will be easiest to find where the parties actually say that that is what they are doing. The courts are much more reluctant to imply an intention which is not made explicit. Two cases can be contrasted. *Re Flavell* (1883) concerned a partner in a firm of solicitors. When he retired, his partners agreed to pay him an annuity. It was also agreed that when Flavell died, the annuity would be paid to his personal representatives, to be applied for the benefit of his widow and children. After Flavell's death, his creditors wanted the annuity to be regarded as part of the general assets of the estate, and therefore available to them. The High Court held, however, that the words used in setting up the annuity had created a trust in Mrs Flavell's favour. She therefore had a prior claim over the creditors.

Sixty years later, in *Re Schebsman* (1944), a different conclusion was reached. Schebsman was the employee of a company. On his retirement, the company agreed to pay him £5,500 pounds in instalments over six years. If he died within that period, certain sums were to be payable to his widow. Schebsman did die within the six years, shortly after having been declared bankrupt. The trustee in bankruptcy claimed that the payments to Mrs Schebsman were made on the basis of a trust, and therefore, under the provisions of the relevant bankruptcy legislation, should form part of Schebsman's estate, and go to pay off his creditors. The Court of Appeal held that the contract between Schebsman and the company was simply that payments should be made direct to Mrs Schebsman. Mr Schebsman would have had no rights over them. But it was a straightforward contract between Mr Schebsman and the company, not a trust. Mrs Schebsman had no right to enforce this contract, but equally the trustee in bankruptcy had no claim. As the company was willing to pay Mrs Schebsman, effectively she won.

The distinction between *Flavell* and *Schebsman* is clearly a fine one. It may well have been important that in *Flavell* the payment was to be made to the personal representatives, rather than direct to Mrs Flavell. This indicated an arrangement more akin to a trust than a straightforward contract.

If the contract is intended to benefit the promisee, then, even if it might incidentally benefit a third party, there will be no trust. Thus in the Canadian case of *Vandepitte v Preferred Accident Insurance* (1933) a father took a policy of car insurance which was stated to be 'available to any person while legally operating the car'. His daughter drove the car with his permission, and injured the plaintiff. The plaintiff sued the daughter and won. The relevant legislation provided that the judgment could be enforced against the daughter's insurer. But the daughter had no insurance contract. The plaintiff argued that the father was the trustee of a promise made for the benefit of the daughter. This argument was rejected by the Privy Council on the basis that the father, in making the contract with the insurers was doing so for his own benefit, not his daughter's. There was no clear intention that she was to benefit, and therefore the trust argument failed.	4.5.2 Need for a clear intention to benefit the third party rather than the promisee
Whereas the parties to a contract are always free to change it by mutual agreement, a trust, once established, is regarded by the courts as irrevocable because it creates rights for the third party beneficiary which the trustee and the promisor are not entitled to change. This requirement has perhaps been the biggest obstacle to the development of the concept of the 'trust of a promise'. For example, in *Re Sinclair's Life Policy* (1938) a policy of life insurance was taken out for the benefit of the insured's godson. There was a clear intention in this case to benefit the third party. The policy, however, contained a provision enabling the policy to be surrendered for the benefit of the insured. It was not, therefore, irrevocable, and so could not be the subject of a trust.	4.5.3 Intention to benefit must be irrevocable

This was an additional reason for the decision in *Re Schebsman*. The court was not prepared to concede that parties to a contract had given up their right to consensual variation.

An element of discretion as regards who is to benefit will not, however, be fatal to a trust. In *Re Webb* (1941), insurance policies were taken out by a father in favour of his children. The policies allowed him to exercise options which would vary the benefits. This was held not to be fatal to a trust. Similarly, in *Re Flavell* (above), where there was a discretion to pay to the widow or daughters, the trust was upheld. So, the existence of a discretion will only defeat the trust if it enables the benefit to be diverted away from the beneficiaries altogether.

4.5.4	Effects of a trust

If a trust is found to exist, the third party can sue but must join the promisee as a party. The third party is entitled to any money paid or payable under the contract: the promisee has no rights to it, unless the trust fails for some reason.

4.5.6	Conclusion on trust device

The trust of a promise is a true exception to the doctrine of privity. The restrictions outlined above mean, however, that it has limited application. Indeed, it was not even considered in *Beswick v Beswick* (1968). The principle has never been denied, however, and if an appropriate case arose again, no doubt the courts would apply it.

4.6   Collateral contracts

A collateral contract generally takes the form of a unilateral contract, under which one party says 'if you enter into contract X, I will promise you Y'. The consideration for the promise, is the entering into contract X. It is quite possible for such an agreement to be made between the two parties to contract X, as in the case of *Esso Petroleum Co v Mardon* (1976), which is discussed below in Chapter 6. In a three-party situation, however, the construction of a collateral contract can be a means of evading the doctrine of privity. In *Shanklin Pier v Detel Products* (1951), the plaintiffs, who were the owners of a pier, were promised by the defendants, who were paint manufacturers, that the defendants' paint, if used to re-paint the pier, would last for seven years. As a result, the plaintiffs instructed the firm of painters who had undertaken the re-painting, to purchase and use the defendants' paint. This they did, but the paint only lasted three months. At first sight, the plaintiffs appeared to have no remedy, since they had provided no consideration for the promise given by the defendants. The only contract which the defendants had made was to sell paint to the painters, and the plaintiffs were not a party to that agreement. It was held, however, that the plaintiffs could recover on the basis of a collateral contract. The consideration for the promise as to the paint's durability was the instruction by the plaintiffs to their painters to purchase the paint from the defendants.

In this case there was a particular 'main' contract in prospect, that is, the purchase of the paint to re-paint the pier. This will usually be the case, but the device can be used even where there is no such contract specified at the time of the promise. In *Wells (Merstham) Ltd v Buckland Sand & Silica Co Ltd* (1965), the plaintiffs, who were chrysanthemum growers bought sand produced by the defendants from a third party on the basis of the defendants' assurances as to its iron oxide content. These assurances turned out to be unreliable, and the plaintiffs sued the defendants' for the resulting loss on the basis of a collateral contract. The court held that, although at the time the assurance was given there was no specific main contact in contemplation, this did not matter as long as it could be said to be made *animo contrahendi*, that is, with a view to a contract being made shortly. The plaintiffs were entitled to succeed.

The collateral contract device is not, of course, a true exception to the doctrine of privity (in the way that the trust is), because in the end the plaintiff and defendant are found to be the parties to a contract, albeit a collateral one. The way that it is used by the courts at times, however, is clearly as a means of avoiding the doctrine of privity, in that they are not over-scrupulous in investigating whether the parties themselves thought that they were entering into a contract of the kind alleged, or had any intention of doing so.

In a number of situations there has been statutory intervention to mitigate the effects of the doctrine of privity. These are generally connected with insurance, and the need to make sure that the intended beneficiary under an insurance contract is enable to enforce his or her rights. Examples include the Married Women's Property Act 1882, s 11, and the Road Traffic Act 1988, s 148(7).

4.7   Statutory exceptions

The exceptions and evasions of the doctrine of privity which we have looked at so far, have all been concerned with the recovery of a benefit by a third party. In this section we are concerned with the possibility of imposing a restriction on a third party's behaviour.

4.8   Restrictive covenants

In land transactions the seller of a piece of land will often wish to restrict the use to which the purchaser can put the land, particularly if the seller is retaining ownership of adjacent land. Of course, as between the original seller and purchaser, this can be achieved by contract. What about someone who buys from the original purchaser, however? Can that person be made subject to the restriction? In *Tulk v Moxhay* (1848) it was held that this could be the case in relation to land, provided that certain conditions were satisfied, in particular, that the original vendor still had an interest to protect (for example, continued ownership of the adjacent land).

4.8.1	Application outside land law

Land law has subsequently developed a complicated set of rules dealing with the enforceability of such 'restrictive covenants'. Outside the land law area, however, the courts have been reluctant to extend this exception to the privity doctrine. In *Taddy v Sterious* (1904), the court refused to apply it to an attempt to restrict the price at which the plaintiff's goods were sold by a third party. There have, nevertheless, been some cases concerned with shipping contracts where it has been used. In *De Mattos v Gibson* (1859), for example, it was held that a charterer of a ship was entitled to an injunction to prevent a subsequent mortgagee from using the ship inconsistently with the charter. The same line was taken by the Privy Council in *Lord Strathcona SS Co v Dominion Coal Co* (1926). The plaintiffs had chartered a ship which had subsequently been sold. It was held that the new owner, the defendant, could be restrained by injunction from using the ship in a way which would prevent the operation of the charter contract made by the previous owner. It was regarded as significant, however, that the new owner had been aware of the existence of the charter at the time that the ship was bought.

4.8.2	The current position

The further development of this exception to privity was halted by the refusal of Diplock J (as he then was) in *Port Line Ltd v Ben Line Ltd* (1958), to accept the earlier decisions as being correctly based on equitable principles analogous to the law relating to 'restrictive covenants'. He took the view that these cases could be more properly viewed as falling within the area where the law of tort (see below, para 4.9), could provide a remedy, rather than as examples of a more general exception to the doctrine of privity. This analysis was apparently accepted for the following 20 years, but in 1979, Browne Wilkinson J, indicated that there might still be some life in the equitable, restrictive covenant approach outside the area of land law. In *Swiss Bank Corporation v Lloyds Bank Ltd* (1979) a loan had been made to buy shares. The lender argued that the borrower was contractually bound to repay the loan and interest out of the proceeds of any dealings with the shares. This was said to be a specifically enforceable obligation. The shares were also subject to a charge by Lloyds Bank (presumably they had been put up as security for a loan). The lender alleged that Lloyds' rights over the shares were subject to the rights of the lender as set out in the original contract of loan. Browne-Wilkinson J held that the obligation to repay the loan out of dealings with the shares was specifically enforceable. This meant that the lender held an equitable interest in the shares, and that Lloyds' rights were subject to this obligation. The Court of Appeal and the House of Lords held that there was no specifically enforceable obligation of the kind alleged, but did not disagree with the judge's analysis of the relationship between the parties if there had been. It seems, therefore, that the equitable approach will still be available in certain appropriate cases, although the tortious action considered in the next section is more likely to work in practice.

The cases and principles discussed in this section are in many ways the proper concern of the law of tort. But this is an area (of which there are several) in which the rigid division drawn between tort and contract is unhelpful. The particular tortious action which we need to consider is that of 'wrongful interference with contractual rights'. A person who knowingly, and intentionally, brings about a breach of contract between two others, thereby commits a tort. Moreover, an injunction will generally be obtainable to prevent the interferer acting in this way. To this extent it can be said that a third party is bound by the provisions of a contract between two other people.

4.9   The role of the law of tort

The existence of this tort was recognised and applied in *Lumley v Gye* (1853). Lumley had engaged a singer, Joanna Wagner, to sing at a series of concerts at his theatre. It was a provision of this contract that she should not sing elsewhere. The defendant, who knew of this, persuaded Ms Wagner to sing at his theatre. Lumley first obtained an injunction against Ms Wagner preventing her from breaking her contract in this way. Her response was to leave the jurisdiction, and refuse to sing at either theatre. Lumley then sued Gye, and was awarded damages on the basis of Gye's intentional interference with the contract between Lumley and Wagner. This remedy has also been held to be available where goods are sold subject to a restriction on their disposal. In *BMTA v Salvadori* (1949) the purchaser of a new car agreed not to sell it for a year without first offering it to the plaintiff. The defendant bought the car with knowledge of this restriction, and with the intention of evading its effects, and was again held liable in tort.

As has been noted above, this is an alternative way of analysing the outcome in cases such as *De Mattos v Gibson*, and *Lord Strathcona SS Co v Dominion Coal Co*. It is, however, more limited than the 'restrictive covenant' approach. Such covenants may, in certain circumstances, bind even those who are unaware of them. The tort of interference with contract, on the other hand, requires intention on the part of the tortfeasor.

It is only where he or she is aware of the other contract, and the fact that rights under it may be affected, that the tortious remedy will be available to restrain, or provide compensation for, the interference.

| 4.10 | **Privity and exclusion clauses** |

One particular situation where the parties to a contract may wish to confer a benefit on a third party is in relation to exclusion clauses. Where some part of the contract is to be performed by employees, or sub-contractors, of one of the parties, that party may wish to extend the benefit of a clause excluding liability to such people. The doctrine of privity stands in the way of this, however. The problem generally arises where some loss or damage has been caused by negligence. If it is the negligence of an employee of a contracting party, then that party may well be protected, as far as breach of contract or vicarious liability in tort is concerned, by an exclusion clause. The employee will not be protected, however, and the injured party may decide to take action directly against him or her in tort (as happened in *Adler v Dickson* (1954)), perhaps relying on the fact that the employer may well feel obliged to make good any damages awarded. This has the effect of negating the benefit of the exclusion clause as regards the contracting party as well, and, if the clause has been specifically worded to try to protect the employee, contradicts the intention of the parties. The courts have therefore sought ways to avoid applying the doctrine of privity in such situations. One possibility, where the plaintiff has specifically promised not to sue the third party, is for the promisee to intervene to seek a stay of the action. This was recognised as a possibility in *Gore v Van der Lann* (1967), and applied (though not in a situation concerning negligence) in *Snelling v Snelling Ltd* (1973). Its limitation, however, is that is dependent on the existence of a specific promise, and also on the willingness of the promisee to intervene on the third party's behalf. Other attempts to avoid the effects of privity in this type of situation have been more broadly based.

| 4.10.1 | Vicarious immunity |

In *Elder, Dempster & Co v Paterson, Zochonis & Co* (1924) the House of Lords allowed shipowners to take the benefit of an exclusion clause (which was stated to apply to them), contained in a contract between the charterers of the ship, and the owner of goods being carried on it. The ratio of the decision is not very clear, but one possible basis for it was a principle of 'vicarious immunity', under which those who perform contracts on behalf of a contracting party can take the benefit of exclusion clauses contained in that contract. This analysis, which would constitute a major exception to the doctrine of privity, was, however, subsequently rejected by the House of Lords in *Scruttons Ltd v Midland Silicones Ltd* (1962). The House ruled that the third party stevedores in this case were unable to rely on an exclusion clause contained in a contract of carriage to which they were not parties. It recognised, however, that it might be possible in some situations for a contracting party to be regarded as the agent of someone who was involved in the performance of the contract, for the purpose of bringing them into a contractual nexus with the other party.

This possibility was developed by the Privy Council in *New Zealand Shipping Company v Satterthwaite & Co (The Eurymedon)* (1975). The case again concerned the liability of stevedores for the negligent unloading of a cargo. The contract of carriage contained a very detailed exclusion clause, which, among other things, specifically stated that the carrier was to be regarded as acting as agent for any independent contractors carrying out any part of the contract, and that such contractors would have the benefit of the exclusion clause. The majority of the Privy Council found this sufficient to enable them to construct a contract between the owner of the goods and the stevedores. It was in the form of a unilateral contract, under which the owners said 'if you agree to unload these goods, we will give you the benefit of the exclusion clause'. The carriers acted as the stevedores' agents for the receipt of this offer. The consideration provided was the unloading of the goods. The stevedores were of course bound to do this anyway, under their contract with the carriers, but, as discussed in Chapter 3, the performance of an existing contractual duty owed to a third party is perfectly good consideration.

There is no doubt that the contract constructed in *The Eurymedon* was a 'fiction' in the sense that it is highly unlikely that any of the parties intended precisely such an arrangement as the Privy Council found to have existed. On the other hand, the result is clearly commercially convenient, since it is the clear desire and expectation of all concerned in contracts of this kind that third parties who perform part of the contract should be able to take the benefit of any relevant exclusion clause. The decision has not opened a up a major exception to the doctrine of privity: indeed, like the collateral contract device, it is not really an exception at all, since the individual who initially looks like a non-contracting third party, is found to be a party to a contract after all. The approach taken in *The Eurymedon* was applied again by the Privy Council in *The New York Star* (1981), and must now be regarded as an established

4.10.2   The agency approach

principle which can be applied wherever the wording of the clause and the relationships between the various parties make it appropriate.

4.10.3	Modification of the duty of care

An alternative way of giving negligent third parties the benefit of an exclusion clause has been recognised in some recent cases. In *Southern Water Authority v Carey* (1985) the negligence of sub-contractors had caused the loss. The main contract contained an exclusion clause purporting to extend to the sub-contractors, and stating that the main contractor contracted on their behalf. The agency argument, based on *The Eurymedon* failed, however, because of the rule of agency that the principal (in this case the sub-contractor) for whom an agent acts must be identifiable at the time of the contract. That was not the case here. The judge decided in favour of the sub-contractors, on the basis that the existence of the exclusion clause negated any duty of care owed by the sub-contractors to the plaintiff. The validity of this approach has subsequently been confirmed by the Court of Appeal in *Norwich City Council v Harvey* (1989). Once again the case concerned the negligence of sub-contractors, who in this case had set fire to the plaintiffs' premises. The main contract, however, contained a clause placing the burden of insuring against fire on the plaintiff. In this context, the Court of Appeal took the view that the sub-contractors were not in breach of any duty of care. As May LJ put it:

> 'I do not think that the mere fact that there is not strict privity between the employer and the sub-contractor should prevent the latter from relying on the clear basis on which all the parties contracted in relation to damage to the employer's building caused by fire, even when due to the negligence of the contractors or sub-contractors.'

4.11	**Proposals for reform**

The doctrine of privity, in particular as it applies to promised benefits, has been the subject of much criticism both judicial and extra-judicial. As Cheshire, Fifoot and Furmston point out, the doctrine has in practice been found to have 'worked injustice and to be inadequate to modern needs' (*Law of Contract*, 12th ed, p 454). As a result, they comment, 'it is not surprising that many and various attempts have been made to induce the courts to sanction evasions of the doctrine'. Over 50 years ago the Law Revision Committee recommended that a third party who is, in express terms, stated to be entitled to a benefit under a contract, should be able to enforce that benefit directly (6th Interim Report, Cmd 5449, 1937). No action was taken, however, and the matter has been considered again more recently by the Law Commission in its Consultation

Paper 121, Privity of Contract - Contracts for the Benefit of Third Parties, November 1991.

The Law Commission refers to the rule that 'a person cannot enforce rights under a contract to which he is not a party' as 'the third party rule', and this phrase will be used here. The Paper also looks at the related rule that contractual remedies are generally designed to compensate the parties to the contract, and not third parties. The Commission rejects, however, the idea that the problems of privity could be solved simply by means of widening the scope of those allowed to be compensated for a breach of contract, as in *Jackson v Horizon Holidays*. The view is taken that a more fundamental reform is desirable, allowing direct enforcement of rights by third party beneficiaries. Otherwise, the beneficiary would be in the hands of the contractual promisee, who in some circumstances might refuse to act. This might well have been the case in *Beswick v Beswick*, for example, if the nephew had been the executor of his uncle's estate. He would hardly have been likely to have brought an action against himself, for the benefit of his aunt!

Because of the need for fairly fundamental reform, the Commission is of the view that this will have to be achieved by legislation. It then has to consider exactly what the scope of the reform should be. Should further specific exceptions to the third party rule be enacted to deal with what are seen as the most pressing areas? Or should there simply be a general legislative provision allowing a third party to sue on a contract made for his or her benefit, which would then be interpreted by the courts? The Commission's view is that tinkering with exceptions, or setting out a general principle to be fleshed out by the courts, would not lead to satisfactory reform. Rather the Commission proposes that reform should take the form of the enactment of a detailed legislative scheme granting third parties the right to enforce contracts made for their benefit. What form should this scheme take?

4.11.1   Reform by legislation

The simplest form would be to say that third parties should be able to sue wherever a contract happens to benefit them. The Commission rejects this as being unacceptably wide, and opening the floodgates to litigation. It should only be where the contracting parties intend to confer a benefit on the third party that a right of action should arise. Even this goes too far, however. The Commission gives the example of a contract between a building company and a highway authority for the construction of a new road. The road may be intended for the benefit of all road-users but it would surely not be acceptable for all of them to have a right of action, for example, in the

4.11.2   The basis of the reform

event of delay in completion of the project. The Commission, therefore, recommends that the range of potential third party plaintiffs should be narrowed to those on whom the parties to the contract intend to confer an enforceable legal obligation. This intention need not be expressly stated, but may be inferred from all the circumstances. It would not be necessary for the parties to name the beneficiary third party, or even for the third party to be in existence at the time of the contract (if, for example, it was a company subsequently incorporated). Difficulties of identification might, however, cast doubt on whether there was in fact an intention to create an enforceable benefit.

The finding of intention will presumably have to be decided on an objective basis, since the defendants in situations such as those in *Beswick v Beswick*, or *Dunlop v Selfridge* would be unlikely to accept that they intended to create an enforceable benefit. The court would have to ask what the reasonable person, looking at the agreement, would have taken the parties to have intended. On this basis, it is submitted, both Dunlop and Mrs Beswick would be likely to be held to have rights under the Law Commission's scheme. The Jackson family, however, might well have more difficulty in establishing their claim.

4.11.3   Relevance of defences

The Commission further suggests that the rights of a third party who brought an action under the scheme would be subject to any defences that the promisor would have had if sued by the other contracting party. Thus an exemption clause, a set-off, or a counter-claim could all be raised by way of defence.

4.11.4   Freedom to change the agreement

An important issue which arises, once third party rights are recognised in this way, is the extent to which the parties to the contract should be free to change, or even cancel, their agreement. In other words, does the third party have a legal right as soon as the contract is made, or only at some later stage. The Commission considers various possibilities, including a requirement that the third party should have to 'adopt' the contract in order to prevent its variation. This approach has been used in some other jurisdictions, such as Western Australia. The Commission was, however, unable to come to a firm conclusion and has invited comment on whether acceptance, adoption or material reliance should be required before the parties are prevented from changing their agreement in a way which affects the third party. The Commission was also unable to reach a decision as to whether the promisee should be able to sue in addition to the promisor.

These proposals, if enacted, would, as has been indicated above, be likely to lead to a different conclusion in the situations which have arisen in some of the leading cases. To that extent they would meet the criticisms that the rights of third parties are being unfairly restricted by the present doctrine. The discovery of 'intention' is not always going to be straightforward, however, particularly where it has to be inferred from the circumstances. Nor will the Commission find it easy to resolve the problem of restricting the freedom of the parties to change their agreement. Deciding on the exact point at which third party rights should crystallise may well prove to be one of the most difficult and controversial issues. As noted above, one of the stumbling blocks for the development of the 'trust of a promise' was the courts' insistence that the creation of the trust must have been intended to be irrevocable. A clear advantage of reform, however, should be that there would no longer be the need to strain other concepts in the attempt to do justice. Once it has been recognised that in certain situations third parties can have rights without needing to be in a contractual relationship, the courts will be able to address directly the problems which arise from such recognition, rather than struggling to adapt existing principles, in order to achieve a result that is felt to be just, and to represent fairly the interests of all concerned.

4.11.5   Effect of the reform

Privity

The doctrine of privity is regarded as one of the fundamental characteristics of the English law of contract.

- The essence of the doctrine is that only those who are parties to a contract can have rights or liabilities under it.

- The doctrine is linked to, but distinct from, the rule that consideration must move from the promisee.

- Development of the doctrine: *Tweddle v Atkinson* (1861) provides the starting point for the modern law: confirmed by the House of Lords in *Dunlop v Selfridge* (1915), and *Beswick v Beswick* (1968).

- Multi-party contracts: these are a special case, eg *Clarke v Dunraven* (1897).

Various attempts have been made to evade the effects of the doctrine.

- Damages on behalf of another was used in *Jackson v Horizon Holidays* (1975), but was disapproved by the House of Lords in *Woodar Investment Development Ltd v Wimpey* (1980).

- Trust of a promise: a true exception to privity, recognised in *Les Affreteurs Reunis SA v Leopold Walford* (1919), and applied in *Re Flavell* (1883). Strict conditions as regards the intention to create an irrevocable trust (as in, eg *Re Schebsman* (1944)), which is meant to benefit the third party alone (*Vandepitte v Preferred Accident Insurance* (1933)), have prevented the development of the concept.

- Collateral contracts: the construction of a collateral contract, with consideration in the form of the making of the main contract, may bring parties who would otherwise appear strangers to the contract into such a relationship: *Shanklin Pier v Detel Products* (1951). This is not a true exception, rather a device used to evade the doctrine by the construction of another contract.

- Statutory exceptions: these mostly concern insurance.

- Restrictive covenants: a means of imposing burdens on third parties, recognised in land law: *Tulk v Moxhay* (1848). These have been used in some shipping cases (eg *De Mattos v Gibson* (1859); *Strathcona v Dominion Coal* (1926)), but were rejected in *Port Line v Ben Line* (1958). There has been no recent use, but note *Swiss Bank Corporation v Lloyds Bank* (1979), which suggests this approach is still possible.

The role of the law of tort

A tort can be committed by:

- intentionally inducing a breach of contract. This was used in *Lumley v Gye* (1853), to restrict the actions of a person who was not party to the contract.

  This provides an alternative explanation of the shipping 'restrictive covenant' cases.

Privity and exclusion clauses

Privity and exclusion clauses

- Sub-contractors and employees included within the scope of exclusion clauses in contracts to which they are not parties will not generally be protected: *Adler v Dickson* (1954).

- Protection may arise if there is a promise not to sue, and the promisee is willing to intervene: *Snelling v Snelling Ltd* (1973).

- The doctrine of 'vicarious immunity' (*Elder, Dempster v Paterson Zochonis* (1924)) was rejected by House of Lords in *Scruttons v Midlands Silicones* (1962).

- Agency, where the promisee is deemed to act as agent for the third party beneficiary, was used by the Privy Council in *The Eurymedon* (1975), and again in *The New York Star* (1981). This involves the construction of a collateral, unilateral contract between promisor and beneficiary.

- In negligence cases, the clause may be taken to have modified or negated the duty of care owed by the third party: *Southern Water Authority v Carey* (1985); *Norwich City Council v Harvey* (1989).

Proposals for reform

Proposals for reform

- Note the 1937 proposals of the Law Revision Committee.

- Most recent proposals: Law Commission Consultation Paper 121, Privity of Contract: Contracts for the Benefit of Third Parties, November 1991.

- Law Commission proposes legislation to give a right to sue to those on whom the parties to the contract intend to confer an enforceable obligation.

Chapter 5

Capacity

In order to make a valid, enforceable, contract, both parties must be regarded as having capacity in law to enter into such an agreement. This is not an issue which causes practical problems with any frequency, and the rules are not particularly complicated. Three aspects of this topic are considered in this chapter, namely minors' contracts, mental disability, and intoxication. The problems which can, on occasion, arise concerning the capacity of companies to make particular contracts are not considered here, being regarded as more appropriately the concern of texts on company law.

5.1 Introduction

The basic rule is such that people who have not reached the age of 18 are regarded in English law as 'minors' and as having limited capacity to enter into contracts. The purpose of the rules is largely paternalistic - that is, it is intended to protect minors from the consequences of their own actions. As a result, the law can sometimes appear to operate harshly against those who contract with minors. In particular, the adult party who is unaware that he or she is contracting with a minor, may still find the contract unenforceable. The law starts with a presumption that all minors' contracts are either void or voidable. There are two main exceptions to this, namely contracts for 'necessaries', and 'beneficial contracts of service'. There are also certain contracts which are classed as 'voidable'. The scope of these various categories will be considered next, before moving on to the consequences of entering into a contract with a minor.

5.2 Minors' contracts

The first major exception to the rule as to unenforceability relates to contract for 'necessaries'. The reasoning here is that a total rule of unenforceability would act to the minor's disadvantage. If traders knew that any contract with a minor would involve the risk of the minor deciding not to honour it, they would be reluctant to enter into such contracts at all. As a consequence the minor might have difficulty acquiring the basic requirements of everyday life, such as food or clothing. In reality, of course, the majority of transactions of this type take place on the basis of the simultaneous exchange of goods and payment, where there is little or no risk to the trader. In relation to more complicated transactions, and particularly those which do not involve payment on the spot, the question of whether the contract concerns 'necessaries' will still be important.

5.2.1 Contracts for necessaries

5.2.2	The definition of 'necessaries'	

The concept of necessaries, which covers both goods and services, was explained in some detail in *Chapple v Cooper* (1844), where it was held that a widow who was a minor was liable in contract for the cost of her husband's funeral. According to Alderson B in this case, 'necessaries' includes not only things which are absolutely necessary for survival, but also all those which are required for a reasonable existence. Food, and clothing are obviously covered, but also medical assistance, and education. Once the goods or services are of a kind which can be put in the general category of 'necessaries' there is then a further question as to whether they are appropriate to the particular minor. Whether a silk dress can count as a necessary will depend on the minor's normal standard of living. Items of 'mere luxury', however (as opposed to 'luxurious articles of utility'), will not be regarded as necessaries. Nor will articles bought as gifts normally be so regarded: *Ryder v Wombwell* (1868). The approach of the common law is confirmed as far as goods are concerned by s 3 of the Sale of Goods Act which states:

> ' "necessaries" means goods suitable to the condition in life of the minor and to his actual requirements at the time of sale and delivery.'

As will be noted, this adds to the test stated above the question of whether the minor is already adequately supplied with goods of this kind: *Nash v Inman* (1908). The same is almost certainly true of services. In *Nash v Inman* the plaintiff was a tailor, and the defendant an undergraduate at Cambridge University, who had ordered 11 fancy waistcoats. When the plaintiff sued for payment, the defendant pleaded lack of capacity. The plaintiff argued that the waistcoats were in the category of necessaries. There was no doubt that they were among the class of things (that is, clothing) capable of being necessaries. It was up to the plaintiff to prove, however, that the defendant was not already adequately supplied with items of this kind, which he was unable to do. It should be noted that this case made it clear that the trader who is ignorant of the minor's situation will not be protected. The decision is made by looking at matters entirely from the minor's point of view.

5.2.3	Beneficial contracts of service	

A person under the age of 18 must have the possibility of being able to earn a living, and so contracts of employment, training, or apprenticeship, will be enforceable. The contract, taken as a whole, must not, however, be oppressive. *De Francesco v Barnum* (1889), for example, concerned a girl of 14 who entered into a contract with the plaintiff as an apprentice dancer. The contract was to last for seven years. During its operation the girl was forbidden to marry, and could not accept any professional engagements without the plaintiff's consent, but, on the other hand, was not guaranteed work by the plaintiff. The plaintiff could decide to terminate the agreement virtually at his discretion. The Court of Appeal held that the stipulations were of an extraordinary and unusual character, which gave the plaintiff inordinate power without any corresponding obligation. The agreement was, as a whole, not beneficial, and was thus unenforceable.

The inclusion of some disadvantageous terms, however, will not necessarily be fatal. In *Clements v London & NW Rly* (1894) C was employed as a porter. Under his contract he agreed to forgo his rights under the Employers' Liability Act . Instead he agreed to join an insurance scheme to which the employer contributed. The Court of Appeal held that although the insurance scheme had some disadvantages (for example, lower rates of compensation), it also had wider coverage than the Act in terms of the types of accident included. On balance the Court was not prepared to say that the contract of employment as a whole was disadvantageous.

The rules about beneficial contracts of service extend to contracts related to the way in which the minor earns a living. Thus in *Doyle v White City Stadium* (1935) a contract between a boxer and the British Boxing Board of Control, under which the boxer received a licence in return for agreeing to abide by the Board's rules, was held to be enforceable, despite the fact that in this particular case the rules operated to the boxer's disadvantage. This decision was relied on in *Chaplin v Leslie Frewin* (1966), where the court upheld a contract relating to the production of the minor's autobiography (he was the son of Charlie Chaplin). The contract enabled the minor to earn money, and to make a start as an author, and for that reason was to be regarded as beneficial.

Trading contracts, on the other hand, will not be enforced. In *Mercantile Union Guarantee v Ball* (1937) the court refused to enforce a hire purchase contract made by a minor who ran a haulage business. The minor business-person is therefore at a considerable disadvantage, as compared with the minor employee. Once the age of the minor is known to others with whom he or she wishes to trade, it is unlikely that any contracts will be forthcoming. The reason for this is in line with the general paternalistic approach taken in this area, in that it is felt undesirable that the minor should enter into contracts carrying the high financial risks which will often be involved in business agreements. On the other hand, it poses severe restrictions on the teenage entrepreneur who wishes to set up a business producing and dealing in, for example, computer software.

5.2.4   Other contracts related to work

UWCC LIBRARY

| 5.2.5 | Voidable contracts | Certain contracts are regarded as being valid, unless the minor repudiates them, either during minority, or within a reasonable time of becoming 18. These are, in general, contracts which involve the minor obtaining an interest in property which involves continuous or recurring obligations. So this rule applies, for example, to contracts involving obligations of shareholding, for example to pay 'calls' (that is a demand to pay money due in relation to a share price payable by instalments): *Dublin & Wicklow Rly v Black* (1852); partnership agreements: *Goode v Harrison* (1821); marriage settlements: *Edwards v Carter* (1893); and contracts relating to interests in land, such as leases: *Davies v Benyon-Harris* (1931). In relation to the last category, it should be noted that the Law of Property Act 1925, s 1(6), prevents a minor from holding a legal estate in land. The interests concerned will therefore always be equitable. |

The repudiation of one of the above contracts during minority is always possible. What constitutes the period after reaching 18 for which this right subsists is not easy to determine. The House of Lords in *Edwards v Carter* (1893) simply felt that repudiation must occur within a 'reasonable' time, and that in the particular case, a period of four years and eight months was too long to be reasonable. It is likely to be regarded as a question of fact in each case as to what is acceptable, and it does not seem possible to lay down any clear rules on this point.

5.3 Effects of entering into a contract with a minor

What are the consequences of entering into a contract with a minor? For example, can property transferred be recovered if the contract is void? And if the contract is for necessaries, is the minor obliged to pay the full contract price? The answers to these questions will be discussed as they operate in relation to void, voidable, and enforceable contracts.

| 5.3.1 | Void contracts | The first point to note is that, since the passage of the Minors' Contracts Act 1987 (repealing s 2 of the Infants Relief Act 1874), it is possible for a void contract to be ratified (expressly or impliedly) on the minor's attaining majority. If this is done then the contract will take effect as normal, with full enforceability on both sides. |

If the contract remains void at the time a dispute arises, the position is more complicated. The Infants Relief Act 1874 declared most such contracts 'absolutely void', but this was an inaccurate representation of reality, and has been repealed by the Minors' Contracts Act 1987. The position now is that a contract which has been fully executed will be effective to transfer the ownership of any money or other property which has changed hands under it. A minor who purchases non-necessary goods for cash is not entitled to demand to be allowed to return them. If the minor has performed, it seems that he or she will be able to claim damages (though not specific performance) from the adult party. Money or property transferred will only be recoverable by the minor, however, if there has been a total failure of consideration: *Valentini v Canali* (1889). If the adult party has performed, in whole or in part, then, if it is services that have been provided, the adult is without a remedy. If property has been transferred, the common law said that it was irrecoverable, but that has been altered by s 3 of the Minors' Contracts Act 1987. This empowers the court, 'if it is just and equitable to do so', to require the minor to transfer to the adult any property transferred, or any property representing it. This is a broad discretion, and the court is given no guidance as to how it should be exercised. But it does provide the opportunity to prevent a minor taking advantage of the situation, and gaining unjust enrichment. Not all such cases are covered, however. As has been noted, the section has no application where it is non-necessary services that have been provided, nor will it provide a remedy where goods, or the proceeds of their sale, have been consumed by the minor.

If a minor repudiates a voidable contract, this will not effect obligations which have already fallen due and have been performed. Money or property transferred by the minor will be irrecoverable, unless there has been a total failure of consideration: *Corpe v Overton* (1833). The position as regards liabilities which have fallen due, but have not been performed at the time of the repudiation is less clear. The point was considered, *obiter*, in *North Western Rail Co v McMichael* (1850). Parke B took the view that a call on shares which had become due was of no effect once repudiation had taken place. In other words, the repudiation was, to that extent, retrospective.

5.3.2   Voidable contracts

Where a minor has received necessary goods and services, what is the obligation as regards payment? As far as goods are concerned the position is governed by the Sale of Goods Act 1979, s 3(2), which states that:

> 'Where necessaries are sold and delivered to a minor ... he must pay a reasonable price for them.'

Two points emerge from this. Firstly, the liability only arises after delivery. The fact that ownership has passed under the rules for 'passing of property' is irrelevant (see below, Chapter 16). Secondly, the liability is only to pay a reasonable price, which is not necessarily the contract price. This was also the line taken on this issue by Fletcher Moulton LJ in *Nash v Inman* (1908).

5.3.3   Enforceable contracts

It seems, however, that the position may be different as regards necessary services. The relevant authority is *Roberts v Gray* (1913). The defendant was an aspiring billiards player who made a contract to go on a world tour with the plaintiff, who was a leading player. The defendant, however, backed out before the tour began. The Court of Appeal regarded this as a quasi-educational contract, and therefore within the scope of a contract for necessaries. The defendant argued that nevertheless, no damages should be payable, because he had received nothing under the contract. By analogy with contracts for necessary goods, only where services had actually been supplied should a liability to pay for them arise. The Court of Appeal refused to accept this. Hamilton LJ commented:

> 'I am unable to appreciate why a contract which is in itself binding, because it is a contract for necessaries not qualified by unreasonable terms, can cease to be binding because it is still executory.'

Damages were awarded to the extent of the plaintiff's full losses in organising the abortive tour. In effect, then, the minor was made liable on the agreement itself, rather than for what had been received under the agreement. This is also the approach taken to beneficial contracts of service. Thus it seems to be only in relation to contracts for the supply of necessary goods that there can be no recovery on an executory contract.

5.4	**Minors' liability in tort**

Although it is perfectly possible for a minor to be liable in tort, there being no age limit in relation to tortious liability, the courts will not allow such an action to be used as a means of indirectly enforcing an otherwise unenforceable contract. The difficulty lies in deciding exactly when that will be the effect of the tortious action.

The first case to consider is *Jennings v Rundall* (1799). The defendant was a minor who had hired a horse for a short journey. In fact it was taken on a long journey, and suffered injury as a result of this over-riding. The plaintiff's action in tort failed on the basis that this was in substance an action for breach of contract, which would not have been sustainable because of the defendant's minority.

This must be contrasted with *Burnard v Haggis* (1863). This again concerned the hire of a horse to a minor. The defendant had said that he did not require a horse for jumping, and indeed was specifically told by the owner 'not to jump or lark with it'. The defendant lent the horse to a friend who used it for jumping with the result that the horse fell and was killed. The defendant was held liable in tort to the owner. The distinction between this case and *Jennings v Rundall* appears from the judgment of Willis J, who commented that the act of riding the mare into the place where she was killed was as much a trespass as if:

> '... without any hiring at all, the defendant had gone into a field and taken the mare out and killed her. It was a bare trespass, not within the object and purpose of the hiring.'

Thus the test is the 'object and purpose' of the contract. Did the tortious act occur as part of the performance of the 'object and purpose'? If so, there will be no liability. So in *Jennings v Rundall* the object and purpose was riding the horse on a journey. In *Burnard v Haggis*, however, jumping was outside the object and purpose, and the defendant was therefore liable.

This approach has been confirmed by later cases. Thus in *Fawcett v Smethurst* (1914) the taking of a hired car on longer journey than indicated at the time of hire was still within the contract's 'object and purpose'. Whereas in *Ballett v Mingay* (1943) the defendant, who had hired a microphone and amplifier and was found to have lent them to a friend was held to be altogether outside the scope of the contract, and the defendant was therefore liable in tort.

Insofar as there is immunity, it extends not only to torts committed in the course of a contract, but also fraud which induces a contract. Thus fraudulent misrepresentation of the minor's age will not stop the minor from pleading lack of capacity, and avoiding the contract. Nor will it give the adult party a right to bring an action in tort for deceit. Where property had been transferred as a result of such fraud, equity had developed remedies in certain situations to allow the adult party to recover it (*Stocks v Wilson* (1913)). Although this equitable remedy is still available in theory, the enactment of the more general provision relating to restitution in s 3 of the Minors' Contracts Act 1987 means that it is of virtually no practical importance, and so is not discussed further here.

The law also provides protection for those who make contracts while under some mental disability. There are, of course degrees of mental disability, unlike the position in relation to minors, where the person is either under 18 or over 18. English contract law recognises three categories. First, there are those whose mental state is such that their affairs are under the control of the court, by virtue of Part VII of the Mental Health Act 1983. Since the court effectively takes over the individual's power to make contracts, any contracts purported to be made by the individual will be unenforceable against him or her. Secondly, there are those whose mental state is such that, although they are not under the control of the court, they are

5.5   Mental disability

unable to appreciate the nature of the transaction they are entering into. Contracts made by people in such a condition will be enforceable against them (even if the contract may in some sense be regarded as 'unfair'), unless it is proved that the other party was aware of the incapacity. This was the view taken in *Imperial Loan Co v Stone* (1892), and has more recently been confirmed by the Privy Council in the New Zealand case of *Hart v O'Connor* (1985). The third category consists of those people who are capable of understanding the transaction, but who are, as a result of some mental disability, more susceptible to entering into a disadvantageous contract. Contracts made by such people are binding, unless affected by the rules relating to 'undue influence', which are discussed in Chapter 9.

The only exception to the above rules relates to contracts for necessaries. The Sale of Goods Act 1979 applies the same rule as to contracts for necessary goods made by those who 'by reason of mental incapacity ... incompetent to contract' as it does to minors. Thus the mentally incapacitated individual is liable to pay a reasonable price for goods sold and delivered. It must also be assumed, although there is no recent authority, that rules equivalent to those which apply to minors will operate in relation to necessary services. These rules will apply to people in both of the first two categories listed above.

5.6   Intoxication

Those who as a result of drunkenness, whether voluntary or involuntary, are 'incompetent to contract', are, by virtue of s 3 of the Sale of Goods Act liable to pay a reasonable price for necessary goods 'sold and delivered'. 'Incompetent to contract' presumably means 'unable to understand the nature of the transaction'. Beyond this there appears to be little authority on contracts made by those who are intoxicated. It is assumed, however, that similar rules apply as in the case of incapacity through mental disability. This means, amongst other things, that, in contrast to the position in relation to minors, there must be an awareness of the incapacity on the part of the other party before the contract will be unenforceable.

Such cases as there are on this topic, are concerned with intoxication through the consumption of alcohol. There seems no reason why the same rules should not apply to a person who is incapacitated through drug-taking.

Capacity

With regard to minors contracts:

- the basic rule is that those under the age of 18 have limited capacity to enter into contracts, and it is irrelevant whether the other party is aware of the minor's age. Exceptions exist in relation to necessaries, beneficial contracts of service, and certain voidable contracts;

- necessaries may be defined as those goods and services which are necessary for a reasonable existence: *Chapple v Cooper* (1844). They may include 'luxurious items of utility' (eg food, clothing). They must be appropriate to the particular minor, and to his or her actual requirements: Sale of Goods Act 1979, s 3; *Nash v Inman* (1908).

- beneficial contracts of service must not be oppressive (*De Francesco v Barnum* (1889)), but the overall effect will be considered, rather than particular terms: *Clements v London & NW Rly* (1894). Rules extend to contracts related to the way in which the minor earns a living: *Doyle v White City Stadium* (1935);

- trading contracts are always unenforceable against the minor;

- voidable contracts are valid unless repudiated before, or within a reasonable time of, reaching majority (*Edwards v Carter* (1893)). Voidable contracts include 'calls' on shares, partnership agreements and leases;

- effects of contract with a minor are as follows:

  (i) void contracts - may be ratified on reaching majority. If not, the adult party cannot enforce against the minor, but may be able to recover property which has been transferred: Minors' Contract Act 1987, s 3. The minor will be able to recover property on a total failure of consideration: *Valentini v Canali* (1889). A contract which has been fully executed will be effective to transfer ownership of property, and will not be rescinded;

  (ii) voidable contracts - repudiation does not effect obligations which have been performed, unless there has been a total failure of consideration from the adult party: *Corpe v Overton* (1893);

(iii) enforceable contracts - the minor must pay a reasonable price for delivered necessary goods: Sale of Goods Act 1979, s 3. May be liable for full compensation in relation to necessary services (*Roberts v Gray* (1913)), and beneficial contracts of service;

- the minor is only liable if tort is outside the 'object and purpose' of the contract: *Burnard v Haggis* (1863). Immunity extends to fraudulent misrepresentation of age.

Mental disability

Note the different categories of mental disability:

- as regards those whose affairs are controlled by the court under the Mental Health Act 1983, all contracts other than for necessaries, are unenforceable;

- as regards those not under the control of the court, but who are incapable of appreciating the nature of the transaction, they will be liable unless the other party was aware of the disability.

Rules as to necessaries apply here in the same way as to minors: note the Sale of Goods Act 1979, s 3.

Intoxication

The rules for intoxication *presumably* apply to all types of intoxication whatever the cause.

- The intoxicated party will be liable unless the other party was aware of the intoxication. Intoxication must be such as to render the person unable to understand the transaction.

- Rules as to necessaries apply in the same way as to minors: note the Sale of Goods Act 1979, s 3.

Chapter 6

The Contents of the Contract

6.1   Introduction

This chapter is concerned with the situation where the parties have fulfilled all the requirements for making a valid contract, as described in the previous chapters. It may then become necessary to determine exactly what the obligations are under the contract. Problems may arise in a number of ways. There may, perhaps, have been a lengthy period of pre-contractual negotiation, and it may not be clear which, if any, of the statements which were made at that stage were intended to form part of the contract. The contract may be in writing, and yet one of the parties may allege that it does not truly represent their intentions. Or the contract may be purely verbal, in which case there may be a dispute as to what was said or promised, and by whom. Some of these problems may be resolved by the rules which the courts have developed to enable terms to be implied into a contract. Moreover, in certain situations terms will be implied by statute, irrespective of the wishes or intentions of the parties.

The order of treatment adopted here is to look first at the question of pre-contractual statements, and the remedies that may be available for them. Secondly, the approach to express terms will be discussed. And finally, the rules relating to the implication of terms, both at common law and by statute, will be considered.

6.2   Distinction between representations and terms

The importance of distinguishing between representations and terms arises from the question of the remedies that will be available in each case. If a statement amounts to a promise which forms part of a contract, then a person who breaks it will be liable for the full range of contractual remedies discussed in Chapter 13. In particular, the plaintiff will normally be entitled to damages which will compensate for any profits that may be been lost as a result of the broken promise. A statement which is not a term, however, and which turns out to be untrue, or which contains a promise which is broken, may still give rise to a remedy, but generally on a more restricted basis. This is discussed in the next section (para 6.3) on remedies for pre-contractual statements.

Where there have been statements made prior to a contract, and there is then a dispute as to whether they were intended to form part of the contract or not, how do the courts resolve the issue? The approach is (as in many other areas of contract law) to try to determine the intentions of the parties. Did they intend the statement to be contractually binding? In looking at this the courts generally adopt an approach based on 'detached objectivity', that is, asking what the reasonable third party would have taken the parties to have intended. The importance apparently attached to the statement by the plaintiff will be very significant in considering this, as in *Bannerman v White* (1861), where a buyer of hops had been assured that sulphur had not been used in their production. He had made it clear that he would not be interested in buying them if it had. When it turned out that sulphur had been used he was entitled to reject them for breach of contract. The courts have also, however, regularly used three more specific tests to help determine this issue. These concern; whether the contract was put into written form; whether the plaintiff was relying on the skill and knowledge of the defendant; the lapse of time between the statement and the contract.

6.2.1	Was the contract put into written form?

As we saw in Chapter 2, there is generally no need for a contract to be put into writing in order for it to be a valid agreement. On the other hand, if the parties have taken the trouble to commit their contract to writing, the courts will be reluctant to find that it does not contain all the terms which were important to either party. Moreover, if a written contract has been signed, the party who has done so may find it virtually impossible to vary its express provisions: *L'Estrange v Graucob* (1934). (This case is discussed further in the context of exclusion clauses, in Chapter 7.) This is often referred to as the 'parol evidence rule', by virtue of which the courts will be reluctant to accept oral evidence in order to add to the terms in what appears to be a complete written contract. This was part of the reason for the rejection of an alleged term (relating to the age of a motorcycle), in *Routledge v McKay* (1954). It is not an absolute rule, however, and if the party can show that the term which was not included was of the utmost importance, then the courts may be prepared to allow it to be added. This is most likely to be the case where the written contract is in a standard form, rather than the result of individual negotiation. An example is *Evans & Son Ltd v Andrea Merzario Ltd* (1976). The plaintiffs had made a contract for the transport of machinery by sea. They had made it clear to the defendants that it was of great importance that the machinery should not be carried on deck. The defendants had given an oral assurance that the plaintiffs' machinery would be carried below deck. The printed standard conditions for the contract, however, allowed for freight to be carried on deck. The plaintiffs' machinery was carried on deck, and was lost overboard. It was held by the Court of Appeal, that in this case the verbal assurance took precedence over the written conditions. The statement that the plaintiffs' goods would be carried below deck was a contractual term, and the plaintiffs were entitled to succeed.

If there is an imbalance of skill and knowledge relating to the subject-matter of the contract as between the plaintiff and defendant, this will be relevant in deciding whether an oral pre-contractual statement should be treated as a contractual term. The fact that the defendant is in a better position to be able to guarantee the truth of a statement will lend weight to its being regarded as part of the contract. If, on the other hand, it is the plaintiff who is the expert, then the reverse will be true.

6.2.2 Was the plaintiff relying on the skill and knowledge of the defendant?

Two cases concerning contracts for the sale of cars conveniently illustrate the two sides of this test. The first case to consider (though the later in time) is *Dick Bentley Productions Ltd v Harold Smith (Motors) Ltd* (1965). The plaintiff had bought a car from the defendants, relying on a pre-contractual statement as to its mileage, which later turned out to be untrue. The Court of Appeal held that the statement as to the mileage was a term of the contract, on the basis that the defendant was a car dealer who should be taken to have better knowledge of such matters than the plaintiff, who was not involved in the motor trade. In reaching this decision, the court distinguished the earlier case of *Oscar Chess Ltd v Williams* (1957). Here the defendant was a private individual who had sold a car to a garage. The relevant pre-contractual statement was that defendant had innocently told the garage that the date of the car was 1948, when in fact it had been first registered in 1939. The garage sued for breach of contract, but the Court of Appeal held that, on the basis of the fact that the plaintiffs here had the greater skill and knowledge of such matters, the statement should not be regarded as a term.

Other cases where the greater skill and knowledge of the defendant has been relevant in giving contractual status to a pre-contractual statement include *Birch v Paramount Estates Ltd* (1956), *Schawel v Reade* (1913), and *Hurling v Eddy* (1951).

The courts generally consider that the closer in time that the statement was made to the conclusion of the contract, the more likely it is that it was a matter of importance to the plaintiff, and should therefore be treated as a contractual term. It is certainly true that if there is no significant gap then the statement may well be treated as being intended to be part of the contract, particularly if the agreement is not put into

6.2.3 Was there a significant lapse of time between the statement and the contract?

writing. It is by no means clear, however, that the mere existence of a delay should be regarded as in itself reducing the significance of the statement. Such delay may well have been caused by matters irrelevant to the statement, and the plaintiff may have felt that having settled the issue which the statement concerned, there was no need to re-state it at the time of the contract. Nevertheless, whatever the true significance of the delay, it is undoubtedly the case that as far as the courts are concerned it will weaken the plaintiff's case.

An example of the application of this test is the case of *Routledge v McKay* (1954). This concerned the sale of a motorbike. The defendant, who was selling the bike, had told the plaintiff that the date of the bike was 1942. In fact it dated from 1930. A week elapsed between the defendant's statement, and the making of the contract of sale (which was put into writing). It was held by the Court of Appeal that the defendant's statement was not a term of the contract. The decision may appear a little harsh, but it may be significant that application of both the other tests outlined above would have gone in favour of the defendant. Thus, the written agreement made no mention of the age of the bike, and neither party had any special skill or knowledge. Both were private individuals, and the defendant in making the statement had innocently relied on false information contained in the bike's registration document.

As this last case shows, it must be remembered that none of the tests discussed here is automatically conclusive of the issue. All may need to be considered, and, if they point in different directions, weighed against each other. The ultimate question is whether the statement, viewed objectively, was intended to form part of the contract. All the other tests are simply matters which may provide guidance to the court in determining this issue.

6.3 Remedies for pre-contractual statements

This section is concerned with the situation where the answer to the question raised in the previous section is that the statement is not a term of the contract. What remedies, if any, are available to a person who has made a contract in reliance on such a statement? Although it may be argued that discussion of this issue is out of place in this chapter, since, by definition, such statements are not part of the 'contents of the contract', it is nevertheless helpful to consider them briefly at this stage, in order to fully understand the importance of deciding whether a statement is part of the contract or not. It is only by considering the consequences of that decision, that its significance can be properly appreciated.

There are three possible forms of action which must be considered: the actions for misrepresentation; for breach of a collateral contract; and for the tort of negligent misstatement.

The common law and equity recognised two remedies for misrepresentation. Provided that there were no complicating factors, such as the involvement of third party rights, rescission of the contract was the main remedy for all types of misrepresentation. If the misrepresentation was made fraudulently, there was, in addition, the possibility of an action in tort for deceit, which would provide for the recovery of damages: *Derry v Peek* (1889). Both these remedies are still available in appropriate cases. In addition, however, there is now the possibility of an action for damages for so-called 'negligent misrepresentation' under s 2 of the Misrepresentation Act 1967.

For any of these remedies to be available, the statement must have been a representation in the strict sense. That is it must have been a statement of existing fact, not a statement of opinion (*Bisset v Wilkinson* (1927)), nor a statement of law, nor a promise to act in a particular way in the future. Thus a statement by a seller of a computer system that a 24-hour service facility will be provided is not a 'representation', but a promise. A statement that the system is ideal for a small business may well be a statement of opinion rather than fact (unless it is based on facts which the maker of the statement knows to be untrue: *Smith v Land and House Property Corporation* (1884)). But a statement that the firm has already sold 1,000 similar systems, or that it has a team of six service engineers, are representations which, if untrue, may give the other party a remedy.

The statement must have induced the contract: *JEB Fasteners v Marks, Bloom & Co* (1983). This rule, together with other aspects of the law relating to misrepresentations, is discussed in more detail in Chapter 8, Mistake and Misrepresentation.

We have already encountered the concept of the collateral contract, as a means of evading the doctrine of privity, by bringing apparent third parties into a contractual relationship, as in *Shanklin Pier v Detel Products* (1951). As noted there, however, the collateral contract can also be used between parties who themselves subsequently enter into a main contract. The collateral contract will take the form of one party expressly, or impliedly, saying to the other 'if you enter into the main contract, I will promise you X'. It can thus provide a remedy for pre-contractual statements which have

6.3.1   Misrepresentation

6.3.2   Collateral contract

not been incorporated into the main contract. It has the advantage over the remedies for misrepresentation in that it is not limited to statements of existing fact. A promise to act in a particular way is clearly covered. Continuing the computer contract example used above, a statement that 'we will answer all service calls within six hours' could not be a misrepresentation, but could found an action for breach of a collateral contract. Statements of fact, or even opinion, may also give rise to a collateral contract, if it can be said that the maker of the statement was guaranteeing its truth.

An example of the use of a collateral contract in a two-party situation is *City of Westminster Properties v Mudd* (1959). A tenant had been in the practice of sleeping in the shop which he rented. When the lease was renewed, the landlord tried to insert a clause stating that the premises should not be used for lodging, dwelling, or sleeping. The tenant objected, but was assured orally that if he signed the lease, he would be allowed to sleep there. In fact, probably due to an oversight, the new clause was omitted, but a provision containing an obligation only to use the premises for the purposes of trade remained. The landlord subsequently tried to rely on this clause to forfeit the lease, claiming that the tenant was in breach of it through sleeping on the premises. It was held that the tenant could rely on a collateral contract, giving him the right to sleep on the premises, which in effect, overrode the clause in the lease itself.

In *Esso v Mardon* (1976) the statement related to the potential throughput of a petrol station, which led the other party to sign a lease. The statement was made by a representative of the petrol company, and, although it was in the form of an expression of opinion, the Court of Appeal nevertheless held that it involved a collateral 'warranty' that the forecast of the throughput had been made with reasonable care and skill. Since this was not the case, the tenant was able to recover damages on the basis of a breach of the collateral contract.

6.3.3   Limitations of the 'collateral contract'

As will be seen from these examples, the collateral contract is a very flexible device. Its disadvantage as compared to the action for misrepresentation is that it will only provide a remedy in damages, and will not allow the plaintiff the possibility of rescinding the main contract. Moreover, the level of damages which can be awarded is more restricted than in the case of actions for deceit, or under the Misrepresentation Act 1967, s 2(1).

In 1963 the House of Lords confirmed that the tortious action for negligence could provide a remedy for negligent misstatements which have resulted in purely economic loss: *Hedley Byrne v Heller* (1963). The development of the law in this area of the past 30 years has been complicated, as the courts have tried to decide exactly when a duty of care as regards such statements can be said to arise. The recent trend, as shown by cases such as *Caparo v Dickman* (1990), has been to limit strictly the number of 'special relationships' which can give rise to such a duty. There is no doubt, however, that a duty of this kind may arise between parties who subsequently enter into a contract. The possibility was recognised in *Esso v Mardon*, for example. In practice, however, the existence of the remedies under s 2(1) of the Misrepresentation Act 1967 (above, para 6.3.1) means that it is not very likely to be needed in this situation. The action under the Act has the advantage that the burden of proof as regards negligence is on the defendant (who effectively has to disprove it), and that more extensive damages are available. The only situation where it might be necessary for a party to a contract to look to the common law negligence action is where the statement is not a representation in the strict sense, and it is also impossible to construct a collateral contract. The situations where this is likely to be the case will be very few, and so this remedy is not discussed further here.

As we have seen there are a variety of actions which may be available in relation to pre-contractual statements. There is nothing to stop a plaintiff relying on more than one, as was pointed out by Lord Denning in *Esso v Mardon*. The decision as to which action will be the most appropriate to press, will depend on the type of statement (is it a statement of fact?), and on the remedy which is being sought (is rescission of the contract required, or will damages be adequate?).

In this section we are concerned with terms that have without doubt been put forward by one or other party as a term of the agreement. There may be disputes, however, as to whether the clause has been incorporated into the contract, as to its proper construction, and as to the consequences of breaking it. In dealing with all these questions the approach of the courts will again be to try to determine the parties' intention, from an objective viewpoint.

We have already discussed the rules which the courts adopt to decide whether pre-contractual statements should be regarded as having been incorporated into a contract. The

6.3.4	Negligent misstatement
6.3.5	Conclusion on pre-contractual statements
6.4	**Express terms**
6.4.1	Incorporation

situation under consideration here is slightly different, and will generally arise in relation to written contracts in a standard form which have not been signed. One party may object that a particular clause should not be regarded as being included in the contract, because they were unaware of it for some reason, and would have objected to it. The rules that operate in this area have mainly developed in relation to the incorporation of exclusion clauses, and detailed discussion of them will be left until Chapter 7. In appropriate cases they can apply to other types of clause, however, as is shown by the case of *Interfoto Picture Library v Stiletto Visual Programmes* (1988).

The defendants were an advertising agency. They needed some photographs for a presentation. On 5 March 1984 they contacted the plaintiffs, who ran a library of photographic transparencies to see if they might have anything suitable. The plaintiffs sent round a packet of 47 transparencies, together with a delivery note. The transparencies were, however, apparently overlooked and not used. They were eventually returned on 2 April, ie nearly a month after they had been received. The plaintiffs then claimed the sum of £3,783,50 from the defendants as a 'holding charge' for the transparencies. This was calculated in accordance with the terms laid down in the delivery note, which stated that in relation to transparencies not returned within 14 days of receipt, a charge of £5 per day plus VAT would be made in respect of each transparency. The issue before the court was thus whether the terms of the delivery note formed part of a contract between the parties; and if so, whether the plaintiffs could enforce these terms against the defendants. The Court of Appeal held that the clause could not be enforced. They did so by reference to the case law on exclusion clauses and when they are deemed to have been incorporated into a contract. In particular they relied on *Parker v South Eastern Rly Co* (1877), and *Thornton v Shoe Lane Parking* (1971). *Parker* established the principle that in order to rely on an exclusion clause in an unsigned contract, the defendant had to have taken reasonable steps to bring it to the attention of the plaintiff. *Thornton* added the gloss that the more unusual and onerous the clause, the more that the defendant had to do to draw it to the plaintiff's attention. The court saw no reason why this approach should not apply to the case before them. The clause was particularly, and unusually, onerous in its effect. The plaintiffs had done nothing to draw it to the defendants' attention. It should be regarded as not having been incorporated into the contract.

Even where there is no dispute as to whether a clause is incorporated, the parties may disagree as to what it was intended to mean. It will be necessary to try to construe the clause in order to give effect to it. The courts will adopt the approach of trying to assess objectively what the parties must be taken to have intended. If the contract is in the form of a written document, the parol evidence rule will apply to restrict the use which can be made of oral statements. Such evidence will be permissible, however, in order to establish a trade or local custom as to the meaning of a particular phrase. In *Smith v Wilson* (1832), evidence was allowed to establish a local custom to the effect that the phrase '1,000 rabbits' meant '1,200 rabbits'. It may also be used to establish the starting-date of the contract (*Pym v Campbell* (1856)), or to explain an ambiguous phrase (*Robertson v Jackson* (1845)). More generally it may be allowed if the court accepts that the written document was not intended to contain all the contractual terms. We have already seen this approach operating in relation to pre-contractual statements in the case of *Evans v Andrea Merzario* (1976).

Further discussion of the approach to the construction of terms will be found in Chapter 7, since a number of cases deal with this issue in the context of the scope of exclusion clauses.

There is a generally accepted hierarchy of terms within a contract, with 'conditions' being more important than 'warranties'. There are also some terms which do not fit easily within either category, and are therefore treated as 'innominate'. The significance of the distinction between terms on this basis, however, only becomes important when the consequences of breach are being considered. Breach of a condition is more serious than breach of a warranty, whereas the consequences of breach of an innominate term may depend on the context in which it occurs, and its effect on the rest of the contract. For this reason, discussion of this topic is left until Chapter 12, which is concerned with the issues of performance and breach.

One or other of the parties to an agreement may wish to claim that although a particular term has not been set out explicitly, either in words or writing, it should nevertheless be implied into the contract. It is also the case that in some situations a term will be implied because Parliament has by statute required that all such contracts should contain such a term.

The order of treatment here will be to look first at terms implied by the courts, which can be further divided into terms implied by custom, terms implied in fact, and terms implied by law. Terms implied by statute will then be considered.

6.4.2   Construction

6.4.3   Conditions, warranties and innominate terms

6.5   Implied terms

6.5.1	Terms implied by the courts	The general approach of the courts is that they are reluctant to imply terms. The parties are generally expected to take the trouble to set out the provisions of their agreement in full. A contract in which certain terms are implicit clearly gives great opportunities for dispute, and the courts have been reluctant to give any encouragement to parties to try to escape from contractual obligations on the basis of some term which was not stated, but which is now alleged to be of great significance. There are certain situations, however, where this reluctance is overcome, and terms are implied. The first of these is where the implication of the term derives from a local or trade custom.
6.5.2	Terms implied by custom	Provided that there is sufficient evidence to establish the custom the courts will be prepared to interpret the contract in the light of it. An early example is *Hutton v Warren* (1836). A tenant claimed to be entitled, on quitting his tenancy, to an allowance for seed and labour. There was nothing in the lease to this effect, but the court accepted that this was a well-established local custom, and implied a term. The issue is thus primarily one of fact. The person wishing to rely on the custom must produce convincing factual evidence of its existence and general acceptance. Assuming that there is sufficient evidence, the courts will imply a term to give it effect.
		Such implication will not be possible, however, if the contract contains an express term which is inconsistent with the custom: *Les Affreteurs Reunis v Walford* (1919). In that case the express term will prevail over the custom.
6.5.3	Terms implied in fact	The approach here is based on the attempt to determine the true intention of the parties. The courts will imply a term if they consider that it represents the true intention of the parties on a particular issue. In other words, the term is implied not as a matter of law, but on the basis that as a matter of fact, this is what the parties had agreed, though the agreement was implicit rather than explicit. The courts will not easily, however, be convinced that such implication should take place. It is certainly not sufficient that a particular clause would appear to be 'reasonable'.
6.5.4	The 'Moorcock' test	The starting point for the law in this area is the case of *The Moorcock* (1889). This concerned a contract which involved the plaintiff's ship mooring at the defendant's wharf in the Thames. The Thames being a tidal river, at low tide the ship, as both parties knew would be the case, settled on the river bed. Unfortunately, the ship was damaged because of ridge of hard ground beneath the mud of the river bed. There was no express term in the contract as to the suitability of the river bed for mooring a ship there. Nevertheless, it was held by the

Court of Appeal that such a term could, and should, be implied. The reason for this was that without such a provision the contract would have effectively been unworkable. It was implicit in the contract for the mooring of the ship, that it would have to rest on the bottom of the river. Both parties must have contracted on the basis that it was safe to do so. On this basis the court felt that it must have been the intention of the parties that the owners of the wharf should warrant that the river bed was suitable for the purpose of the contract.

Note that the test being applied here is a stringent one. It is not based on the reasonable expectation of the owner of the ship, but rather on what is necessary in order to make the contract work at all. The fact that a contract might work better with a particular term implied would not be sufficient. *The Moorcock* can thus be characterised as having established a test of 'necessity' in relation to the implication of terms.

| The reason why necessity is a good test for the implication of terms is that it must be regarded as a sure guide as to what the parties intended. If a contract will not work without the inclusion of a particular term, it is a reasonable assumption that the parties intended that term to be included. The courts have been prepared, however, to consider other tests of intention. One of the most commonly used is the test of the 'officious bystander.' This derives from the case of *Shirlaw v Southern Foundries* (1939). MacKinnon LJ suggested that a term may be implied where it is so obvious that it 'goes without saying', so that: | 6.5.5 | The 'officious bystander' test |

'... if while the parties were making their bargain, an officious bystander were to suggest some express provision for it in the agreement, they would testily suppress him with a common "Oh, of course!".'

The operation of both *The Moorcock* and the 'officious bystander' tests were considered by Gatehouse J in *Ashmore v Corporation of Lloyd's (No 2)* (1992). The case arose out the problems of Lloyd's 'names' who had made substantial losses out of insurance contracts. The plaintiffs were arguing that Lloyd's had a duty to alert names about matters of which Lloyd's became aware which might seriously affect their interests. One basis for the action was that the duty should be based on an implied term in the names' contracts with Lloyd's. Gatehouse J, however, was unable to find that either of the tests outlined above helped the plaintiffs. Looking first at *The Moorcock* test of business efficacy, many thousands of people had been or were names with Lloyd's under the same contractual arrangements as the plaintiffs. It could not be said that these contracts would not work without the suggested implied term.

As to the officious bystander, Gatehouse J found the suggested question too complicated to be answered by a simple 'yes'. The question was set out in this way by the plaintiff:

> 'If at the Rota meeting to admit a new Member, an officious bystander interrupted the proceedings and said, "You Lloyd's are asking this applicant to engage in a high risk business and, in effect, entrust his entire personal fortune to an underwriting agent approved by you with whom he is not to interfere, and whom you know he relies upon and is by the system you impose forced to rely on: [Question] what if something professionally discreditable is or becomes known to Lloyd's about the underwriting agent which might prejudice the member's underwriting interests, other than matters which in Lloyd's reasonable opinion are not capable of being seriously prejudicial to the member's underwriting interests, would you Lloyd's be obliged to take reasonable steps to alert the applicant, if thought necessary, in confidence, and tell the underwriting agent within a reasonable time thereafter what you have done?" Surely the answer would be "of course".'

On the contrary, the response of Lloyd's to such a question, thought Gatehouse J, would have been to refer the question to their lawyers, following which the most likely answer would have been an uncompromising 'no'.

This case illustrates the reluctance of the courts to imply a term, and that the tests to be satisfied are applied quite strictly.

6.5.6   Terms implied by law

The distinction between terms implied in fact, and terms implied by law, was well-explained by Lord Denning in *Shell v Lostock Garage* (1977). The case concerned a contract under which a garage owner agreed to buy petrol exclusively from Shell. The garage owner was arguing that a term should be implied to the effect that Shell would not discriminate against him in the terms on which it supplied the petrol. The majority of the Court of Appeal (Bridge LJ dissenting) held that no such term could be implied. In coming to this conclusion, Lord Denning emphasised the difference between terms implied in fact, and by law. As regards the first category, as we have seen, this involves deciding what the parties themselves would have put into the contract had they addressed themselves to the issue. Lord Denning thought that the required term could not be implied on this basis, because it was highly unlikely that Shell would have agreed to the inclusion of such a term if this had been requested by the garage owner. Terms implied by law, however, do not depend on determining the intention of the parties. The court in this case will impose the term on them, whether they would have agreed to it or not. Two conditions need to be satisfied before this can be done, however. First, the contract has to be of a sufficiently common type (eg seller/buyer, owner/hirer, employer/employee, landlord/tenant) that it is possible to identify the typical obligations of such a contract. Secondly, the matter to which the implied term relates must be one which the parties have not in any way addressed in their contract. There must be a clear gap to be filled. In *Shell v Lostock Garage* the garage owner failed on the first test. Lord Denning was not prepared to hold that exclusive dealing contracts of this kind were sufficiently common that typical terms could be identified.

This type of implication of terms derives from the House of Lords' decision in *Liverpool City Council v Irwin* (1976). The contract in this case was a tenancy agreement in relation to a block of flats. The agreement said nothing about who was to be responsible for the maintenance of the common parts of the block, and in particular the lifts and rubbish chutes. The tenants argued that a term should be implied that the City Council was responsible. It would clearly not have been possible to imply such a term using *The Moorcock*, or the 'officious bystander' tests. It would have been quite possible to have a workable tenancy agreement in which, for example, the responsibility for the common parts was shared among all the tenants of the block. An officious bystander suggesting that a term should be included imposing liability on the landlord alone would have been unlikely to have been considered to be stating the obvious, at least as far as the City Council were concerned. The House of Lords nevertheless decided that it was possible to imply a term to the effect that the landlord should take reasonable steps to keep the common parts in repair. What the House was in effect doing was to say that:

- the agreement was incomplete, in that it was mainly concerned with the tenant's obligations, and contained very little about those of the landlord;

- it was an agreement of a type that was sufficiently common that the court could decide that certain terms would normally be expected to be found in it;

- the term implied was one which the House thought was reasonable in relation to the normal expectations of the obligations as between landlord and tenant.

Despite the fact that Lord Wilberforce insisted on referring the test as one of 'necessity' rather than 'reasonableness', it is clear that in practice it is the latter word which indicates the approach being taken.

6.5.7   *Liverpool City Council v Irwin*

The possibility of implying a term in law was also raised in *Ashmore v Corporation of Lloyd's*, as an alternative to implication in fact. The plaintiff argued that there were many contracts in identical terms between 'names' and Lloyd's, and that therefore this was an appropriate situation in which to use the *Liverpool City Council v Irwin* approach. Gatehouse J disagreed. What was important was not the number of contracts. Rather there needed to be a broad category or type of relationship, even though within that type the detailed terms might vary on particular points. The fact that in this case each contract was in identical terms did not create a category, or genus, or contracts, for which typical terms could be found. The plaintiff's attempt to imply a term by this means failed once again.

6.5.8	Terms implied by statute	

There are two reasons why it may be appropriate for parliament to enact that certain provisions should be implied into all contracts of a particular type. One relates to efficiency. If it is virtually universal practice for certain terms to be used, in particular contractual relationships, there is no need for the parties to state them specifically every time. Rather than having to agree an appropriate wording on each occasion, they can rely on the statutory formulation as representing their obligations. In such a situation, however, there should be the possibility of the parties being able to agree to depart from the statutory wording, if they so wish.

The second reason why terms might need to be implied by statute is for the protection of one of the parties. It may be thought that a particular type of contractual relationship is likely to involve inequality of bargaining power, so that, unless protective provisions are implied, the weaker party may be forced into a very disadvantageous bargain. If this is the reason for the implication, then it may well be that the obligation to include the term should be absolute, without any possibility of its being excluded, or amended, in particular contracts.

Examples of both these bases for implying terms by statute can be found in the implied terms as to quality under the Sale of Goods Acts. The original Sale of Goods Act 1893, was intended to represent a codification of current commercial law and practice. Thus the implied terms as to quality, contained in ss 13–15 were those which merchants of the time would have expected to appear in any contract for the sale of goods. This, then was an example of the first ground for implying terms. In line with this approach, s 55 of the 1893 Act allowed the parties to agree to different terms as to quality, or to exclude them altogether, if they so wished. By the time of the enactment of the revised version of the Act in 1979, however, the atmosphere had changed. The provisions as to quality had come to be regarded as important elements in the law of consumer protection. Their role was therefore at least in part to provide protection for the weaker party in a sale of goods contract. As a result, the Unfair Contract Terms Act 1977 made it impossible in situations where the contract is made between a business and consumer, for the business to exclude the implied terms. Even as between business parties, the exclusion will be subject to a test of 'reasonableness'.

The details of the terms implied by the Sale of Goods Act 1979, and the restrictions on exclusion of them under the Unfair Contract Terms Act 1977, are discussed in detail in Chapter 16.

Another example of a term implied on the grounds of protection is to be found in the Equal Pay Act 1970. Section 3 of this Act implies into every employment contract an 'equality clause' which has the effect of ensuring that as between men and women employed on 'like work' there is equal treatment in relation to all terms of their contracts.

The implication of terms on this basis runs counter to the normal philosophy of English contract law, which is to make the intentions of the parties paramount. Here the clause is imposed on the parties, whether they like it or not. Even if they expressly agree that it is not to operate, the courts will still give effect to it.

The Contents of the Contract

The distinction between representations and terms is important because of remedies. These are more limited as regards representations.

The principal test is the intention of the parties, and the courts will consider:

- the importance of the issue to the parties: *Bannerman v White* (1861);

- whether the contract was put into writing: *Routledge v McKay* (1954); but compare *Evans v Andrea Merzario* (1976);

- relative skill and knowledge of parties: compare *Dick Bentley v Harold Smith* (1965), with *Oscar Chess v Williams* (1957).

- lapse of time between statement and contract: *Routledge v McKay* (1954) - here, one week was too long.

The remedies for pre-contractual statements may be based on:

- misrepresentation - this may be innocent, fraudulent (*Derry v Peek* (1889), or negligent (Misrepresentation Act 1967, s 2(1)). Remedies are rescission, and for negligent and fraudulent misrepresentation, damages. To be available the statement

  (i) must be of existing fact; not opinion (*Bisset v Wilkinson* (1927)), nor law;

  (ii) must have induced the contract: *JEB Fasteners v Marks, Bloom & Co* (1983);

- collateral contract - this will cover promises as to future action (*City of Westminster Properties v Mudd* (1959)); guarantees of statements of fact; or warranties that a statement has been made with reasonable care and skill: *Esso v Mardon* (1976);

- negligent misstatement - tortious action developed from *Hedley Byrne v Heller* (1963). It covers a wide range of types of statements, but it may be difficult to establish the existence of a duty of care: *Caparo v Dickman* (1990).

Express terms

Express terms are identified by:

- incorporation - a clause may be rejected if it is very unusual, and if insufficient notice is given: *Interfoto Picture Library v Stiletto Visual Programmes* (1988). See also the case law on exclusion clauses;

- construction - an objective approach will be taken to interpretation. Only restricted use will be made of parol evidence, eg to establish a custom (*Smith v Wilson* (1832)), or resolve an ambiguity (*Robertson v Jackson* (1845)). Compare also *Evans v Andrea Merzario* (1976).

Implied terms

Terms may be:

- implied by the court

    (i) by custom - if custom is established as a question of fact, the court will apply it (*Hutton v Warren* (1836)), unless there is an express term which is inconsistent (*Les Affreteurs Reunis v Walford* (1919)).

    (ii) in fact - courts attempt to decide what the parties intended. Courts will use the test of necessity ('does the contract work without the clause?') derived from *The Moorcock* (1889), or the 'officious bystander' test (*Shirlaw v Southern Foundries* (1939)). Neither is easy to satisfy: *Ashmore v Corporation of Lloyd's (No 2)* (1992).

    (iii) by law - this approach derives from *Liverpool City Council v Irwin* (1976). It can be used where the contract is of a 'common type' (eg sale of goods, employment, landlord/tenant), and there is a clear gap which needs filling: *Shell v Lostock Garage* (1977). The fact that a lot of contracts have similar provisions does not make them of a 'common type': *Ashmore v Corporation of Lloyd's (No 2)* (1992).

- implied by statute - they can be used to incorporate terms which are generally accepted, but may be excluded (Sale of Goods Act 1893); or terms which are designed to protect the weaker party (Sale of Goods Act 1979; Equal Pay Act 1970), irrespective of the parties' intentions (see further Chapter 16).

Chapter 7

Exclusion Clauses

It will very often be the case that a contract will include a clause exempting or excluding one of the parties from liability in the event of certain types of breach. The exclusion may be total, or may limit the party's liability to a specified sum of money. There is nothing inherently objectionable about a clause of this kind. Provided that it has been included as a result of a clear voluntary agreement between the parties, it may simply indicate their decision as to where certain risks involved in the transaction should fall. If the contract involves the carriage of goods, for example, it may have been agreed that the owner should be responsible for insuring the goods while in transit. In that situation it may be perfectly reasonable for the carrier to have very restricted liability for damage to the goods while they are being carried. The inclusion of the clause is simply an example of good contractual planning.	**7.1 Introduction**

Many exclusion clauses, however, are not of this type. They appear in standard form contracts, which the other party has little choice as to whether to accept or not, and may give the party relying on them a very broad exemption from liability, both in tort and contract. (Note that it is quite possible for an exclusion clause in a contract to restrict tortious liabilities, particularly for negligence in the performance of the contract). When such inequitable clauses began to appear with some frequency in the 19th Century the courts devised ways of limiting their effectiveness. More recently Parliament has intervened to add a statutory layer of control on top of the common law rules (ie Unfair Contract Terms Act 1977 (UCTA), below, para 7.3). The common law is still very important, however, not least because its rules apply to *all* contracts, whereas UCTA only applies in certain situations.

The approach of the courts to exclusion clauses has not been to assess them on their merits. In other words, they have not said 'we think this clause is unreasonable in its scope, or unfair in its operation, and therefore we will not give effect to it'. Such an approach would have run too directly counter to the general ideas of 'freedom of contract' which were particularly important to the courts of the 19th Century. So instead, the courts developed and adapted formal rules relating to the determination of the contents of the contract, and the scope of the clauses contained in it. These are issues which we touched	**7.2 Common law rules**

on in Chapter 6, but it is in the context of exclusion clauses that they have been most fully developed, and that is why they need to be considered in detail here. The main rules which are used are those of 'incorporation' and 'construction', though we will also need to note the so-called 'doctrine of fundamental breach'.

7.3   Incorporation

A clause cannot be effective to exclude liability if it is not part of the contract. As part of the control of exclusion clauses, therefore, the courts have developed fairly strict rules as to the incorporation of terms. The rules are based on the general principle that a party must have had reasonable notice of the exclusion clause at the time of the contract in order for it to be effective. If, however, the contract containing the clause has been signed by the plaintiff, there will be little that the courts can do. In *L'Estrange v Graucob* (1934), for example, the clause was in small print, and very difficult to read, but because the contract had been signed, the clause was held to have been incorporated.

7.3.1   Relevance of time

If a contract containing the clause has not been signed, then the *time* at which it is put forward will be important. If it is not put forward until after the contract has been made then it clearly cannot be incorporated. All the main terms of the contract must be settled at the time of acceptance. Thus in *Olley v Marlborough Court Hotel* (1949), the plaintiff made the contract for the use of a hotel room at the reception desk. A clause purporting to exclude liability for lost luggage was displayed in the room itself. It was held that this came too late to be incorporated into the contract. The position might have been different if the plaintiff had been a regular user of the hotel, and therefore as a result of a long and consistent 'course of dealing' could be said to have had prior notice of the clause: *Hardwick Game Farm v Suffolk Agricultural, etc, Association* (1969). The defendant would be entitled to assume that the plaintiff had read the clause, even if this was not in fact the case.

7.3.2   Requirement of 'reasonable notice'

More commonly, the clause will be presented as part of a set of standard terms, which the other party will be given or referred to at the time of making the contract. In that situation the test is whether 'reasonable notice' of the clause has been given: *Parker v South Eastern Rly* (1877). In this case the clause was contained on a cloakroom ticket, given in exchange for the deposit of a bag. The front of the ticket, which contained a number and date, also said 'See back'. On the other side of the ticket were various clauses, including one excluding liability for goods exceeding the value of £10. The plaintiff's bag, worth £24.50 had been lost. The jury had found that the plaintiff had not read the ticket, nor was he under any obligation to do so. On that basis the judge had directed that judgment should be given for the plaintiff. The Court of Appeal, however, ordered a new trial, on the basis that the proper test was whether the defendants had given reasonable notice of the conditions contained on the ticket.

The standard to be applied is what is reasonable as regards the ordinary adult individual, capable of reading English. Thus in *Thompson v London, Midland and Scottish Rly* (1930), the fact that the plaintiff was illiterate did not help her. The Court of Appeal in addition held that stating on a ticket 'Issued subject to the conditions and regulations in the company's time-tables and notices' was sufficient to draw the other party's attention to the existence of the terms, and thereby to incorporate them into the contract. The contractual document itself, therefore, does not need to set out the exclusion clause, if it gives reasonable notice of the clause's existence, and indicates where it can be read.

The *Thompson* decision is clearly helpful to the defendant. More recently the courts have adopted an approach which requires an assessment of the nature of the clause alongside the amount of notice given. Thus, the more unusual or more onerous the exclusion clause, the greater the notice that will be expected to be given. In *Spurling v Bradshaw* (1956), for example, Lord Denning commented that:

> 'Some exclusion clauses I have seen would need to be printed in red ink on the face of the document with a red hand pointing to it before the notice could be held to be sufficient.'

In *Thornton v Shoe Lane Parking Ltd* (1971), this approach was applied, so that a clause displayed on a notice inside a car park, containing extensive exclusions, was held not to be incorporated into a contract which was made by the purchase of a ticket from a machine. In addition, as we saw in Chapter 6, the same rule operated in *Interfoto Picture Library v Stiletto Visual Programmes* (1989) to prevent the incorporation of a clause which was not an exclusion clause, but which was nevertheless exceptional, and unusually onerous.

In order to be effectively incorporated the exclusion clause must generally be contained, or referred to, in something which can be regarded as a contractual document. This is an aspect of the rule that reasonable notice must be given. Notice is unlikely to be regarded as reasonable if the clause appears in something which would not be expected to contain contractual

7.3.3   Incorporation and unusual exclusions

7.3.4   Need for a 'contractual' document

terms. Thus in *Chapelton v Barry UDC* (1940) a ticket which was given in exchange for the hire of a deckchair was held to be a mere receipt. It was not a document on which the customer would expect to find contractual terms, and the exclusion clause printed on it was therefore not incorporated. In fact in this case, the ticket was in any case provided too late, as it was held that the contract was formed when the deckchair was first taken for use, whereas the ticket was not handed over until some time later.

7.4   Construction

Once it has been decided that a clause has been incorporated into the contract, the next issue is whether it covers the breach that has occurred. In other words, the wording of the clause must be examined to see if it is apt to apply to the situation which has arisen. This is the called the rule of 'construction', but might equally well be called the rule of 'interpretation'. The clause is being 'constructed' or 'interpreted' to determine its scope.

7.4.1   *Contra proferentem* rule

The rules of construction, like the rules for incorporation, are of general application, and can be used in relation to all clauses within a contract, not just exclusion clauses. It is in relation to exclusion of liability, however, that most of the case law has arisen. In this context the courts have traditionally taken a strict approach. The rule of construction has been used as a means of limiting the effect of exclusion clauses, and a person wishing to avoid liability has been required to be very precise in the use of language to achieve that aim. One aspect of this is the *contra proferentem* rule, whereby if there is any ambiguity in an exclusion clause then it is interpreted against the person putting it forward. Thus in *Andrews v Singer* (1934) a clause excluding liability in relation to *implied* terms was ruled ineffective to exclude liability for breach of an *express* term. Particular difficulty can arise where the defendant seeks to exclude liability for negligence in the performance of a contract. In *Hollier v Rambler Motors* (1972) the plaintiff's car was at the defendant's premises when it was damaged by fire, caused by the defendant's negligence. There was a clause in the contract which stated 'the company is not responsible for damage caused by fire to customers' cars on the premises'. In the Court of Appeal the view was taken that customers would assume that this clause related to fires which arose without negligence on the part of the defendant (though as a matter of law there would in fact be no liability in such a case). If the defendant wanted to exclude liability for negligence then this should have been done explicitly. This is possible by using a general phrase, such as 'no liability for any damage, *howsoever caused*'.

Note, however, that the position is different if the only basis of liability which the plaintiff would think existed is negligence liability: *Alderslade v Hendon Laundry* (1945). In that case the courts will be prepared to allow exclusion without any specific reference to negligence, or the use of a general phrase clearly including negligence: *Rutter v Palmer* (1922). In the end it is a matter of attempting to assess the intentions and reasonable expectations of the parties.

The position as regards exclusion of liability for negligence has been significantly affected by the Unfair Contract Terms Act 1977 (UCTA - below, para 7.3). More generally, the existence of stricter statutory controls over exclusion clauses has encouraged the courts to take the line that there is no need for the rule of construction to be used in an artificial way to limit their scope. The consumer and the standard form contract are dealt with by UCTA. Businesses negotiating at arms length should be expected to look after themselves. If they enter into contracts containing exclusion clauses they must be presumed to know what they are doing. Thus on three occasions since the passage of UCTA (ie in *Photo Production v Securicor* (1980), *Ailsa Craig Fishing Co v Malvern Fishing Co* (1983), and *Mitchell (George) v Finney Lock Seeds* (1983)) the House of Lords has criticised an approach to the interpretation of exclusion clauses in commercial contracts which involves straining their plain meaning in order to limit their effect.

7.4.2   Relexation of the rule

At one time the view was taken by some courts, and in particular the Court of Appeal, that some breaches of contract are so serious that no exclusion clause can cover them. This was expressed in the so-called doctrine of fundamental breach. This doctrine found its origins in shipping law, where there is strong authority that if a ship 'deviates' from its agreed route, there can be no exclusion of liability in relation to events which occur after the deviation: eg *Joseph Thorley Ltd v Orchis SS Co Ltd* (1907). Applied more generally to the law of contract it took two forms. One was that there are certain terms within the contract which are so fundamental that there cannot be exclusion for breach of them. Such would be the situation where the contract stipulated for the supply of peas, and beans were provided instead: *Chanter v Hopkins* (1838). This involves the 'breach of a fundamental term'. The second form arises where the breach which occurs, or its effects, are so serious that it must be taken effectively to have destroyed the whole contract, so that exclusion of liability is no longer possible. This is, in other words, a 'fundamental breach'. The Court of Appeal took the view that this is what had occurred in *Photo Production v Securicor* (1980). The plaintiffs owned a factory, and engaged

7.4.3   Fundamental breach

the defendants to provide security services, including a night patrol. Unfortunately, one of the guards employed by the defendants to carry out these duties, started a fire on premises which got out of control, and destroyed the entire factory. Thus, rather than protecting the plaintiffs' property, as they had been contracted to do, the defendants could be said to have achieved the exact opposite. The contract, however, contained a very broadly worded exclusion clause, which, on its face, seemed to cover even the very serious breach of the agreement which had occurred. The Court of Appeal took the view that this could not protect the defendants. There had been a fundamental breach, and the exclusion clause was ineffective. The House of Lords, however, took a different view. In an earlier case, *Suisse Atlantique Société d'Armemente SA v NV Rotterdamsche Kolen Centrale* (1967) the House had expressed disapproval of the doctrine of fundamental breach. The Court of Appeal, however, had regarded it as still available in *Harbutt's Plasticine v Wayne Tank and Pump Co Ltd* (1970), and again in *Photo Production v Securicor*, as we have seen. The House of Lords took this opportunity to state its position with no possible ambiguity. It ruled that there was no rule of law that a fundamental breach of contract prevented an exclusion clause from being effective. The so-called doctrine of fundamental breach was in fact no more than an aspect of the doctrine of construction. Of course it was the case that the more serious the breach of contract, the clearer the words would need to be which would exclude liability for it. But if two businesses had negotiated an agreement containing a clause which on its plain wording covered such a breach, there was no reason why the courts should not give effect to it. In the present case, the House, while noting the breadth of the exclusion clause, also noted that the plaintiffs were paying a very low rate for the defendants' services. It was therefore not unreasonable that the defendants should have a low level of liability. The ratio of the case was not, however, that the clause was reasonable in all the circumstances, but that on its true construction it covered the breach.

7.4.4   The current position

The demise of the doctrine of fundamental breach as a rule of law (and there has been no attempt to revive it since the *Photo Production* decision) has to some extent simplified the law in this area. It may be still be difficult to decide in particular cases, however, what to do where a breach effectively negates the whole purpose of the contract. It is a matter of looking at the precise wording of the exclusion clause, and trying to determine the intentions of the parties in relation to it. The likelihood of exclusion being effective will decrease with the seriousness of the breach, but it is now always a question of balance, rather than the application of a firm rule.

Where the contract involves a consumer, this process is generally rendered unnecessary because of the statutory provisions contained in the Unfair Contract Terms Act, to which we now turn.

The Unfair Contract Terms Act 1977 (UCTA) has had a very significant effect on the law relating to exclusion clauses. Where it applies it has to a large extent replaced the common law rules. Although strictly speaking the rules of incorporation and construction are logically prior to any consideration of the statutory provisions, so that if a clause is not incorporated or does not cover the breach it can have no effect at all, and UCTA is irrelevant, the Act will in practice often be looked at first. The student of contract law must, of course, always be prepared to discuss both common law and statute. It must be remembered, too, that UCTA does not apply to all contracts. The first point for discussion here is therefore the precise scope of the Act.

7.5 Unfair Contract Terms Act 1977 (UCTA)

There are certain contracts, listed in Schedule 1 to the Act, which are not within the scope of ss 2 to 4 (which are the main protective provisions) at all. These include:

7.5.1 Scope of UCTA

- contracts of insurance;

- contracts concerning the creation or transfer of interests in land;

- contracts concerning the creation or transfer of intellectual property rights (copyright, patent, etc);

- contracts relating to the formation, dissolution, or constitution of a company, partnership, or unincorporated association;

- contracts relating to the creation or transfer of securities.

The Act also has only limited application in relation to various types of shipping contract, including carriage of goods by sea, and contracts of employment. In relation to contracts of this type, it is always important to check the provisions of Schedule 1.

The next limitation on the scope of the Act which must be noted appears in s 1(3). This states that ss 2 to 7 apply only to:

7.5.2 'Business' liability

'... business liability, that is liability for breach of obligations or duties arising (a) from things done or to be done in the course of a business ...; or (b) from the occupation of premises used for the business purposes of the occupier.'

In general, therefore, the non-business contractor is free to include exclusion clauses, without their being controlled by UCTA (though the scope of s 6, which deals with sale of goods contracts, is wider - see Chapter 16, below). In many situations the test of whether obligations arise in the course of a 'business' will not give rise to problems, but it is perhaps unfortunate that the Act does not contain a comprehensive definition of what is meant by 'business'. Section 14 states that '"business" includes a profession and the activities of any government department or local or public authority'.

This leaves open the position of organisations such as charities, or universities, which may engage in business activities, but might not be thought to be contracting 'in the course of a business'. The protective policy of the Act would suggest that such situations ought to be covered. The phrase 'in the course of a business' has, however, been interpreted fairly restrictively in relation to its use in another context within the Act. Section 12 uses it as part of the definition of whether a person 'deals as a consumer' for the purposes of buying goods, which is an important consideration in relation to the application of s 6. In *R & B Customs Brokers v UDT* (1988) the plaintiff was a private company involved in the export business. A car was bought by the company for the personal and business use of the directors. It was held by the Court of Appeal that it was not bought 'in the course of a business', because the plaintiff's business was not that of buying and selling cars. If this approach is taken in relation to s 1(3) it would mean, for example, that a university which provides car-parking facilities on its site in return for payment, or a charity which makes money by organising a 'car-boot' sale, and selling 'pitches', would not be covered by the Act. It is difficult to see, however, why the other contracting party should be any less protected in such a situation than if dealing with a commercial organisation, which might well be in no better position to meet financial liabilities, or to ensure against them, than the university or charity. For the time being, however, the decision in *R & B Customs Brokers v UDT* must be regarded as the governing authority.

7.3.3   Disclaimers

The final issue in relation to the scope of the Act concerns the type of clauses which are covered. In drawing up a contract it is possible to attempt to avoid liabilities in a number of ways. The most obvious is by an exclusion clause which states that in the event of a breach there will be no liability, or that it will be limited to a particular sum. It is also possible, however, to attempt to achieve the same objective by clauses which define the obligations arising under the contract restrictively ('disclaimers'), or make the enforcement of a liability subject to restrictive conditions (eg 'all claims must be made within 48 hours of the conclusion of the contract'). Section 13 makes it clear that all clauses of this kind which have the effect of excluding or restricting liability are caught by the Act's provisions. In *Smith v Bush* (1989) the House of Lords confirmed that s 13 extends s 2 of the Act to a clause which is in the form of a disclaimer, which in this case was given by a surveyor providing a valuation of a property to the plaintiff, via a building society. The valuation was stated to be given without any acceptance of responsibility as to its accuracy. This was held to be an 'exclusion clause' within the scope of UCTA, and to fall foul of its requirement of 'reasonableness' (discussed below, para 7.8). (See also *Stewart Gill v Horatio Myer & Co Ltd* (1992) where the Court of Appeal held that a clause restricting a right of set-off or counterclaim could be regarded as an exclusion clause, and therefore within the scope of UCTA.)

Section 2 of UCTA is concerned with clauses which attempt to exclude business liability for 'negligence', which is defined for the purposes of the Act in s 1(1) to cover the breach:

7.6 Exclusion of negligence under UCTA

'(a) of any obligation, arising from the express or implied terms of a contract, to take reasonable care or exercise reasonable skill in the performance of the contract;

(b) of any common law duty to take reasonable care or exercise reasonable skill (but not any stricter duty);

(c) of the common duty of care imposed by the Occupiers' Liability Act 1957.'

Thus it applies to negligent performance of a contract (subsection (a)), the tort of negligence independent of any contract (subsection (b)), and the statutory duty of care imposed on occupiers towards lawful visitors (subsection (c)).

The level of control imposed by s 2 depends on the consequences of the negligence. To the extent that the exclusion clause attempts to limit liability for death or personal injury resulting from negligence it will be totally ineffective (s 2(1)). As regards any other types of loss or damage the clause will be effective to the extent that the clause satisfies the 'requirement of reasonableness' set out in s 11 of UCTA (s 2(2)). This is discussed further below, para 7.8. It is not clear what the approach of the courts will be towards a clause which attempts to exclude or limit liability for all loss or damage (including death or personal injury) resulting from negligence by the use of a general phrase such as 'no liability for any loss, injury or damage, howsoever caused'. Clearly the clause will not be effective in relation to death or personal injuries resulting from negligence. This does not mean that the clause is totally without effect, however. The Act does not invalidate a clause altogether simply because it attempts to exclude liability for personal injuries. It may be arguable, however, that in relation to other losses the breadth of the clause makes it unreasonable. The answer to this will depend on the precise interpretation of the requirement of reasonableness, and we will return to this issue in the context of that discussion.

| 7.7 | **Standard terms and consumer contracts** |

Whereas s 2 is only concerned with the exclusion of negligence liability, s 3 covers all types of liability arising under a contract, including strict liability, but is limited in the types of contract which it effects. The section is directed at situations where there is inequality of bargaining power, and the plaintiff may have effectively been forced to accept a wide ranging exclusion clause, which may appear to operate unfairly. The section operates in relation to two types of contract. First it covers contracts where the plaintiff 'deals as a consumer' . The definition of 'dealing as a consumer' is to be found in s 12. A party 'deals as a consumer' if:

'(a) he neither makes the contract in the course of a business nor holds himself out as doing so; and

(b) the other party does make the contract in the course of a business'.

| 7.7.1 | Meaning of 'in the course of a business' |

The scope of the phrase 'in the course of a business' as defined in *R & B Customs Brokers v UDT* (1988) has been discussed above. As we have seen it means that it is not simply the private individual who can claim to deal 'as a consumer'. Businesses will apparently be able to do so in relation to contracts which do not form a regular part of their business. Whether this is what was intended by Parliament must be open to doubt, but it represents the position as currently indicated by the Court of Appeal. A person claiming to deal as a consumer does not have to prove this: the burden of proof is on the party claiming that a person is *not* dealing as a consumer (s 12(3)).

| 7.7.2 | Standard terms of business |

The second type of contract which is covered by s 3 is one which is made on the basis of the defendant's 'written standard terms of business'. This phrase is not further defined, but it is to be assumed that the individual negotiation of some of the terms of the agreement will not prevent them from being 'standard'. The exclusion clause itself will, however, presumably have to be part of the standard package. It is important to remember that this provision is not concerned directly with inequalities in bargaining power. It is likely in practice (because of the way in which the requirement of reasonableness operates) to benefit the weaker party more frequently, but there is no reason in theory why it should not be relied on by a large corporation which happens to have made a contract on the basis of a much smaller and less powerful business's standard terms. It is also important to note that this category is unlikely to be needed to be used by the private individual, despite the fact that many contracts between individuals and businesses are made on the business's standard terms. The reason for this is, of course, that the private individual will contract 'as consumer', and will therefore be within the other category covered by s 3.

The effect of s 3 is that in relation to any contract within its scope, any attempt to exclude or restrict liability by the non-consumer, or the party putting forward the standard terms, will be subject to the requirement of reasonableness (s 3(2)(a)). Moreover, s 3(2)(b) goes on to make it clear that this extends also to any contractual term by virtue of which such a party claims to be entitled:

7.7.3   Effect of s 3

'(i)   to render a contractual performance substantially different from that which was reasonably to be expected of him, or

(ii)   in respect of the whole or any part of his contractual obligation, to render no performance at all ...'

The point of the provisions in s 3(2)(b) is similar to that of s 13. It is trying to anticipate attempts to exclude liability indirectly by the use of clauses which define a party's obligations very restrictively. Such clauses are permissible, but only to the extent which they satisfy the requirement of reasonableness. This enables a court to distinguish clauses which are genuine and legitimate attempts to set out the parties' contractual obligations, from those which are being used to escape any substantial liability at all. The test of legitimacy, as indicated by s 3(2)(b)(i) above, is likely to be the reasonable expectations of the other party.

The overall effect of s 3 is that, because the vast majority of exclusion clauses will be in either a consumer contract, or one which is on standard terms, there will be very few situations in which an exclusion clause is not at least subject to the requirement of reasonableness. It gives the Appeal Courts the opportunity to indicate the acceptable limits of exclusion of liability, though as will be seen below, para 7.8, it is not one which they have shown any great willingness to accept.

7.8 The requirement of reasonableness

The test to be applied to determine whether a clause meets the requirement of reasonableness is set out in s 11 of UCTA. The central element of the test is stated in s 11(1) as being whether the clause was:

> '... a fair and reasonable one to be included having regard to the circumstances which were, or ought reasonably to have been, known to or in the contemplation of the parties when the contract was made.'

This very general test imposes no very significant restrictions on the exercise of a court's discretion in relation to a clause, and therefore makes things difficult for the parties in terms of contractual planning. It will be very difficult to predict whether a particular clause is likely to fall foul of this test. A few guidelines to its operation can be found, however, both within the Act itself and from case law.

7.8.1 Interpretation of reasonableness

Starting with the wording of s 11, it is clear that the point at which the clause should be assessed is when the contract was created, and that the test is directed at the clause itself, not at any particular application of it. Thus the issue is whether the clause is one which at the time the parties made the contract could be regarded as fair and reasonable. Subsequent events should not be relevant in deciding this issue. In particular, the actual breach which has occurred and for which the clause is claimed to provide exclusion or limitation of liability, should not, in theory, be considered. The strict reading of the section makes it clear that it is quite possible for a court to feel that it would be reasonable for the defendant to have excluded liability for the particular breach which has occurred, but that the clause is too widely worded to be reasonable, and should therefore fail. This is in line with a policy which aims to discourage the use of unnecessarily wide clauses, rather than simply trying to provide a just solution to individual disputes. The Court of Appeal in *Stewart Gill v Horatio Myer & Co Ltd* (1992) confirmed that it is the reasonableness of a clause as a whole, rather than the part of it which is being relied on in the particular case, that must be considered.

Where the clause is one which attempts to limit liability to a specific sum of money, rather than excluding it altogether, s 11(4) directs the court to take into account, in assessing the reasonableness of the clause:

> '(a) the resources which [the defendant] could expect to be available to him for the purpose of meeting the liability should it arise; and
>
> (b) how far it was open to him to cover himself by insurance.'

This recognises that it may be quite reasonable for a contracting party who is impecunious, or is engaging in a particularly risky activity, to put a financial ceiling on liability.

Finally, s 11(5) makes it clear that the burden of proof as regarding reasonableness lies on the party seeking to rely on the clause.

The only other part of UCTA which provides guidance on the operation of the reasonableness test is Schedule 2. Strictly speaking, the 'guidelines' which it contains are only to be used in relation to exclusion clauses which attempt to limit liability for breach of the statutorily implied terms under sale of goods and hire purchase contracts. In practice, however, the considerations set out are likely to be regarded as relevant whenever reasonableness is in issue. There are five listed, covering the following areas:

- The relative strength of the bargaining position of the parties - in particular, did the plaintiff have any option about contracting with the defendant, or were there other means by which the plaintiff's requirements could have been met.

- Whether the plaintiff received an inducement (eg a discount) to agree to the term; could the same contract have been made with other persons without the exclusion clause?

- Whether the plaintiff knew or ought reasonably to have known of the existence and extent of the term. (Note that there is a clear overlap here with the common law requirement of incorporation.)

- Whether at the time of contract it was reasonable to expect that compliance would be practicable with any condition which, if not complied with, leads to the exclusion or restriction of liability.

- Whether goods were manufactured, processed or adapted to the special order of the customer. (Note that this consideration is specifically linked to contracts for the supply of goods: put into general terms it would require the court to consider whether the contract was specially negotiated to meet the plaintiff's requirements.)

The weight to be given to any of these considerations is left entirely to the discretion of the court. Moreover, since they are only 'guidelines' there is no obligation to look at them at all. It is unlikely, for example, that the Court of Appeal would overturn a judge's decision on the reasonableness issue simply because one of the above guidelines had not been considered, even in relation to a contract for the supply of goods. The list is not exclusive, and other matters may be taken into consideration, if the court feels that this is appropriate.

7.8.3   Judicial approach to 'reasonableness' - pre-UCTA

As far as the case law on 'reasonableness' is concerned there are two House of Lords decisions which are worth noting, one applying a test of reasonableness which pre-dated UCTA, the other dealing with UCTA itself.

The first case is *George Mitchell v Finney Lock Seeds* (1983). This concerned a contract for the sale of cabbage seed which turned out not to match its description, with the result that the entire crop failed, and the purchaser suffered a loss of £63,000. The contract contained an exclusion clause, limiting the liability of the seller to the price of the seed, which was under £200. The clause was subject to the test of reasonableness (now superseded by UCTA) contained in s 55(4) of the Sale of Goods Act 1979 (as set out in Schedule 1), which required the court to decide whether it was fair and reasonable to allow reliance on the clause. The trial judge and the Court of Appeal held that the clause did not on its true construction cover the breach. The House of Lords differed on the construction issue, holding that the wording was apt to cover the breach, and so had to go on to consider the question of reasonableness. The House emphasised that it was best on this issue, wherever possible, for the appeal courts to accept the judgment of the trial judge, who had the benefit of hearing all the witnesses. (This point was also made in the later case of *Phillips v Hyland* (1987)). Since that was not possible here, however, the House went on to determine the 'reasonableness' issue itself. It approached it as an exercise in 'balancing' various factors against each other. On the one hand the clause was a common one in the trade, and had never been objected to by the National Union of Farmers. Moreover, the magnitude of the damage in proportion to the price of the goods sold also weighed in the defendants' favour. Lord Bridge, however, found three matters to put into the other side of the balance. First, the fact that the wrong seed was supplied was due to negligence (albeit of the defendants' sister company, rather than the defendants themselves). Secondly, the trial judge had found that the defendants would have been able to take out insurance against crop failure, without needing to increase the price of the seeds significantly. Thirdly, and in Lord Bridge's view most importantly, there was evidence from a number of witnesses (including the chairman of the defendants) that it was general practice in the trade *not* to rely on this clause in cases like the one which the House was considering, but to negotiate more substantial compensation. As Lord Bridge put it:

'This evidence indicates a clear recognition by seedsmen in general, and the [defendants] in particular, that reliance on the limitation of liability imposed by the relevant condition would not be fair and reasonable.'

This indicates that where the courts are dealing with a common type of contract within a particular area of business activity, the practices of the trade or business are likely to be of considerable relevance. In addition the fact that *all* the circumstances must be considered, and that the appeal courts' are reluctant to interfere with decisions of the trial judge, means that it is not necessarily the case that because a particular exclusion clause has been found unreasonable in one situation, that it will be precluded from use in others. This element of uncertainty will pull in two directions. It will make those who wish to include exclusion clauses cautious, and may encourage them to word clauses narrowly and precisely. On the other hand, the plaintiff who wishes to challenge a clause may well be deterred by the fact that the outcome of such a challenge will be very unpredictable.

The second House of Lords case which has discussed the concept of 'reasonableness' is *Smith v Bush* (1989). The case concerned a 'disclaimer' of liability for negligence put forward by a surveyor carrying out a valuation of a property for a building society, which was relied on by the purchaser of the property. Having decided that this disclaimer did constitute an exclusion clause, by virtue of s 13 of UCTA (see above, para 7.5.3), the House then had to consider whether it satisfied the requirement of reasonableness. The factors which were considered relevant to this issue were set out most clearly in the speech of Lord Griffiths. He thought that there were four matters which should *always* be considered in deciding this issue. They were:

7.8.4   UCTA in the
          House of Lords

• Were the parties of equal bargaining power? (This also appears in the guidelines in Schedule 2 to UCTA.)

• In the case of advice, would it have been reasonably practicable to obtain the advice from an alternative source taking into account considerations of costs and time? In this case, although the purchaser could have obtained another survey, it was relevant that the house was 'at the bottom end of the market', which made it less reasonable to expect the purchaser to pay for a second opinion.

• How difficult is the task being undertaken for which liability is being excluded? The more difficult or dangerous the undertaking, the more reasonable it is to exclude liability.

• What are the practical consequences of the decision on reasonableness? For example, if the risk is one against which a defendant could quite easily have insured, but which will have very serious effects on a plaintiff who is required to bear the loss, this will suggest that exclusion is unreasonable. It might be otherwise if a finding of liability would 'open the floodgates' to claims.

With these considerations in mind, and in addition, the fact that this was an individual private house purchase, not a deal in relation to commercial property, the House decided that the disclaimer of liability did not meet the requirement of reasonableness.

Two Court of Appeal decisions, *Phillips Products v Hyland* (1987) and *Thompson v Lohan (Plant Hire)* (1987), have also involved consideration of the test, but the cases (which involved differing interpretations of the same clause), do not add significantly to the guidelines on how the test should be applied as indicated by the *Mitchell v Finney Lock*, and *Smith v Bush* decisions.

7.9	**Indemnities**	Section 4 deals with attempts to impose liability on a person dealing as a consumer by way of an obligation to indemnify another for liability for negligence or breach of contract. This can only be done insofar as the clause satisfies the requirement of reasonableness.

This might be attempted where, for example, a consumer sues in tort an individual employee who has acted negligently in the course of employment. The employee may well be entitled to be indemnified by his or her employer, and the employer may in return have provided for an indemnity in the contract with the consumer. By virtue of s 4, this will only be enforceable if it satisfies the requirement of reasonableness.

7.10	**Guarantees of consumer goods**	A 'guarantee' provided by the manufacturer of goods, for example, may try to limit a consumer's rights, by giving, for example, a right to replacement, but denying any other liability. Where the goods have proved defective while 'in consumer use' (ie other than exclusively for the purposes of a business (s 5(2)(a)), and this results from the negligence of the defendant, then the limitation of liability will be ineffective (s 5(1)).

Note that this section does not apply to guarantees given by a seller, or hirer, of goods. The effect of such provisions in these contracts is covered by ss 6 and 7 of UCTA, which are discussed below.

There are special provisions under the Act in relation to contracts for the supply of goods (ss 6 and 7) and liability for misrepresentations (s 8). These are dealt with in the chapters concerned with these topics (ie 16 and 8 respectively).

7.11   Other cases - sale, hire purchase, misrepresentation

It should be noted that with effect from 31 December 1994, English law will be required to comply with the provisions of the European Directive on Unfair Contract Terms in Consumer Contracts (Directive 93/13). UCTA goes some way towards meeting this obligation, but does not do so completely, since, among other things, the Directive extends beyond exclusion of liability. It is not clear at the moment how the British government intends to amend the law, but some legislation will be needed.

A full discussion of the provisions of the Directive may be found in Meryll Dean, 'Unfair Contract Terms: The European Approach' (1993) 56 MLR 581.

7.12   European Directive on Unfair Terms in Consumer Contracts

Exclusion Clauses

The Common Law developed formal rules to protect the 'weaker party' from exclusion clauses.

Common law rules

- Incorporation

  If the contract is not signed (*L'Estrange v Graucob* (1934)), reasonable notice must be given, at or before the time of contract (*Olley v Marlborough Court Hotel* (1949); *Parker v South Eastern Rly* (1877)).

  The degree of notice required will vary according to the scope of the clause: *Spurling v Bradshaw* (1956); *Thornton v Shoe Lane Parking* (1971); *Interfoto Picture Library v Stiletto Visual Programmes* (1989). The clause must be contained in a 'contractual' document: *Chapelton v Barry UDC* (1940).

- Construction

  Clauses will be construed *contra proferentem*: *Andrews v Singer* (1934). Negligence liability may need to be specifically excluded (*Hollier v Rambler Motors* (1972)), unless it is the only type of liability possible (*Alderslade v Hendon Laundry* (1945)). UCTA has led to some relaxation in the rule of construction.

- Fundamental breach

  This was rejected as a rule of law by the House of Lords in *Photo Production v Securicor* (1980). It now exists simply as an aspect of the rule of construction.

The Unfair Contract Terms Act 1977 (UCTA) has in practice replaced the common law in many areas, though it does not apply to all contracts.

Unfair Contract Terms Act 1977 (UCTA)

- Scope of UCTA

  Some types of contract (eg concerning land) are altogether outside its scope (Schedule 1). In other cases it generally only applies to 'business liability' (s 1(3)). This concept has been narrowly defined in *R&B Customs Brokers v UDT* (1988).

  Disclaimers, and other attempts to avoid liability by narrowing obligations, are to be treated as exclusion clauses: s 13, and *Smith v Bush* (1989).

- Negligence liability

  This is dealt with by s 2. There can be no exclusion in relation to liability for death or personal injury (s 2(1)). Other losses caused by negligence can be excluded, if the clause is 'reasonable' under s 11.

- Standard term and consumer contracts

  These are dealt with by s 3. All attempts to exclude or restrict liability, or to re-define obligations so as to avoid liability, will be subject to the requirement of reasonableness in s 11.

The requirement of reasonableness

The clause must be a 'fair and reasonable one to be included' in the contract, at the time it was made. The burden of proof is on the defendant: s 11(5).

The clause must be assessed as at the time of contract: *Stewart Gill v Horatio Myer & Co* (1992).

If it restricts liability to a specific sum the defendant's resources, and the availability of insurance must be considered: s 11(4).

- Guidelines under Schedule 2

  These strictly only apply to contracts concerned with the supply of goods, but are likely to be more generally referred to. They cover such things as the relative bargaining strength of the parties, and the plaintiff's knowledge of the term.

- Reasonableness in the courts

  In *George Mitchell v Finney Lock Seeds* (1983) (pre-UCTA), the House of Lords was strongly influenced by commercial practice in deciding what was 'reasonable'.

  In *Smith v Bush* (1989) the House of Lords set out some guidelines as to what should be considered, which included bargaining strength, availability to the plaintiff of alternatives, the difficulty of the task, and the availability of insurance.

Other clauses within UCTA

Note that the Act also contains provisions dealing with indemnities (s 4), guarantees of consumer goods (s 5), contracts for the sale or hire purchase of goods (ss 6 and 7), and liability for misrepresentations (s 8).

European Directive on Unfair Terms in Consumer Contracts

The European Directive on Unfair Terms in Consumer Contracts will not come into force until 31 December 1994, but will then have a significant effect on the English law relating to consumer contracts.

Chapter 8

Misrepresentation and Mistake

8.1 Introduction

A party to a contract which has been validly formed, and in which all the terms are clearly agreed, may nevertheless decide that it has turned out not to be quite what was anticipated when it was made. This may be the result of a misrepresentation by the other party, or of a mistake made by either or both parties. In such a situation the party may wish to escape from the agreement altogether, or to seek compensation of some kind. This chapter discusses the situations where English law allows this to occur, on the basis of the rules relating to 'misrepresentation' or 'mistake'. These two topics, while not co-terminous, have sufficient degree of overlap to justify dealing with them both in the same chapter. (Note that some aspects of misrepresentation have been touched on in Chapter 6, at 6.3.1).

The rules covering this area impose fairly heavy burdens on the plaintiff, particularly in relation to mistake. This is not surprising. It would not be satisfactory if a party to a contract could simply, by saying 'I'm sorry, I made a mistake', unstitch a complex agreement, without any thought for the consequences to the other party, or any third parties who might be involved. On the other hand, there are some contractors, such as certain large chain stores, who feel able (presumably because of their volume of business, and their strength of position in the market) to allow customers who have changed their minds to exchange or return goods which are in no way defective. These arrangements are, however, exceptions to the general position, which will only allow a party to undo the agreement in a limited range of circumstances.

We shall consider first misrepresentation, and then mistake.

8.2 Misrepresentation

The basic requirements that are necessary in order for there to be a remedy for a pre-contractual misrepresentation are as follows. The statement must have been made by one of the contracting parties to the other; it must be a statement of fact, not opinion or law; and the statement must have induced the other party to enter into the contract.

8.2.1 Statement by one party to the other

If a person has entered into a contract on the basis of a misrepresentation by a third party, this will have no effect on the contract, or on the person's legal relationship with the other contracting party. A person who buys shares in a company on the basis of a third party's statement that it has just made a substantial profit, cannot undo the share agreement if the statement turns out to be untrue. This general principle may have been affected in limited circumstances, however, by the House of Lords decision in *Barclays Bank v O'Brien* (1993). This is discussed in Chapter 9, 'Duress and Undue Influence'.

8.2.2	Statement of existing fact	The statement must be one of fact, not opinion or law. This has already been discussed in Chapter 6, 6.3.1. One further point should be noted here. A statement of an intention to act in a particular way in the future may be interpreted as a statement of fact, if it is clear that the person making the statement did not, at that time, have any intention of so acting. In *Edgington v Fitzmaurice* (1885) a company prospectus, designed to attract subscribers, contained false statements about the uses to which the money raised would be put. It was held this statement of intention could be treated as a representation as to the directors' state of mind at the time that the prospectus was issued, and could thus be treated as a statement of fact. As Bowen LJ put it:

'... the state of a man's mind is as much a fact as the state of his digestion. It is true that it is very difficult to prove what the state of a man's mind at a particular time is, but if it can be ascertained it is as much a fact as anything else. A misrepresentation as to the state of a man's mind is, therefore, a misstatement of fact.'

8.2.3	Misrepresentation by silence	In general there is no misrepresentation by silence. Even where one party is aware that the other is contracting on basis of a misunderstanding of some fact relating to the contract there will generally be no liability. There are, however, some exceptions to this. First, the maker of the statement must not give only half the story on some aspect of the facts. Thus in *Dimmock v Hallett* (1866) the statement that flats were fully let, when in fact the tenants had given notice to quit, was capable of being a misrepresentation. Secondly, if a true statement is made, but then circumstances change, making it false, a failure to disclose this will be treated as a misrepresentation: *With v O'Flanagan* (1936). Thirdly, certain contracts, such as those for insurance, are treated as being 'of the utmost good faith' (*uberrimae fidei*), and requiring the contracting party to disclose all relevant facts. In an insurance contract this obligation is placed on the person seeking insurance. A similar obligation applies to contracts establishing family settlements: *Gordon v Gordon* (1816). Finally, there are come contracts which involve a fiduciary relationship, and this may entail a duty to disclose. In

this category are to be found contracts between agent and principal, solicitor and client, and a company and its promoters. Other similar relationships which have a fiduciary character will be treated in the same way, and the list is not closed.

It is not enough to give rise to a remedy for misrepresentation, for A to point to some false statement of fact made by B prior to a contract which they have made. It must also be shown that that statement formed some part of the reason why A entered into the agreement. In *JEB Fasteners Ltd v Bloom* (1983), for example, which was concerned with this issue of reliance in the context of an action for negligent misstatement at common law, it was established that the plaintiffs took over a business having seen inaccurate accounts prepared by the defendants. Their reason for taking over the business, however, was shown to have been the wish to secure the services of two directors. The accounts had not induced their action in taking over the business.

8.2.4 Misrepresentation must induce the contract

On the other hand it is not necessary for the misrepresentation to be the *sole* reason why the contract was entered into. In *Edgington v Fitzmaurice* (1885), the plaintiff was influenced not only by the prospectus, but also by his own mistaken belief that he would have a charge on the assets of the company. His action based on misrepresentation was nevertheless successful.

Nor does it matter that the party deceived has spurned a chance to discover the truth. In *Redgrave v Hurd* (1881) false statements were made by the plaintiff about the income of his practice as a solicitor, on the strength of which the defendant had entered into a contract to buy the plaintiff's house. He had been given the chance to examine documents which would have revealed the true position, but had declined to do so. This did not prevent his claim based on misrepresentation.

Related to this is the question of whether the reliance on the statement has to be 'reasonable'. This issue was considered in *Museprime Properties Ltd v Adhill Properties Ltd* (1990). Property owned by the defendant was sold by auction to the plaintiffs. There was an inaccurate statement in the auction particulars, which was re-affirmed by the auctioneer, to the effect that rent reviews of three leases to which the properties were subject had not been finalised. The plaintiffs sought to rescind the contract for misrepresentation. *Inter alia*, the defendants argued that the misrepresentation was not material because no reasonable bidder would have allowed it to influence his bid. Scott J held, approving a passage to this effect in Goff and Jones, *The Law of Restitution* (3rd ed (1986) p 168), that the materiality of the representation was not to be determined by whether a reasonable person would have been induced to contract. As long as the plaintiff was *in fact* induced, as was the case here, that was enough to entitle him to rescission. The reasonableness or otherwise of his behaviour was relevant only to the burden of proof: the less reasonable the inducement, the more difficult it would be for the plaintiff to convince the court that he had been affected by the misrepresentation.

8.3   Remedies for misrepresentation

The remedies for misrepresentation depend to some extent on the state of mind of the person making the false statement. If it is fraudulent the remedies will be more extensive than if it is made negligently or innocently. There are remedies available under common law and equity and also under the Misrepresentation Act 1967.

8.3.1   Rescission

The principal remedy under English law for a misrepresentation was for a long time the equitable remedy of rescission. This allows the parties to be restored to their original position. Thus, if the contract is one for the sale of goods, both the goods, and the price paid for them, must be returned. It is still available in relation to all types of misrepresentation. It does not matter now whether or not the misrepresentation has become a term of the contract: Misrepresentation Act 1967, s 1. Because the remedy is equitable, however, certain bars operàte in relation to it, however. The remedy will be lost in the following situations:

- Affirmation of the contract by the other party - ie the party, having knowledge of the other side's misrepresentation nevertheless continues with the contract: *Long v Lloyd* (1958).

- Lapse of time: *Leaf v International Galleries* (1950) - attempt to rescind when a misrepresentation came to light five years after the contract. The test will be that of what is a 'reasonable' time.

- Restitution impossible - as for example where goods have been destroyed, consumed, or irretrievably mixed with others. A decline in value will not, however, be sufficient to bar rescission: *Armstrong v Jackson* (1917). (*Cf Cheese v Thomas* (1993) discussed at para 9.10.)

- If rescission would affect the rights of third parties. This is a major limitation where goods obtained on the basis of a (probably fraudulent) misrepresentation have been sold on to an innocent third party. See, for example, *Phillips v Brooks* (1919), discussed below, para 8.3.3.

At common law damages are only available in relation to fraudulent misrepresentations, under the tort of deceit: *Derry v Peek* (1889). For a misrepresentation to be treated as fraudulent it must be proved that the statement was made knowing that it was false, or with a reckless disregard for the truth. This goes beyond mere negligence, or carelessness. If fraud is established, the damages may be extensive, since in *Doyle v Olby (Ironmongers) Ltd* (1969) it was held that the defendant will be liable for all losses which can be shown to be the consequences of the false statement, without being limited by the normal rules of 'remoteness' (for which, see Chapter 13, para 13.4.1). Moreover, in *East v Maurer* (1991) it was held that this included lost profits, which would normally only be recoverable in an action for breach of contract.

It should be noted here that in certain situations damages for the tort of negligence may be recoverable in relation to misstatements: *Hedley Byrne v Heller* (1963). For this to be available a duty of care must be shown to exist between the maker of the statement and the person who has acted on it. The House of Lords decision in *Caparo v Dickman* (1990) has severely restricted the circumstances in which such a duty will now be found to exist. It had previously been accepted that it could arise in relation to statements made by one contracting party to the other (*Esso Petroleum v Mardon* (1976)), and this is still presumably the case (see, for example, *Gran Grelato v Richcliff* (1992)). One advantage of the *Hedley Byrne* action is that it applies to *all* types of statement, not just statements of fact. However, it is not intended to discuss this complex area further here, since it is more appropriately dealt with in texts which are concerned more generally with the law of tort.

The Misrepresentation Act 1967 introduced a statutory remedy in damages (whether or not rescission is also granted) for what is commonly referred to as 'negligent misrepresentation'. In fact s 2(1) does not use this phrase, but makes the remedy available where the person making the misrepresentation would have been liable if it had been made fraudulently:

> '... unless he proves that he had reasonable ground to believe and did believe up to the time the contract was made that the facts represented were true.'

The test of what is a misrepresentation will be as set out above, para 8.2. As will be noted, this action is advantageous to the plaintiff in that, once it is established that a false statement was made, the burden of proof shifts to the defendant to establish that there were reasonable grounds for believing it to be true. Moreover, the courts seem to be

8.3.2   Damages at common law

8.3.3   Damages under the Misrepresentation Act 1967, s 2(1)

prepared to be fairly strict as to what will be regarded as reasonable grounds. In *Howard Marine Dredging v Ogden* (1978) the Court of Appeal held that an incorrect statement as to the weight of a vessel gave rise to an entitlement to damages under s 2(1) because, even though the incorrect figure appeared in usually authoritative publication (Lloyd's Register) the defendant had previously seen the correct figure in the shipping documents.

8.3.4	Measure of damages under s 2(1)

One difficulty which has arisen with s 2(1) is the measure of damages - should it be contractual or tortious? In *Watts v Spence* (1976) there was some suggestion that it should be contractual. The Court of Appeal, however, in *Sharneyford v Edge* (1987), ruled that it should be tortious. The issue was considered further in *Royscot Trust Ltd v Rogerson* (1991). A car dealer misrepresented to the plaintiff finance company the amount of a deposit paid by a customer in connection with a hire purchase agreement. The finance company would not have been prepared to lend as much as it did had it known of the true value of the deposit. The finance company suffered a loss when the customer defaulted on his payments, after having sold the car to an innocent third party (who obtained good title under the Hire Purchase Act 1964). In an action by the plaintiff against the dealer for non-fraudulent misrepresentation, the only dispute was as to the amount of damages payable. The measure used by the judge at first instance was supported by neither party in the appeal, so that the Court of Appeal effectively had to decide the matter *de novo*. It confirmed that in an action for misrepresentation under s 2(1) of the 1967 Misrepresentation Act the correct measure of damages is tortious rather than contractual. Moreover, since the wording of s 2(1) makes liability conditional on the situation where 'the person making the misrepresentation would be liable to damages in respect thereof had the misrepresentation been made fraudulently', damages should be assessed in the same way as for fraudulent misrepresentation. This meant that the defendant was liable for *all losses* flowing from the defendant's misrepresentation (as is the case with the tort of deceit: *Doyle v Olby* (1969) above), and not simply for those losses which are reasonably foreseeable. Although the wording of the section itself gives rise to the so-called 'fiction of fraud' alluded to above, the weight of academic opinion, as evidenced by all the leading contract textbooks, has been in favour of applying the negligence remoteness rules, because to apply the deceit rule would operate too harshly in a situation where the defendant has been negligent rather than deliberately fraudulent. The

Court of Appeal, in this case, however, was not prepared to be swayed by these arguments of policy. They found that s 2(1) aligned liability under it with liability for fraud. The wording of the section was clear and the Court saw no reason to depart from its literal meaning. This presumably also means that, assuming the decision in *East v Maurer* (1991) is followed, that lost profits will be recoverable. In other words, the form of the remedy will be tortious, but the effect will be that the plaintiff will be able to recover expectation losses (for which see Chapter 13, para 13.3.1), as if suing for breach of contract, but without the restriction of the rules of remoteness.

Section 2(2) of the 1967 Act allows a court to award damages in lieu of rescission, whether or not they are also awarded under s 2(1). This power is to be exercised if the court is:

8.3.5   Damages under Misrepresentation Act 1967, s 2(2)

'... of opinion that it would be equitable to do so, having regard to the nature of the misrepresentation and the loss that would be caused by it if the contract were upheld, as well as to the loss that rescission would cause to the other party.' (emphasis added)

The power is presumably lost where the right to rescission has been lost, for example by lapse of time, or the intervention of third party rights (above, para 8.3.1). The measure of damages to be used under this section is unclear, and there is so far no authority on its use.

Section 3 of the Misrepresentation Act, as amended by s 8 of the Unfair Contract Terms Act 1977, restricts the possibility of exclusion of liability for misrepresentation. As regards any contract term which attempts to restrict either liability for misrepresentation, or any remedy available in relation to it, this will only be effective insofar as it satisfies the requirement reasonableness under s 11 of UCTA (see Chapter 7, para 7.8).

8.4   Exclusion of liability for misrepresentation

As pointed out by Lord Atkin in *Bell v Lever Bros* (1932), there are two types of mistake which may affect a contract, those which 'nullify consent' and those which 'negative consent' ('consent' meaning here 'agreement'). A mistake which has the effect of nullifying consent means that although the parties were in agreement, they were both labouring under the same misapprehension relating to an important element of the contract (eg the existence of the subject-matter) which means that the agreement should be set aside. Cheshire and Fifoot refer to this type of mistake as a 'common' mistake. A mistake 'negativing' agreement occurs where the mistake has the effect of preventing the parties ever reaching an agreement. It may take two forms. First, the parties may simply be at cross-

8.5   Mistake

purposes, as where they have each assumed that they were contracting about a different item. Cheshire and Fifoot label this as 'mutual mistake'. Secondly, one of the parties may be aware of the other's mistake, but nevertheless keep quiet (as for example where the innocent party is mistaken as to the identity of the other party). This may be described as a 'unilateral mistake' (Cheshire and Fifoot). It is in relation to this type of mistake that there is most likely to be an overlap with misrepresentation.

In what follows, the Cheshire and Fifoot division into common, mutual, and unilateral mistakes will be adopted.

8.6   Common mistake

The clearest type of common mistake which will be regarded as rendering the contract void for mistake is where the parties have made a contract about something which has ceased to exist at the time the contract is made. (Where the subject matter ceases to exist *after* the contract is made the doctrine of 'frustration', which is dealt with in Chapter 11, applies, rather than mistake.) If, for example, the contract concerns the hire of a boat which, unknown to either party, has been destroyed by fire the day before the contract was made, the agreement will undoubtedly be void for common mistake. The parties have reached agreement, but that agreement is nullified by the destruction of the subject matter. This type of common mistake is sometimes referred to by the Latin tag of *res extincta*. An example from the cases is *Galloway v Galloway* (1914). The parties, who thought they had been married to each other, made a separation agreement. It was then discovered that their supposed marriage was invalid, because the husband's previous wife was still alive. As a result, the separation agreement was void, and the 'husband' had no liability under it.

As regards contracts for the sale of goods, the common law rule is give statutory effect by s 6 of the Sale of Goods Act 1979. This states that:

> 'Where there is a contract for the sale of specific goods, and the goods without the knowledge of the seller have perished at the time when the contract is made, the contract is void.'

The word 'perished' almost certainly encompasses more than simply physical destruction, as is shown by the pre-Sale of Goods Act case of *Couturier v Hastie* (1856). The contract concerned a contract for the purchase of a cargo of corn. At the time of the contract the cargo had, because it was starting to deteriorate, been unloaded and sold to someone else. The purchaser was held to have no liability.

The cases we have been considering deal with the situation where the subject-matter *did* exist at one point, but have ceased to do so by the time of the contract. The position is more difficult where the subject-matter has *never* existed. There seems no logical reason why the contract should not equally be void for mistake in such a case, but this was not the view of the High Court of Australia in *McRae v Commonwealth Disposals Commission* (1951). The Commission had invited tenders for a salvage operation in relation to an oil tanker, said to be 'lying on the Jourmand Reef'. The plaintiffs were awarded the contract, but on arrival found that neither the tanker, nor the reef existed. The Commission claimed that the contract was void for mistake, and that they therefore had no liability. The Court held, however, that there was a contract, in that the Commission had to be taken to have warranted the existence of the tanker. The plaintiffs were entitled to damages to compensate for their costs in putting together the abortive enterprise. In reaching this conclusion, the Court did not accept that the decision in *Couturier v Hastie* was truly based on 'mistake'. It was simply that the plaintiff's claim in that case that the price was payable simply on production of the shipping documents could not be upheld as being part of the contract.

8.6.1   Subject-matter which never existed

An operative common mistake may also arise where, although the subject-matter of the contract has not been destroyed, performance is, and always was, impossible. This may result from a physical impossibility (as in *Sheikh Bros v Ochsner* (1957): land not capable of growing the quantity of crop contracted for), or legal impossibility (as where the contract is to buy property which the purchaser already owns: *Cooper v Phibbs* (1867)). There is also one case, *Griffith v Brymer* (1903), where a contract was found void for what Treitel refers to as 'commercial impossibility'. The contract was to hire a room to view an event which, at the time of the contract, had already been cancelled. Performance of the contract was physically and legally possible, but would have had no point. (Compare the frustration cases on similar situations, Chapter 11, para 11.2.3.)

8.6.2   Impossibility of performance

Can there be an operative common mistake where the parties are mistaken as to the quality of what they have contracted about? Suppose A sells B a table, both parties being under the impression that they are dealing with a valuable antique, whereas it subsequently turns out to be a fake? Can B avoid the contract on the basis of mistake? (Often this type of situation will in practice be dealt with by the provisions of the Sale of Goods Act - see Chapter 16 - but that does not prevent

8.6.3   Mistake as to quality

us using the example as a means of exploring the principles of mistake). The leading House of Lords authority is *Bell v Lever Brothers* (1931). The plaintiffs (Lever Brothers) had reached an agreement for compensation with the defendant over the early termination of contract of employment. This termination agreement was itself a contract, providing for the payment of £50,000. The plaintiffs then discovered that the defendant had previously behaved in a way which would have justified termination without compensation. They therefore argued that the compensation contract should be regarded as being void for mistake. The House was reluctant to allow a mistake as to the quality, or value, of what had been contracted for to be regarded as an operative mistake. As Lord Atkin put it:

'In such a case a mistake will not affect assent unless it is the mistake of both parties and is as to the existence of some quality which makes the thing without the quality essentially different from the thing as it was believed to be.'

This would not be the case in an example such as that of the antique which turns out to be a fake. Lord Atkin again comments:

'A buys a picture from B: both A and B believe it to be the work of an old master, and high price is paid. It turns out to be a modern copy. A has no remedy in the absence of representation or warranty.'

Applying this approach to the case before them, the conclusion was that there was no operative mistake. The plaintiffs had obtained exactly what they had bargained for, that is the release of the contract with the defendant. The fact that the plaintiffs could have achieved the same result without paying compensation by relying on the defendant's earlier conduct was immaterial.

8.6.4	Effect of *Bell v Lever Brothers*

This conclusion has sometimes been regarded as indicating that there can never be an operative mistake as to quality. But the decision does not go quite that far, as the first quotation from Lord Atkin, above, shows. This point was noted by Steyn J in *Associated Japanese Bank Ltd v Credit du Nord SA* (1988). He held that a contract of guarantee which was given on the basis of the existence of certain gaming machines, was void at common law when it turned out the gaming machines did not exist at all. It should be noted that this was not a case of *res extincta*, though it comes close. The gaming machines were not the subject-matter of the contract under consideration. The subject-matter was in fact a contract in relation to the gaming machines the performance of which had been supported by a guarantee given by the defendant. Steyn J concluded:

'For both parties the guarantee of obligations under a lease with non-existent machines was essentially different from a guarantee of a lease with four machines which both parties at the time of the contract believed to exist.'

The position would seem to be that some mistakes as to the quality, or value, of the subject-matter of the contract can give rise to an operative mistake provided that the mistake has a sufficiently serious effect in relation to matters which are fundamental to the contract. There are *obiter* statements in *Nicholson and Venn v Smith-Marriott* (1947) (mistake as to the provenance of antique table linen) which would support such a view, though equally in *Leaf v International Galleries* (1950) (mistake as to whether a picture was painted by Constable) there are *obiter* statements which envisage a very limited role for this type of mistake.

The effect of an operative common mistake at common law is to render the contract void *ab initio*. It is as if the contract had never existed, and therefore, as far as is possible, all concerned must be returned to the position they were in before the contract was made. This applies equally to third parties, so that the innocent purchaser of goods which have been 'sold' under a void contract will be required to disgorge them, and hand them back to the original owner. These powerful and far-reaching consequences perhaps explain why the courts have shown a reluctance to extend the scope of common mistake too far, preferring to allow the flexible application of equitable remedies to pick up the pieces in the majority of cases (below, para 8.10).

8.6.5 Effect of an operative common mistake

'Mutual mistake' refers to the situation where the parties are at cross-purposes. This may relate to the subject-matter of the contract, or the identity of the other contracting party. If the mistake is sufficiently fundamental that it means in effect that there was no agreement between the parties (ie a mistake 'negativing' agreement), then there can be no contract, and any actions taken on the basis that there was a contract will have to be undone.

8.7 Mutual mistake

A classic example of a situation which can give rise to this kind of mistake is to be found in *Raffles v Wichelhaus* (1864). The alleged contract was for the purchase of a cargo of cotton due to arrive in England on the ship *Peerless*, from Bombay. There were two ships of this name carrying cotton from Bombay, one which left in October, the other in December. The court held that, in the absence of agreement between the parties as to which ship was meant, and since there was no objective evidence which would determine the issue, the contract could not stand.

8.7.1	Subjective or objective approach?	The case shows the courts using a combination of a subjective and objective approaches to the agreement. No doubt if the parties had in fact been in agreement about which ship was meant then the contract would have been upheld. In the absence of such agreement, the question to be asked is what would a reasonable third party, looking at what was said and done, think that they had intended, or what would a reasonable offeror have thought was being offered. In *Raffles v Wichelhaus* (1864) the confusion was such that it was not possible to give a definite answer to such questions. A similar result occurred in *Scriven Bros v Hindley* (1913), where there was confusion as to the nature of two lots in an auction, one being 'hemp', the other being much less valuable 'tow'. The defendant who had bid an unusually high price for the tow, in the mistaken belief that it was hemp, was allowed to avoid the contract. In *Smith v Hughes* (1871), however, which again concerned an alleged mutual mistake in relation to the subject matter of the contract, a different view was taken. The plaintiff had offered to sell oats to the defendant. The defendant thought that he was buying 'old' oats. When delivered they turned out to be 'new', and of no use to the defendant. The trial judge directed the jury that if they thought that the defendant believed that he was contracting for old oats, they should give a verdict for the defendant, which they did. On appeal, however, the Queen's Bench held that it was not enough that the defendant had made a mistake. To allow him to escape from the contract it would be necessary to show that the defendant thought that it was a *term of the contract* that the oats were 'old', *and that the plaintiff was aware that the defendant thought this* (ie a 'unilateral', rather than 'mutual', mistake). Looked at objectively, it appeared to be simply a contract for the sale of a specific parcel of oats, about which there was no ambiguity.

The approach here, therefore, as in general with issues as to the creation of an agreement, is to concentrate on what can be deduced objectively from what the parties have said or done, rather than to try to determine their precise state of mind at the time of the alleged agreement.

8.8	**Unilateral mistake**	As we have seen, the court in *Smith v Hughes* thought that the result would have been different if the plaintiff had been aware that the defendant was acting on the basis of a mistake as to a term of the contract. In such a situation there will often have been a misrepresentation which will provide the other party with a remedy. If there was no such misrepresentation, however, or the remedies available for misrepresentation are inadequate, there may be a remedy on the basis of a 'unilateral mistake'. Where one party knowingly takes advantage of the

other's mistake, this will lead to the contract being held either void at common law, if it is a mistake such as would be regarded as an operative common mistake, or non-existent if it is of a kind which would prevent an agreement arising on the basis of mutual mistake.

Many of the cases concerning unilateral mistake deal with mistakes as to who the other contracting party is. The general rule is that the mistake to be operative must relate to the *identity* of the person with whom you are contracting, not his or her *attributes*. For example, you cannot back out of a contract simply because you mistakenly thought the other party was wealthy, and therefore creditworthy.

8.8.1   Mistaken identity

The courts have been more willing to treat mistakes of identity as operative where the contract has been made through the post, or via an agent, rather than in person. In *Boulton v Jones* (1857), for example, the defendant had sent an order to one 'Brocklehurst' with whom he had dealt regularly. Brocklehurst had, however, just transferred the business to his foreman, who fulfilled the order. The defendant resisted a claim for payment by the foreman on the basis that he had a 'set-off' against Brocklehurst, arising out their previous dealings. The court accepted that the existence of this set-off made the identity of the other party of crucial importance to the defendant, and the contract was set aside.

This result may appear a little harsh to the plaintiff in *Boulton v Jones* who, while aware of the defendant's mistake, was not trying to take any unfair advantage. This was not the case, however, in *Cundy v Lindsay* (1878). A fraudulent individual named Blenkarn placed large orders for handkerchiefs with the plaintiffs. Blenkarn was trading from Wood Street, and the plaintiffs thought that they were dealing with a reputable firm by the name of Blenkiron & Co, which also had its business in Wood Street. Blenkarn deliberately contributed to this mistake by the manner in which he signed his order. The goods were supplied, and sold on to the defendant, who was an innocent third party. The House of Lords confirmed that there was no contract between the plaintiffs and Blenkarn. As Lord Cairns put it:

'Of him [Blenkarn] they [the plaintiffs] knew nothing, and of him they never thought. With him they never intended to deal. Their minds never for an instant of time rested upon him, and as between him and them there was no consensus of mind which could lead to any agreement or any contract whatever.'

As will be noted, this introduces a rather more subjective element, concerned with the fact of agreement, than is usually the case in this area. Even from an objective point of view, however, the fact that the plaintiffs had addressed the orders, and other correspondence, to 'Messrs Blenkiron', indicated that they had been under a misapprehension about whom they were dealing with, and had not intended to contract with Blenkarn. The consequences of the decision, however, were serious for the innocent defendants, who had to return the handkerchiefs (for which they had paid) to the plaintiffs, and were left to seek compensation from the fraudulent Blenkarn.

8.8.2 Need for intended party to exist

For the mistake as to identity to be operative the mistaken party must be able to show who it was that was the intended contracting party. Thus in *King's Norton Metal Company v Edridge, Merrett & Co* (1897), although once again a contract was induced by fraudulent person (Wallis), who was pretending to be a firm called 'Hallam & Co', the contract was upheld. This was because 'Hallam & Co' was a pure invention, created by Wallis. There was no genuine firm of that name with whom the plaintiffs could have thought they were dealing. The mistake was therefore not one of identity, but of attributes. The plaintiffs thought that they were dealing with a firm, though in fact they were dealing with a private individual, Wallis.

8.8.3 Contracts *inter praesentes*

It becomes much harder to argue for mistake where the contract is made in person or *inter praesentes*. The courts are reluctant to accept that you did not intend to contract with the person who is standing in front of you, even though you may have been under a misapprehension as to their attributes, or qualities.

In *Phillips v Brooks* (1919) a person went into a jeweller's shop. He selected various valuable items, including a ring. As he was writing a cheque in payment, he said 'You see who I am, I am Sir George Bullough', giving an address in St James Square. The plaintiff checked this information in a directory, and then allowed the man to take the ring with him. The cheque was dishonoured, and the man turned out not to be Sir George at all. He had in the meantime, however, passed the ring to the defendants, who had taken it in all innocence. The court held that the contract was with the person in the shop. The plaintiff had failed to establish that the identity of the person was a crucial element in the contract.

This approach was confirmed in *Lewis v Averay* (1972) in which the fraudulent party pretended to be a famous television actor, and on that basis induced the plaintiff to part with his car in return for a worthless cheque. It was held that the contract, while probably voidable for misrepresentation, was not void for mistake, so that the innocent third party who was now in possession of the car was entitled to retain it.

It is difficult, however, to reconcile with these two cases the decision in *Ingram v Little* (1961). Here the contract was, as in *Lewis v Averay*, for the sale of a car. It was owned by three women who lived together. A man calling himself Hutchinson answered their advertisement. He offered a sum which was acceptable to the women, but then produced a cheque book. The woman who was conducting the negotiations at that point indicated that in no circumstances would they accept payment by cheque. The man then gave a full name and an address. One of the other women then left the house to visit the post office and consult a telephone directory, which confirmed that a person of that name lived at the address given. They then allowed him to take the car in exchange for the cheque. The man was not, however, Mr Hutchinson, and the cheque proved worthless. The women brought an action to recover the car from an innocent third party purchaser. The Court of Appeal confirmed the view of the trial judge that they should succeed. The response to the offer of a cheque, and the procedure of checking in the directory, indicated that the identity of the other contracting party was of the utmost importance, and the contract was therefore void for mistake.

8.8.4   A conflicting decision

The principle applied is the same in all three of the cases just discussed, ie the mistake must relate to identity, rather than attributes. It is difficult to see, however, that there really was that much difference in the situation in *Ingram v Little* to justify applying the principle differently from the way in which it was applied in *Phillips v Brooks* and *Lewis v Averay*. Indeed, the decision was not unanimous, since Lord Devlin dissented. In the course of his judgment he expressed the view that it was unfortunate that the rules relating to mistake meant that if it was operative at common law, and the contract was void, it often meant that, as in *Ingram v Little*, one of two innocent parties had to suffer, and there was no good basis for choosing between them. He suggested that it would be better to have some system whereby the losses could be apportioned in such a case. This suggestion, which would be likely to produce a fairer result in many cases, has not, however, been taken up.

8.8.5   Principle clear:
problems of
application

It will be easier for a plaintiff to convince a court that the identity of the other party is important, if the plaintiff has sought the person out. If you advertise goods to the general public, it may be difficult then to suggest that you really wanted to contract with one person in particular. If, however, you have gone to that person's place of business, specifically to enter into a contract, then the argument that the identity of the other party was important is likely to be much more convincing. This may be illustrated by *Hardman v Booth* (1863). The plaintiff had approached a firm, Thomas Gandell & Sons. They dealt with Edward Gandell, a member of the family who they thought was acting for the firm, though in fact he was acting on his own account. He intercepted goods sent by the plaintiffs and sold them to the defendant. It was held that the plaintiffs never intended to deal with Edward, but only with the firm, and the contract was therefore void for mistake.

| 8.9 | Mistake in equity |

As we have seen, the common law rules for identifying an operative mistake are very restrictive. The courts have allowed a more flexible approach under equity. The main limitation on equity, however, is that the courts will not allow it to be used to defeat the position of a bona fide purchaser of goods, who is not aware of any 'mistake'. Thus, where goods have been supplied under a contract induced by a mistake, but have then been sold on to an innocent third party, the original owner will only be able to recover them from the third party if a mistake which the common law will recognise as operative can be shown to have existed. If the goods are still in the hands of the original 'purchaser', however, or if the contract is of a type which has not led to third party involvement, the courts may well be prepared to allow equitable remedies to be applied.

In *Solle v Butcher* (1950) there had been a mistake as to whether the rent payable in relation to a particular property was subject to control under the Rent Restriction Acts. This was held not to be sufficiently serious to render the contract void. But, as Lord Denning put it:

'A contract is also liable in equity to be set aside if the parties were under a common misapprehension either as to facts or as to their relative and respective rights, provided that the misapprehension was fundamental, and that the party seeking to set it aside was not himself at fault.'

This makes it clear that it is not every mistake which will give rise to equitable relief. It must be 'fundamental' - but this seems to be wide enough to include serious mistakes as to the quality or value of the subject-matter of the contract.

Even in equity, however, the mistake must be made at the time of contract. In *Amalgamated Investment and Property Co v John Walker & Sons* (1976), a property was listed as a building of special interest by the Department of the Environment. This placed serious restrictions on the ways in which it could be used, and reduced its value by £1.5 million. This is clearly a mistake of the kind which might allow equitable relief, but unfortunately the 'listing' of the building had taken place two days after the contract for its sale had been concluded. The mistake was not operative at the time of the contract, and so there could be no relief on this basis either under common law or in equity.

Once it is established that equity will take account of the mistake, what remedies are available? There are basically three: refusal of specific performance; rescission on terms; and rectification.

8.10   Forms of equitable relief

As we will see in Chapter 13, the order of specific performance is a discretionary remedy. In deciding whether to order it the court can take into account any hardship which might be caused by so doing. For example, the buyer of a painting which, between contract and performance, is discovered not to be by Constable, as had been thought, may well be able to resist specific performance (though there may still be a liability to pay compensatory damages). Thus in *Malins v Freeman* (1837), where a buyer at an auction mistakenly bid for one lot, thinking that it was another, this mutual mistake was held to be sufficient to allow the buyer not to be made to go through with the contract. In contrast, in *Tamplin v James* (1880) where the defendant bid for an inn and shop, incorrectly thinking that a garden was included, the contract was enforced. The mistake as to the *extent* of the property was distinguishable from a case where the mistake was as to the *identity* of the property.

8.10.1   Refusal of specific performance

If the contract has been performed, but on the basis of a mistake which is operative in equity, the court may order the contract to be rescinded. It may at the same time, however, impose conditions on the grant of rescission, in order to ensure justice as between the parties. Thus in *Solle v Butcher* (above), the lease was rescinded, but on condition that the tenant could remain, provided that he paid rent at the maximum which the landlord could have asked for under the rent control legislation. Similarly in *Grist v Bailey* (1967) a house was sold for £850 on the basis that it had a sitting tenant. In fact the tenant had died, which increased the value of the house to £2,250. The contract was not void at law, but could be rescinded in equity, provided that the vendor gave the purchaser the opportunity of buying for a 'proper vacant possession price'.

8.10.2   Rescission on terms

Rescission on terms is therefore a very powerful remedy, in that effectively it allows the court to substitute what it considers to be a just and fair arrangement for the contract as made by the parties. This degree of judicial intervention is unusual in contract law, and has the potential for giving rise to great uncertainty. It will often be hard to predict on precisely what conditions a court may be prepared to grant rescission. It may also in some cases be prepared to grant rescission without imposing conditions.

<table>
<tr><td>8.10.3</td><td>Rectification</td></tr>
</table>

8.10.3   Rectification

Where an agreement is contained in a document which contains an inaccuracy, in the form of either an error, or an omission, the equitable remedy of rectification may be granted. It is clearly available where both parties miss the error (ie a common mistake), or if one party knows of the other's mistake (ie a unilateral mistake). Thus in *Roberts v Leicestershire County Council* (1961) a construction contract which contained a completion date which was a year later than the contractors believed it to be, was rectified, because there was clear evidence that representatives of the other party were well aware of the basis on which the contractors were undertaking the project. If the mistake is simply a mutual mistake, however, the courts will not grant rectification. A sufficiently serious mistake of this kind will allow the contract to be rescinded, of course, but rectification will not be available: *Riverlate Properties Ltd v Paul* (1975).

It follows from this that if an oral agreement, though based on a mistake, is accurately reproduced in a subsequent document, rectification is not appropriate, and will not be granted: *Rose v Pim* (1953).

8.10.4   Bars to rescission or rectification

Because these remedies are equitable, they may be lost by virtue of:

- lapse of time;

- the intervention of third party rights; or, in the case of rescission,

- the impossibility of reversing the contract - for example, where it concerns goods which have been consumed.

If this is the case, then the plaintiff will have to argue for common law mistake in order to obtain any remedy.

8.11   **Contracts signed under a mistake**

The courts are not inclined to be sympathetic towards people who put their names to contracts without reading or understanding them. In general, then, a person will be taken to have notice of, and to be bound by, all the provisions of a contract which has been signed, whether they have been read or not: *L'Estrange v Graucob* (1934) (see above, para 7.3). There are some exceptional circumstances, however, where the courts will allow a plea of *non est factum* - 'it is not my deed'. The mistake must be such that the document as a whole is 'radically different' from what the person thought they were signing. Moreover, the person must not have been 'careless' in signing the document. These principles are derived from the House of Lords decision in *Gallie v Lee* (1971) (also reported as *Sauders v Anglia Building Society*), which is discussed further below.

The result of these principles, and in particular the second one, is that the doctrine will rarely be available to literate adults, of full capacity. The courts will, however, make the remedy available to those who are tricked into signing the contract. And it may also operate to protect those who from 'defective education, illness, or innate incapacity' (as Lord Reid put it in *Gallie v Lee*), fail to understand what they are signing.

8.11.1   Availability of the plea

A recent (fairly rare) example of the successful use of the plea is to be found in *Lloyd's Bank Plc v Waterhouse* (1990). Here the defendant, who was illiterate, signed a guarantee as regards his son's future liabilities to the plaintiffs. The father thought that this guarantee related solely to the son's purchase of a farm, whereas in fact it covered all the son's liabilities. The trial judge found that this did not amount to a fundamental difference, and that the defendant had been careless in not having the document read to him. He gave judgment for the plaintiff. The defendant appealed.

The majority of the Court of Appeal regarded the mistake as to the extent of the guarantee as being sufficient to support the plea of *non est factum*. The evidence showed that the father would not have signed it if he had known its true nature, even though he was aware of the financial value of the guarantee. As to carelessness, although the bank was unaware of the defendant's illiteracy, and there was no suggestion of impropriety on their part, the defendant had clearly taken steps (by asking questions of the bank's officials) to ascertain his liability. The plea of *non est factum* was made out.

At one time the difference in the extent of the guarantee would not have been regarded as sufficient, as it was thought that the document had to be of a different 'character' for the defence to be available. That test was rejected, however, in *Gallie v Lee* in favour of the more broadly based question of whether the document was 'radically' or 'fundamentally' different. In this case an elderly widow had been tricked by her nephew into signing an assignment of the lease of her house to a third party. She thought she was signing a deed of gift to her nephew. The reason why she had failed to read the document was that she had broken her reading glasses. The House of Lords regarded this as an acceptable reason for failing to read

8.11.2   Nature of the mistake

the document, and held that it did not amount to 'carelessness'. The widow failed, however, on the first test, relating to the nature of the document. Although it involved a different transaction from what she thought, the purpose of the assignment was, albeit indirectly, to provide financial assistance to her nephew. This is what she had wished to achieve by the deed of gift. The document was not, therefore, sufficiently different for the plea to succeed.

If the plea is successful then the transaction is void, and unenforceable.

Misrepresentation and Mistake

For a misrepresentation to give rise to a remedy it must:

- be a statement by one contracting party to another;

- be a statement of existing fact, not opinion or law. But a false statement of intention is a statement of fact: *Edgington v Fitzmaurice* (1885);

- induce the contract: *JEB Fasteners Ltd v Bloom* (1983). It need not be the *only* reason for contracting (*Edgington v Fitzmaurice* (1885)), and the reliance need not be 'reasonable' (*Museprime Properties Ltd v Adhill* (1990)).

Misrepresentation

Remedies depend on the state of mind of the misrepresentor. A range of remedies exist at common law, in equity, and under the Misrepresentation Act 1967.

Remedies for misrepresentation

- Rescission

  This is the principal remedy. It requires the parties to be restored to their original positions. The remedy is equitable, and will be lost by:

  (i) affirmation: *Long v Lloyd* (1958);

  (ii) lapse of time: *Leaf v International Galleries* (1950);

  (iii) impossibility of restitution - eg where goods have been destroyed;

  (iv) involvement of third party rights.

- Damages at common law

  These are only available in relation to fraudulent misrepresentations (ie made with knowledge or recklessness as regards the falsehood). They will cover all consequential losses (*Doyle v Olby (Ironmongers) Ltd* (1969)), including lost profits (*East v Maurer* (1991)).

- Damages under the Misrepresentation Act 1967, s.2(1)

  These are available as regards 'negligent' misrepresentations (ie the misrepresentor had no reasonable grounds for believing the statement to be true). The measure of damages is the same as for fraudulent misrepresentation (*Royscot Trust Ltd v Rogerson* (1991)).

- Damages under the Misrepresentation Act 1967, s.2(2)

  These are available at the court's discretion in lieu of rescission. The measure is uncertain.

- Exclusion of liability for misrepresentation

  By virtue of s 3 of the 1967 Act, this is only permissible where the exclusion clause satisfies the requirement of reasonableness under s 11 of UCTA.

Mistake

A mistake may 'nullify' or 'negative' an agreement. Mistakes may be categorised as 'common', 'mutual', and unilateral.

Common mistake

The clearest example of a common mistake is *res extincta*: *Galloway v Galloway* (1914); Sale of Goods Act 1979, s 6. Note also *Coutourier v Hastie* (1856) as an example of 'commercial' rather than physical perishing.

- Subject-matter never existed

  This will not render the contract void, if the existence has been *warranted*: *McRae v Commonwealth Disposals Commission* (1951).

- Impossibility of performance

  This may take the form or physical (*Sheikh Bros v Ochsner* (1957), legal (*Cooper v Phibbs* (1867), or commercial (*Griffith v Brymer* (1903) impossibility.

- Mistake as to quality

  The leading authority is *Bell v Lever Bros* (1931), which suggests little scope for this. But note *Associated Japanese Bank Ltd v Credit du Nord SA* (1988) which identifies some cases where such a mistake may be operative.

- Effect of an operative common mistake

  The effect is to render the contract void *ab initio*, and require the parties to be restored to their original position. This will override even third party rights.

Mutual mistake

In the case of mutual mistake the parties are, unknowingly, at cross-purposes: *Raffles v Wichelhaus* (1864). The approach is primarily objective: *Smith v Hughes* (1871). The effect of such a mistake is to lead to a finding that there never was a contract.

Unilateral mistake

In the case of unilateral mistake one party is aware that the other party has made a mistake as to some *term of the contract*: *Smith v Hughes* (1871). The contract will be rendered void, if the mistake is serious.

- Mistake as to identity

  The courts will allow this to avoid a contract where it is shown that the identity was of fundamental importance, and relates to the person's *identity*, rather than *attributes*. This is easier where the parties are contracting at a distance (eg *Cundy v Lindsay* (1878)), rather than *inter prasentes*, provided that there is a genuine confusion between two distinct people (*King's Norton Metal Company v Edridge, Merrett & Co* (1897)).

- Contracts *inter praesentes*

  The courts are reluctant to find an operative mistake as to identity (*Phillips v Brooks* (1919), *Lewis v Averay* (1972)), but will do so in appropriate circumstances (*Ingram v Little* (1961), *Hardman v Booth* (1863)).

Where a mistake is not operative at common law, but still relates to an important aspect of the contract, equitable remedies may be available: *Solle v Butcher* (1950).

Mistake in equity

Forms of equitable relief are:

Forms of equitable relief

- refusal of specific performance: *Malins v Freeman* (1837) (*cf Tamplin v James* (1880));

- rescission on terms: *Solle v Butcher* (1950), *Grist v Bailey* (1967);

- rectification of a document: *Roberts v Leicestershire County Council* (1961).

Bars to recission or rectification:

These remedies may be lost by lapse of time, intervention of third party rights, or, in relation to rescission, the impossibility of restitution.

The plea of *non est factum* will only be allowed where the document signed is 'radically different' from that which the person thought they were signing, and the signer has not been 'careless': *Gallie v Lee* (1971).

Contracts signed under a mistake

Chapter 9

Duress and Undue Influence

This chapter is concerned with situations in which an agreement which appears to be valid on its face is challenged because it is alleged that it is the product of improper pressure of some kind. This may take the form of physical coercion or threats, economic pressure, or psychological influence. The problem with the last two categories lies in establishing the boundaries of acceptable behaviour of this kind, because both may be argued to have a legitimate place within business dealings. If impropriety is established under any of the heads, the resulting contract is rendered voidable. The courts may be regarded as intervening either because there is no true agreement between the parties, or simply because it is unacceptable on grounds of public policy that agreements of this kind should be enforced. The latter argument is probably the one which best represents the approach of the modern courts to this issue.

9.1 Introduction

Although it is possible that a person could be physically forced to sign a contract, by someone holding their arm and moving it, the most obvious form of duress is where a contract is brought about as a result of a threat of physical injury. A fairly modern example is to be found in *Barton v Armstrong* (1975), where the managing director of a company was threatened with death if he did not arrange for his company to make a payment to, and buy shares from, the defendant. The Privy Council held that the contract was voidable for duress.

9.2 Duress by physical threats or coercion

The threat need not be of serious physical violence - any illegality in the form of a crime or tort against the person (such as false imprisonment) will apparently be sufficient. Moreover, the threat can relate to a third party, as in *Williams v Bayley* (1866), where the threat, although issued to the plaintiff, related to his son.

Threats in relation to goods were at one time held not to amount to duress sufficient to avoid an agreement: *Skeate v Beale* (1840). It must be doubted, however, whether this doctrine, which was in any case apparently subject to the exception that money paid under duress of goods could be recovered (*Astley v Reynolds* (1731)), has survived the modern development of the concept of 'economic duress', which is dealt with in the next section.

The cases on duress are full of references to the plaintiff's will being 'overborne'. In many cases this will be an inaccurate description of what has happened. The plaintiff has not been forced to act as an automaton. The decision to make the contract has been taken as a matter of choice. It is simply that the threat which has led to that choice is regarded by the courts as illegitimate, and justifies allowing the party threatened to escape from the consequent contract.

9.3   Economic duress

The first recognition of economic duress is probably to be found in the *obiter* statements of Kerr J in *The Siboen and The Sibotre* (1976). The case concerned a renegotiation of charters of two vessels, under the threat that otherwise the charterers would go out of business. It was recognised that this could in some circumstances have amounted to duress sufficient to render the agreement voidable. On the facts, however, the other party had not agreed to the renegotiation under duress, but simply as a result of ordinary commercial pressures. In *North Ocean Shipping Company v Hyundai Construction* (1979) the devaluation of the dollar led to a demand for an increase in the price payable under a ship construction contract. Mocatta J held that this did amount to duress, but that the right to rescind had been lost through lapse of time. These two cases, therefore, recognised the possibility of duress based on improper commercial pressure, but did not in fact apply it to the facts before them. The test of impropriety seems to be that the threat involves the commission of a tort, or breach of contract. In other words an act which is, in the broadest sense, unlawful.

9.3.1   Industrial action

The cases which have subsequently developed and applied the concept of economic duress have often been concerned with industrial action. A trade union threatens to encourage its members to break their contracts with a particular employer, unless the employer agrees to act in a certain way. To carry out the threatened action would (subject to the applicability of any protective trade union legislation) amount to the tort of inducement of breach of contract. This may well be regarded as going beyond legitimate pressure, and thus amount to duress. For example, in *Universe Tankships Inc v International Transport Workers Federation* (1983), the union 'blacked' a ship owned by the plaintiffs, by instructing its members not to deal with it, and therefore preventing it from leaving port. In order to escape from this, the owners, *inter alia*, made a payment to the union's welfare fund. They later brought an action to recover this as a payment made under duress. It was held that the threatened industrial action was unlawful under English law, and the payment was recoverable. Subsequent changes in English employment law, extending the scope of unlawful industrial action, have had the effect of extending the scope of economic duress. This is shown by *Dimskal Shipping Co SA v International Transport Workers' Federation* (1991), which also confirmed that the question whether the actions of a party amount to economic duress must be judged by English law, not the law of the country where the actions took place. The ITF had, through industrial action, persuaded the respondents to agree to contracts involving the payment of large sums of money in respect of back pay to its crew. This was to bring the respondents' terms of employment in line with those approved by the ITF. The respondents sought to have these contracts, which were expressed to be governed by English law, avoided for duress. The judge at first instance refused, since the actions of the ITF were legal where they took place (in Sweden). The Court of Appeal overturned this judgment, and the ITF appealed to the House of Lords which held, with Lord Templeman dissenting, that the issue of what amounted to duress had to be determined by English rather than Swedish law. Since the actions of the ITF would have been unlawful under English employment law, the respondents were entitled to avoid the contracts made as a result of them.

Where the unlawful action threatened is simply a breach of contract, rather than a tort, which may well be the case outside the industrial context, it may be more difficult to identify the boundaries of legitimate pressure. Some assistance is provided by the opinion of Lord Scarman in the Privy Council case of *Pao On v Lau Yiu Long* (1980). In this case the plaintiff had threatened not to proceed with a contract for the sale of shares, unless the other side agreed to a renegotiation of certain subsidiary arrangements. The defendant agreed, but when the plaintiff later tried to enforce these arrangements, claimed that they had been extracted by duress, and were therefore voidable. Lord Scarman identified the following factors as being relevant to whether a person acted voluntarily, or not, and therefore under duress:

9.3.2   Breach of contract

- did the person alleged to have been coerced protest at the time?

- did that person have an alternative course open, such as an adequate legal remedy?

- was the person independently advised?

- did the person take steps to avoid the contract, after entering into it?

On the facts of the case the claim for duress failed, because the defendant had had an alternative course open. That is, he had an adequate legal remedy in an action for specific performance in relation to the original agreement. Lord Scarman referred to this test again in *Universe Tankships v ITF* (1983) where he referred to the victim having 'no practical choice but to submit to the duress'.

9.3.3	No alternative to compliance

A clear example of a person being faced with no alternative but to apply, in a case not concerned with industrial action, is to be found in *Atlas Express v Kafco* (1989). The defendants, Kafco, were a small manufacturing company who had a very valuable contract with Woolworths, a store with branches throughout the country. Kafco employed Atlas, a national firm of carriers, to make deliveries to Woolworths. Atlas found that they had, through their own miscalculation of the quantities of Kafco's goods which could be carried on their lorries at one time, entered into the contract on uneconomic terms. They told Kafco that they must agree to an increase in the charge for carriage, or else Atlas would not make the deliveries. Kafco could not risk being in breach of their contract with Woolworths, and so agreed to the increased charge, under protest. When Atlas brought an action to recover the increased charges, Kafco resisted on the grounds of duress. The court accepted the argument that losing the contract with Woolworths, or being sued by them, would have been so disastrous for Kafco that they had no real alternative but to go along with Atlas's suggestion. An action for damages against Atlas for breach of the original contract would not have been able to provide compensation sufficient to counter-act the effects of the destruction of their business relationship with Woolworths. Kafco were not obliged to pay the additional carriage costs.

The major test for the illegitimacy of the threat of economic pressure, which turns it into duress, thus seems to be that the action threatened would not only be unlawful, but also leaves the person threatened with no realistic alternative to compliance.

9.4	**Remedies for duress**

The remedy that the victim of duress will be seeking is to escape from the agreement that has resulted from the duress - in other words rescission. As has been noted in relation to mistake and misrepresentation (above, paras 8.3.1 and 8.10.4), however, rescission is an equitable remedy, and therefore may be lost through:

• lapse of time (see *North Ocean Shipping v Hyundai Construction* (1978) (above, para 9.3);

- impossibility of restitution; or

- the intervention of third party rights.

Duress is essentially a common law concept. Alongside it must be placed the equitable doctrine of 'undue influence'. This operates to release parties from contracts that they have entered into, not as a result of improper threats, but as a result of being 'influenced' by the other party, whether intentionally or not.

9.5   Undue influence: the concept

The difficulty here, as with duress, is to find the limits of legitimate persuasion. If it were impermissible to seek to persuade, cajole, or otherwise encourage, people to enter agreements, then sales representatives would all be out of a job. The basic test in English law is that it is only where there is some relationship between the parties (either continuing, or in relation to a particular transaction) which leads to an inequality between them that the law will intervene. An initial task is therefore to identify which relationships will give rise to this inequality. Once they have been identified, then further questions will arise as to precise scope of the doctrine.

The whole area of undue influence has recently been given a thorough re-examination by the House of Lords in *Barclays Bank PLC v O'Brien* (1993). In the leading speech Lord Browne-Wilkinson confirmed the analysis of the Court of Appeal in *Bank of Credit and Commerce International ('BCCI') v Aboody* (1988), that there are two main categories of undue influence, the second of which must be divided into two further separate sub-categories. The categories are:

- actual undue influence; and

- presumed undue influence;

    which may be divided into

    (i) relationships (such as solicitor/client) which will always give rise to a presumption of influence;

    (ii) relationships which may, *de facto*, be such that influence should be presumed.

    These three categories will now be considered in turn.

In relation to actual undue influence the plaintiff must prove, on the balance of probabilities, that in relation to a particular transaction, the defendant used undue influence. There is no need here for there to be a previous history of such influence. It can operate for the first time in connection with the transaction which is disputed. A recent example of this type of influence is to be found in *BCCI v Aboody* (1989). Mrs Aboody

9.6   Actual undue influence

was 20 years younger than her husband. She had married him when she was 17. For many years she signed documents relating to her husband's business, of which she was nominally a director, without reading them, or questioning her husband about them. She signed guarantees, and charges relating to the matrimonial home, in order to support loans by the bank to the business. She had taken no independent advice, though the bank's solicitor had at one meeting attempted to encourage her to take legal advice. During that meeting Mr Aboody, in a state of some agitation, came into the room, and managed to reduce his wife to tears. It was held that, although Mr Aboody had not acted with any improper motive, he had unduly influenced his wife.

The Court of Appeal in this case, following *dicta* of Lord Scarman in *National Westminster Bank plc v Morgan* (1985), held that Mrs Aboody's claim to set aside the transaction nevertheless failed, because it was not to her 'manifest disadvantage'. The House of Lords, in *CIBC Mortgages plc v Pitt* (1993), has now indicated that this is not a requirement in cases of actual, as opposed to presumed, undue influence. It may, however, be relevant in considering the effect of undue influence exercised by a third party to the transaction (see below, para 9.9.9).

9.7   **Presumed undue influence: recognised relationships**

There are certain relationships which will be presumed to give rise to undue influence. Here there is no need for the party seeking to escape from a contract to prove that the particular transaction was affected by such influence. The burden of proof will be on the other party to show that no such influence in fact operated in this case. This could be done by showing, for example, that the allegedly influenced party only acted after receiving independent legal advice.

The relationships which fall into this category include parent/child, doctor/patient, solicitor/client, religious adviser/disciple (see eg *Goldsworthy v Brickell* (1987)). It does not include husband/wife (*Midland Bank plc v Shephard* (1988)). The relationships are ones where a person has placed trust and confidence in another, and so is liable to act on their suggestions without seeking independent advice. Other relationships (other than husband/wife) which have these characteristics could be added to the list in the future.

An example of this category of undue influence is *Allcard v Skinner* (1887). The plaintiff had entered a religious order of St Mary at the Cross, and had taken vows of poverty, chastity, and obedience. The defendant was the lady superior of the order. Over a period of eight years during which she was a member of the order, the plaintiff gave property to the value of £7,000 to the defendant, most of which was spent on the purposes of the order. It was held that the property was *prima facie* recoverable as having been given under the undue influence of membership of the order, which required obedience to the defendant. This was so, even though no direct pressure had been placed on the plaintiff. The influence was presumed from the relationship itself. The plaintiff's action to recover her property did not succeed, however, as she did not initiate her action until some six years after she had left the order. This lapse of time was held to operate as a bar on recovery.

For there to be recovery under this heading, the transaction which the plaintiff seeks to undo must have been to his or her 'manifest disadvantage': *National Westminster Bank plc v Morgan* (1985). This requirement is discussed further in the next section.

Even where a relationship does not fall into one of the categories listed in the previous section, it may in fact have developed in a way which indicates that one person is in a 'dominant' position over the other. The dominated person will be likely in such a situation to act on the advice, recommendation, or orders, of the other, without seeking any independent advice, and without properly considering the consequences of his or her actions. If that is so, then the courts will presume that *any* disadvantageous transaction entered into at the instigation of the dominant party will be affected by undue influence, unless the contrary is shown. A number of cases in this area concern the relationship of the dominant husband and the subservient wife, but the presumption does not only arise in this context, as is shown by *Lloyds Bank Ltd v Bundy* (1975).

Mr Bundy was an elderly farmer. He had provided a guarantee and a charge over his house to support the debts of his son's business. He was visited by his son and the assistant manager of the bank. The assistant manager told Mr Bundy that the bank could not continue to support the son's business without further security. Mr Bundy then, without seeking any other advice, increased the guarantee and charge to £11,000. When the bank, in enforcing the charge, subsequently sought possession of the house, Mr Bundy pleaded undue influence. It was held that the existence of long-standing relations between the Bundy family and the bank was important. Although the visit when the charge was increased was the first occasion when this particular assistant manager had met Mr Bundy, he was, as

9.8   Presumed undue influence: other relationships

Sir Eric Sachs put it in the Court of Appeal, 'the last of a relevant chain of those who over the years had earned or inherited' Mr Bundy's trust and confidence. The relationship between Mr Bundy and the bank was therefore one which gave rise to a presumption of undue influence. This was not rebutted, and Mr Bundy was not bound by the charge over his house.

Although the period of time over which a relationship has developed is clearly relevant to deciding whether there should be a presumption of undue influence, it need not be all that long. In *Goldsworth v Brickell* (1987), for example, where the relationship existed between an elderly farmer and his neighbour, it had only been for a few months that the plaintiff had been relying on the defendant. Nevertheless, it was held that the relationship involved sufficient trust and confidence for the undue influence to be presumed.

9.8.1   Requirement of 'manifest disadvantage'

As noted in the previous section, it is a requirement in relation to either type of presumed influence that the transaction which is to be set aside is to the 'manifest disadvantage' of the plaintiff. Not every transaction which is entered into by parties who are in a relationship of presumed influence will therefore be vulnerable. This principle derives from the case of *National Westminster Bank plc v Morgan* (1985). Here Mrs Morgan had agreed to a legal charge over the matrimonial home as part of an attempt to re-finance debts which had arisen from her husband's business. She had been visited at home by the Bank Manager and had thereupon signed the charge. Lord Scarman, with whom the rest of House agreed, held that her attempt to have the charge set aside for undue influence failed for two reasons. First, the bank manager's visit was very short (only about 15 minutes in total), and there was no history of reliance as in *Lloyd's Bank v Bundy*. Secondly, for the presumption to arise, the transaction had to be to the 'manifest disadvantage' of Mrs Morgan. This was not the case here. The charge 'meant for her the rescue of her home on the terms sought by her: a short-term loan at a commercial rate of interest'. Thus although any transaction which puts a person's home at risk must in one sense be regarded as 'disadvantageous', this cannot be sufficient on its own to render a contract voidable. If it were, every mortgage agreement would have to be so regarded. In looking for disadvantage, it is necessary to consider the context in which the transaction took place. If it is clear, as it seemed to be in *Morgan*, that the risks involved were, as far as the plaintiff was concerned, worth running in order to obtain the potential benefits of the transaction, and there is no other indication of unfairness, then the courts will be quite prepared to enforce it.

As has been noted above, some of Lord Scarman's comments in *Morgan* were interpreted by the Court of Appeal in *BCCI v Aboody* as applying the requirement of manifest disadvantage to situations of actual, rather than presumed, influence. This interpretation has been rejected by the House of Lords in *CIBC Mortgages plc v Pitt* (1993).

It is not uncommon for a wife to be persuaded by her husband to enter into a contract with a bank or other creditor, under which she will put property which she partly or wholly owns at risk, in order to secure her husband's personal or business debts. In such a situation, if the husband's actions amount to undue influence, does this affect the wife's transaction with the creditor? The husband is not a party to that transaction, and so the standard answer under the doctrine of privity would be 'no'. Nevertheless, in some situations of this kind (not necessarily involving husband and wife), the courts have been prepared to find that the transaction with the creditor can be set aside.

9.9 Undue influence and third parties

In some cases, eg *Coldunell v Gallon* (1986) (which concerned a son taking advantage of his elderly parents), this was done by treating the debtor (ie the son) as agent for the creditor in getting the other person (ie his parents) to sign the agreement. If that is the case, then the creditor, as principal, would be infected with any wrongful acts of the debtor, as agent, in obtaining the agreement. As was pointed out, however, by Scott LJ in the Court of Appeal in *Barclays Bank v O'Brien* (1992), the analysis of such cases in terms of agency is likely to be 'highly artificial'.

9.9.1 Agency

Another possible analysis, which was preferred by Scott LJ, was to treat married women as being able to take advantage of a 'special equity'. This consists of a recognition by the courts that many wives are still in a position where the husband exercises considerable influence in relation to business decisions taken for the family. In such situations there is therefore an obligation on the creditor, where the wife is entering a transaction which puts her home at risk, to ensure that the she is given full information, and is recommended to seek independent advice.

9.9.2 Special equity

The House of Lords, however, in *Barclays Bank v O'Brien* (1993) was not inclined to adopt either of the analyses identified by Scott LJ. The facts of the case were as follows. Mr O'Brien persuaded his wife to sign a guarantee in relation to an overdraft facility provided by a bank, using the jointly-owned matrimonial home as security. He had told her that the security was limited to £60,000 whereas in fact it was for

9.9.3 The current analysis

£130,000. The employee of the bank who presented the documents for the wife's signature failed to follow a superior's instructions to explain the transaction, and to suggest that the wife took independent legal advice if she had any doubts about it. The papers were presented to the wife open at the place for signature, and she did not read them before signing. When the Bank tried to enforce the security, Mrs O'Brien claimed that she was only bound, at most, up to the £60,000 which her husband had told her was the limit of the liability.

It was found by the Court of Appeal, and not disputed in the House of Lords, that Mrs O'Brien was an intelligent and independent-minded woman, who had not been unduly influenced by her husband. The case, therefore, turned on her husband's misrepresentation of the extent of the liability, and whether this affected the bank. Although the case is therefore not strictly one which is concerned with undue influence, it was accepted in both the Court of Appeal and the House of Lords, that the same principles should apply irrespective of whether the wife was claiming that it was her husband's undue influence, or his misrepresentation, which had led her to enter into the transaction.

Lord Browne-Wilkinson, who gave the only substantive speech in the House of Lords, found that the law in this area had been built on a rather obscure Privy Council decision, *Turnbull v Duval* (1902). Building on this uncertain foundation, it had subsequently developed 'in an artificial way, giving rise to artificial distinctions and conflicting decisions'. As a result he sought to 'restate the law in a form which is principled, reflects the current requirements of society and provides as much certainty as possible'.

9.9.4   The doctrine of notice

The basis on which he felt able to do this was by a proper application of the doctrine of 'notice', which he felt lies at the heart of equity. Where for example, it is necessary to decide between the conflicting rights of two innocent parties, the issue may well be determined by asking whether the holder of the later right had actual or constructive notice of the former right. Looking first at the position of wives, Lord Browne-Wilkinson felt that the fact that many wives place confidence and trust in their husbands in relation to their financial affairs, and that the informality of business dealings between spouses raises a substantial risk of misrepresentation, meant that creditors should in certain circumstances be put on inquiry. These circumstances arose where:

'(a) the transaction is on its face not to the financial advantage of the wife; and (b) there is substantial risk in transactions of that kind that, in procuring the wife to act as surety, the husband has committed a legal or equitable wrong that entitles the wife to set aside the transaction.'

The creditor who ignores the risk, and does not take steps to ensure that the wife is acting with fully informed agreement and consent, will be deemed to have constructive notice of the wife's rights, as against her husband, to set aside the transaction on the basis of misrepresentation or undue influence.

Turning to the broader application of these principles, Lord Browne-Wilkinson saw no reason to confine them to wives. The special position of wives is not based on that status as such, but because of the emotional and sexual ties that arise from the marriage relationship. Such ties exist between all cohabitees, both heterosexual and homosexual, whether married or not. Moreover, the principles will also apply to any situation where the creditor is aware that the surety places trust and confidence in the debtor (as in *Avon Finance Co Ltd v Bridger* (1985) - son and elderly parents). The difference here is that whereas with cohabitees the risk of undue influence or misrepresentation can be inferred, as indicated above, from the combination of the relationship and the nature of the transaction, as regards other relationships it would need to be shown that the creditor had actual knowledge of the surety's reliance on, and trust in, the debtor.

9.9.5   Relationships covered

Summarising the position in the context of cohabitees, where one cohabitee has entered into an obligation to stand surety for the other, and the creditor is aware that they are cohabitees, Lord Browne-Wilkinson outlined the factors which will lead to the obligation being unenforceable, as follows:

9.9.6   Application of doctrine of notice

- there must be undue influence, misrepresentation, or some other legal wrong by the principal debtor;

- the creditor will have constructive notice of such a wrong, and the surety's right to set aside the transaction, unless the creditor has taken reasonable steps to be satisfied that the surety entered into the obligation freely and in knowledge of the true facts;

- the creditor will normally be regarded as taking such steps by (a) warning the surety (not in the presence of the principal debtor) of the amount of the potential liability, and the risks involved, and (b) advising the surety to take independent legal advice.

Applying these guidelines to the facts of the case, Lord Browne-Wilkinson concluded that Mrs O'Brien, having been misled by her husband, and not having received proper advice from the bank, was entitled to set aside the legal charge on the matrimonial home.

9.9.7 Consequences for creditors

The House of Lords decision in this case places a burden on creditors to ensure that they do give proper advice to a surety in any situation where there is a risk of undue influence. It should be noted, however, that if the bank's own procedures had been followed by its employees in this case, the steps advocated by the House of Lords would have been fulfilled. It does not seem, then, that the House of Lords' approach will place unreasonable burdens on creditors, particularly those large organisations which will have standard procedures for dealing with such situations. The safest approach will be to ensure that any private individual standing as surety is advised along the lines suggested by the House of Lords. In terms of contractual principle, however, the case opens another fairly broad exception to the doctrine of privity, in that the actions of a third party are allowed to affect the relationship between creditor and surety.

9.9.8 Application of the doctrine of notice to actual undue influence

Barclays Bank v O'Brien was, as we have seen, dealt with not as a case of undue influence, but of misrepresentation. On the same day as it gave its opinion on this case, the House of Lords also ruled on another husband and wife case, which was agreed to have involved actual undue influence: *CIBC Mortgages plc v Pitt* (1993). Mrs Pitt sought to set aside a mortgage over the matrimonial home granted by the plaintiffs, on the basis that she had been induced to agree to it by the undue influence of her husband. She was unaware of the amount of the mortgage (which was £150,000), though she was aware that her husband was borrowing money to finance share dealings. The trial judge found that Mr Pitt had not been acting as the creditor's agent, but that he had exercised actual undue influence over Mrs Pitt in persuading her to sign the mortgage. Moreover the judge ruled that the mortgage agreement was to Mrs Pitt's manifest disadvantage. Nevertheless, he rejected Mrs Pitt's claim, because he held that the 'special equity' applying to wives only operated where the wife was standing surety, and not to a situation where there was a joint advance to both husband and wife by way of a loan. The Court of Appeal rejected Mrs Pitt's appeal, on the basis that the transaction was not to her manifest disadvantage. Mrs Pitt appealed to the House of Lords.

Lord Browne-Wilkinson again gave the leading speech. He, of course, applied the same approach as had been taken in *Barclays Bank v O'Brien* in relation to the effect of Mr Pitt's behaviour on the contractual relationship between Mrs Pitt and the creditor, ie an approach based on notice. Before considering this, however, the Lord Browne-Wilkinson ruled that the requirement of 'manifest disadvantage' did not apply to cases of actual undue influence. Mrs Pitt would, therefore, have been able to set aside the transaction as against Mr Pitt. As far as the creditor was concerned, however, it had no direct knowledge of the influence Mr Pitt had exercised. Should it be regarded as having constructive notice? The House of Lords thought not. To the creditor it appeared to be a straightforward mortgage transaction:

> 'There was nothing to indicate to the [creditor] that this was anything other than normal advance to a husband and wife for their joint benefit.'

The situation of a joint advance could be distinguished from one involving a surety, because in the latter case:

> '... there is not only the possibility of undue influence having been exercised but there is also the increased risk of it having in fact been exercised because, at least on its face, the guarantee by a wife of her husband's debts is not for her financial benefit. It is the combination of these two factors that puts the creditor on inquiry.'

We see then, that the emphasis in these cases is now on actual, or constructive, notice. Note however, that the concept of 'manifest disadvantage' still has a minor role to play in cases of actual undue influence. It will not be relevant in two party situations, so that the party exercising the influence cannot claim to be able to enforce the agreement simply because it is not disadvantageous. Nor will it be relevant in the three-party situation, if the creditor has actual knowledge of the undue influence. If, however, in such a situation, the creditor does not have actual knowledge, then the fact that the transaction is, or is not, to the other party's disadvantage, will be relevant in deciding whether or not the creditor should be regarded as having constructive notice of the influence.

9.9.9   Relevance of 'manifest disadvantage'

The primary remedy for undue influence in cases such as those discussed in the previous section is the refusal of the courts to enforce the agreement against the person influenced. In other words, that person will often be in the position of defendant, and will use the alleged influence to escape from obligations.

In some cases, however, rescission may be sought (as in *Allcard v Skinner* (above, para 9.7)), and the usual limitations on this equitable remedy (such as lapse of time, involvement of third party rights, and impossibility of restitution) will apply.

9.10   Remedies for undue influence

9.10.1	Change in value of property

Where restitution is ordered, however, but the value of property has changed, it may be difficult to find the just result as to who should get what. This problem arose in *Cheese v Thomas, The Times*, 24 August 1993. C, the plaintiff, and his great-nephew, T, the defendant, had bought a house for £83,000, C contributing £43,000, and T providing £40,000, by means of a mortgage for that amount. The house was in T's name, and C accepted that it would belong to T exclusively after C's death, but in the meantime it was agreed that C was to be entitled to have sole use of the house for the rest of his life. C became worried that T was not keeping up the mortgage repayments, and sought to withdraw from the arrangement. The trial judge ruled that the agreement could be set aside for undue influence. The issue before the Court of Appeal was the amount of money that C should receive, since the house had been sold for £55,400, ie a loss of over £27,500. Should he recover his full £43,000, or only, as the judge held, the appropriate proportion of the selling price? The Court of Appeal upheld the judge's view. The basic principle in applying a restitutionary remedy was that the parties were to be restored as closely as possible to the position they were in before the transaction was entered into. In general, if a plaintiff was able to return to the defendant property which had been transferred under the transaction, it did not matter that the property had meanwhile fallen in value. This case was different, however. The plaintiff had paid the defendant £43,000 not outright, but as part of a purchase price of a house in which both would have rights. Each had contributed a sum of money to buying a house in which each was to have an interest. In that situation the appropriate course was for the loss on the value of the house to be shared. This was even more so where, as the judge had held, the personal conduct of the defendant was not open to criticism, in that he had acted as an 'innocent fiduciary', rather than in any morally reprehensible way.

This case was clearly a difficult one in which to do justice between the parties. It is not entirely convincing, however, on the need to depart from the basic principle of full restitution of cash paid for property, which would be the normal rule. It is not clear why the fact that the parties both had a continuing interest in the property should make such a difference. If the property had increased in value, would the plaintiff have been entitled to a share in that profit? The logical answer must be 'yes'.

9.11	**Unconscionability**

Does the approach of the courts to the issues of duress and undue influence simply reflect a general reluctance to enforce transactions which are so unfair as to be regarded as 'unconscionable'? Is this the underlying principle in these cases?

In *Lloyd's Bank Ltd v Bundy* (1974) Lord Denning based his decision in favour of Mr Bundy on a broader principle than that adopted by the other members of the Court of Appeal. He identified this as 'inequality of bargaining power'. By virtue of this, he claimed:

> 'English law gives relief to one who, without independent advice, enters into a contract on terms which are very unfair or transfers property for a consideration which is grossly inadequate, when his bargaining power is grievously impaired by his own needs or desires, or by his own ignorance or infirmity, coupled with undue influences or pressure brought to bear on him by or for the benefit of the other.'

As will be seen, this puts the emphasis on the nature of the transaction, and its substantive fairness, and probably comes as close as any English judge has done to recognising a general principle of 'unconscionability'. Lord Denning's approach has not been followed, however, and indeed was specifically disapproved by Lord Scarman in *National Westminster Bank v Morgan* (1985), who felt that the fact that Parliament had intervened to deal with many situations of unequal bargaining power (eg by the Consumer Credit Act 1974, Supply of Goods and Services Act 1982) meant that the courts should be reluctant to assume the burden of formulating further restrictions.

The English law relating to both duress and undue influence is still, therefore, primarily concerned with procedural rather than substantive fairness. Unconscionability would require it to focus more directly on the nature of the contract itself, rather than the events which led to it being formed. As we have seen, the requirement of 'manifest disadvantage' does have a minor role to play in cases of presumed undue influence, but it is subsidiary to the issue of whether there was influence in the first place. If there was no such influence, it does not matter how disadvantageous the contract is, the courts will still allow it to stand.

Duress and Undue Influence

A contract which results from threats of physical violence (*Barton v Armstrong* (1975)), or the commission of any crime or tort against a person, will be voidable.

Duress by physical threats or coercion

The concept of economic duress involves 'improper' commercial pressure. First recognised in *The Siboen and The Sibotre* (1976), and *North Ocean Shipping Company v Hyundai Construction* (1979). Applied in *Universe Tankships Inc v International Transport Workers Federation* (1983).

Economic duress

'Impropriety' requires the threat of an unlawful act, in the form of a tort, or breach of contract. Further tests set out by Lord Scarman in *Pao On v Lau Yiu Long* (1980), viz was there a protest at the time? Was there an alternative course of action? Was the person independently advised? Did the person seek to avoid the contract?

'No alternative to compliance' is one of Lord Scarman's tests - it means that the person must have 'no practical choice but to submit to the duress'. See, for example, *Atlas Express v Kafco* (1989), where non-compliance would have led to the collapse of the defendant's business.

Where duress is not being used as a defence to a claim for damages or specific performance, the remedy sought will be rescission. This is subject to the usual restrictions of lapse of time, impossibility of restitution, or the intervention of third party rights.

Remedies for duress

Undue influence is an equitable concept, which divides into actual and presumed undue influence. The presumption may arise from a standard, or a particular, relationship.

Undue influence

The plaintiff must prove that a particular transaction was affected by undue influence. An example is *BCCI v Aboody* (1989) - husband intimidating much younger wife.

Actual undue influence

The burden of proof will be on the defendant to disprove the influence. Relationships covered include parent/child, doctor/patient, solicitor/client, religious adviser/disciple, but not husband/wife (*Midland Bank plc v Shephard* (1988)). Examples include *Allcard v Skinner* (1887).

Presumed undue influence: recognised relationships

Recovery requires that the transaction is to the 'manifest disadvantage' of the person influenced: *National Westminster Bank plc v Morgan* (1985).

Presumed undue influence: other relationships

Once it is shown that a person is in a 'dominant' position, *any* disadvantageous transaction will be presumed to have been affected by undue influence. This has been applied between bank manager and client (*Lloyds Bank Ltd v Bundy* (1975)), neighbouring farmers (*Goldsworthy v Brickell* (1987)), and may also arise between husband and wife (*Barclays Bank plc v O'Brien* (1993) - though no such influence existed in that case).

With regard to the requirement of 'manifest disadvantage' the presumption will not arise unless the agreement is disadvantageous. Thus a short term loan taken out to rescue the husband's business is not manifestly disadvantageous to the wife, even if it uses the matrimonial home as security: *National Westminster Bank plc v Morgan* (1985).

Undue influence and third parties

Undue influence in the case of third parties should generally be dealt with, not by artificial agency arguments, or by a 'special equity' in favour of wives, but by the doctrine of notice: *Barclays Bank plc v O'Brien* (1993). If a surety has been affected by undue influence (or misrepresentation) by a third party (eg her husband), the creditor will only be affected if he or she had actual or constructive notice.

Constructive notice will arise from knowledge of the relationship between the parties (eg cohabitees), and the nature of the transaction (is it disadvantageous?).

The creditor will be protected by advising the surety of the risks involved, and the need to take independent advice.

The same principle of notice applies to actual undue influence by a third party: *CIBC Mortgages plc v Pitt* (1993).

Remedies for undue influence

The primary remedy for undue influence is the refusal to enforce.

Rescission may sometimes be sought, subject to the usual limitations (time, third parties, impossibility of restitution). Note the sharing of losses in *Cheese v Thomas* (1993).

Unconscionability

Note Lord Denning's attempt in *Lloyd's Bank Ltd v Bundy* (1974) to identify an underlying 'unconscionability' principle based on inequality of bargaining power, which has been rejected by the House of Lords (*National Westminster Bank v Morgan* (1985)).

Currently, the English approach concentrates more on procedural rather than substantive fairness, and therefore does not amount to a restriction on 'unconscionable' transactions as such.

Chapter 10

Illegality

This chapter, like the previous one, is concerned with situations where the courts will intervene to prevent the enforcement of an agreement which on its face has all the characteristics of a binding contract. The general heading is that of 'illegality', but it is important to note that this extends far beyond agreements that involve a criminal element. An important area, for example, is agreements which involve an unacceptable restraint on trade (below, para 10.9) such as a restriction on where a person may work. The linking factor between this type of contract, and an agreement to commit a crime, is that both are considered contrary to 'public policy'. This concept permeates the whole area under discussion in this chapter, though at times it is a concept the boundaries of which it is difficult to define.

We start by looking at contracts which involve the commission of a legal wrong.

10.1 Introduction

There are two aspects to contracts which have a criminal element, namely:

- Contracts which constitute a criminal offence

- Contracts which are *performed* in a way which contravenes a statute.

10.2 Contracts having a criminal element

In some circumstances the making of the contract itself will be a criminal act. The most obvious example is an agreement to commit a crime, such as murder, or theft. If A asks B to kill C for a payment of £5,000, and B agrees, then their agreement has all the characteristics of a binding contract, in the form of offer, acceptance and consideration. It also amounts to the criminal offence of conspiracy to murder (under Criminal Law Act 1977), and so will be unenforceable. Any agreement to commit any crime will be treated in the same way.

Certain contracts are made illegal by statute. Under the Obscene Publications Act 1959, for example, it is illegal to sell an 'obscene article'. Here (unlike conspiracy) the offence is only committed by one party, that is the seller, but nevertheless the contract is illegal and will be unenforceable by either party.

10.2.1 Contracts which constitute a criminal offence

10.2.2	Performance is contrary to statute

Performance which contravenes a statute involves contracts which are *prima facie* legal, and which are concerned with the achievement of an objective which is legal, but which contravene a statute by the way in which they are performed. In *Re Mahmoud and Ispahani* (1921), for example, the contract was to sell linseed oil. It was a statutory requirement that both seller and buyer should be licensed. The seller was licensed, but the buyer was not. It was held that the contract was unenforceable for illegality.

The principles which should govern this area were considered by Devlin J in *St John Shipping Corp v Joseph Rank* (1957), which concerned a shipping contract where performance had involved overloading the ship, contrary to the Merchant Shipping Regulations. He said it was necessary to ask:

- does the statute prohibit contracts *as such*, or only penalise certain behaviour?

- if the answer to the first question is that it prohibits contracts, does this contract belong to the class which the statute is intended to prohibit?

In answering the first question he suggested that it was helpful, though not conclusive, to ask whether the object of the statute was to protect the public. If so, then the contract was likely to be illegal. If on the other hand, the purpose was to protect the revenue (as, for example, in a requirement that those who sell television sets pass the names of the purchasers to the Post Office), then it would be likely to be legal. This test is difficult to apply, as was shown by the case itself, where despite the fact that the Merchant Shipping Regulations are clearly not designed simply to protect the revenue, the contract was held to be enforceable.

10.2.3	Relevance of knowledge

In *Archbolds v Spanglett* (1961) it was suggested that the knowledge of the parties might be important, so that if both parties know that the contract can only be performed in a way that will involve the breach of the statute, then it will be illegal. This test is not conclusive either, however, as is shown by *Ailion v Spiekerman* (1976). The contract was for the assignment of a lease, for which a premium was to be paid. This was illegal under the Rent Act 1968, and both parties were aware of this. Nevertheless, the court ordered specific performance of the contract of assignment (though without the illegal premium).

In *Anderson Ltd v Daniel* (1924) both the issue of the protection of the public, and the knowledge of the parties were considered relevant. The contract was for the sale of artificial manure, made up of sweepings of various fertilisers from the holds of ships. Regulations required that the seller should specify the contents of the fertiliser, and the proportions of each chemical it contained. This was impractical as far as sweepings were concerned. The Court of Appeal held the contract for sale unenforceable by the seller, because the statute was intended to protect purchasers. As Scrutton LJ put it:

> 'When the policy of the Act in question is to protect the general public or a class of persons by requiring that a contract shall be accompanied by certain formalities or conditions, the contract and its performance without these formalities or conditions is illegal, and cannot be sued upon by the person liable to the penalties.'

This seems to suggest that the answer might have been different if the purchaser had sued, rather than the seller.

To sum up, the overriding questions are:

- Does the statute prohibit contracts? In deciding this it may be helpful to consider if it is intended to protect the public, or a class of the public.

- Is this particular contract illegal? Here it may be relevant to look at the knowledge of the parties, and the guilt or innocence of the party suing.

The second issue inevitably overlaps with the more general issue of the enforceability of illegal contracts, which is considered further below (paras 10.13-10.14).

A contract to commit an intentional tort, such as assault or fraud, will be illegal in the same way as a contract to commit a crime. On the other hand, a contract which involves the unintentional commission of a tort will not generally be illegal. If, for example, there is a contract for the sale of property which belongs to a third party, but which both the buyer and seller believes to belong to the seller, this will involve the tort of conversion, but the contract itself will not be illegal.	**10.3** **Contract to commit a tort**
The parties may wish to make a type of insurance contract, whereby if one of them commits a crime or tort, the other will pay the amount of any fine or damages imposed, or otherwise provide compensation. Is such an agreement enforceable?	**10.4** **Contract to indemnify**
It will generally be illegal to attempt to insure against criminal liability. There appears to be an exception, however, as regards strict liability offences (that is, where the prosecution does not need to prove any 'guilty mind' on the part of the defendant in order to obtain a conviction). Provided the court is satisfied that the defendant is morally innocent, then it seems the contract will be upheld: *Osman v J Ralph Moss Ltd* (1970).	**10.4.1** Criminal liability

10.4.2 Civil liability	A contract to indemnify will be illegal as regards torts which are committed deliberately, such as deceit, or an intentional libel: *WH Smith & Sons v Clinton* (1909). It is regarded as perfectly acceptable, however, to have such an arrangement as regards the tort of negligence, or where a tort is committed innocently (such as an unintentional libel): *Daily Mirror Newspapers Ltd v Exclusive News Agency* (1937).

Where civil liability arises out of a crime, a contract which would provide compensation may be unenforceable. Thus in *Gray v Barr* (1971), Barr who had been cleared of manslaughter by the criminal courts was sued in tort by the widow of his victim. He admitted liability, but claimed that he was covered by his Prudential 'Hearth and Home' insurance policy, which covered sums he became liable to pay as damages in respect of injury caused by accidents. The Court of Appeal held (in effect ignoring the verdict in the criminal court) that Barr's actions did amount to the criminal offence of manslaughter, and that he therefore could not recover under the insurance policy.

A similar refusal to allow reliance on an insurance contract was shown in *Geismar v Sun Alliance* (1978), where the plaintiff was seeking compensation for the loss of goods which had been brought into the country without the required import duty having been paid.

This approach does not apparently apply, however, where the crime is one of strict liability, or in relation to 'motor manslaughter' (causing death by dangerous driving): *Tinline v White Cross Insurance* (1921). The rules in the motoring area are affected by the need to uphold the effectiveness of the system of compulsory insurance, so that the victims, and families of victims, of road accidents receive proper compensation. The exception in relation to motor manslaughter will not, however, apply if the offence was deliberate: *Gardner v Moore* (1984).

10.5 Contracts contrary to public policy	The following sections concern contracts which are not 'illegal' in the sense that they amount to, or are linked to, the commission of a crime or a tort. Nevertheless, they have been held to be contrary to public policy, and therefore void, and unenforceable. The categories of public policy appear to be closed, so that the courts will not apply this approach to a type of contract to which it has not been applied previously. This rule exists for reasons of certainty, and because public policy claims need to be kept within limits.
10.6 Contracts concerning marriage	The courts regard it as being in the interests of society to preserve the status of marriage. Certain types of contract which are regarded as threatening to the institution of marriage are therefore treated as illegal.

A contract between spouses agreeing to separate at some point in the future is invalid if it is made either before the marriage or during cohabitation. In *Brodie v Brodie* (1917) Mr Brodie only agreed to marry the woman who was carrying his child if a written agreement to separate was drawn up. This, *inter alia*, precluded the woman from bringing legal proceedings against him. The agreement was held to be contrary to public policy, and so did not act as restraint on the woman's action.

This rule does not apply, of course, to an agreement which does not relate to the future, but is followed by immediate separation. Nor does it affect arrangements made by spouses who have been separated, and are then reconciled: *Harrison v Harrison* (1910).

10.6.1   Future separation

A contract by someone which imposes liability on them if they marry is void. Thus a promise by A that if he marries he will pay a sum of money to C is unenforceable: *Baker v White* (1690). Similarly a promise by A to make a payment if he marries anyone else other than B will also be unenforceable: *Lowe v Peers* (1768).

10.6.2   Restraint of marriage

Marriage brokage concerns a contract whereby A promises to procure a marriage for B. The rule is not limited to contracts to procure marriage with a particular person. Thus in *Hermann v Charlesworth* (1905) Miss H entered into an agreement under which if the defendant introduced her to someone whom she married, Miss H would pay the defendant £250. She paid a deposit which, after several unsuccessful introductions, she sought to recover. The Court of Appeal held that the contract was illegal, as being contrary to public policy. As Treitel has commented, however (*Law of Contract*, 8th ed, p 390), 'the harmful tendencies of such contracts are by no means self-evident'.

10.6.3   Marriage brokage

Contracts promoting sexual immorality will include any contracts for sex outside marriage, and would presumably cover otherwise lawful homosexual, as well as heterosexual activities. Such activities, while not constituting criminal offences, or civil wrongs, may still be regarded as immoral, and contracts which involve them will be treated as contrary to public policy.

The rule is not limited to contracts which directly concern sexual activity, as is shown by *Pearce v Brooks* (1866). Here there was a contract under which the plaintiffs supplied the defendant with an ornamental brougham (a type of carriage), which was to be paid for by instalments. After one instalment had been paid the brougham was returned in a damaged condition. The plaintiffs sued for £15 compensation which was payable under

10.7   Contracts promoting sexual immorality

the agreement if the brougham was returned. The defendant, however, was a prostitute, and there was evidence that she intended to use the brougham to attract customers. Moreover, it seems that at least one partner in the plaintiffs' firm was aware of this. On this basis the court held that this would be an illegal contract, so that the plaintiffs would be unable to recover either under the contract, or for the damage.

The knowledge of the plaintiffs was relevant here, but not every contract with a known prostitute will be illegal. In *Appleton v Campbell* (1826), the action was for the recovery of board and lodging in relation to a room rented from the plaintiff. The court held that the plaintiff could not recover if he knew that the defendant was a prostitute, *and* that she was using the room to entertain her clients. But

> '... if the defendant had her lodgings there, and received her visitors elsewhere, the plaintiff may recover, although she be a woman of the town, because persons of that description must have a place to lay their heads.'

There are thus two factors which are necessary for the contract to be unenforceable:

- knowledge that the other party is a prostitute; and

- knowledge that what was supplied under the contract is to be used for the purposes of prostitution.

The same approach will presumably apply to other 'immoral' contracts.

10.8 Contracts to oust the jurisdiction of the court

The courts are very jealous of any attempt in a contract or other agreement to try to take away their powers to oversee the agreement, interpret it, and decide on its validity. They will hold any such agreement to be void as being contrary to public policy. For example, in *Baker v Jones* (1954) the rules of the British Amateur Weightlifters' Association provided that the association's central council was to be 'the sole interpreter of the rules', and that the council's decision was to be final. It was held that although it was perfectly in order to give a tribunal or council the power to make final decisions on questions of fact, the same could not be done as regards questions of law. These provisions in the rules were to that extent contrary to public policy, and void.

There are two exceptions to this general approach, which should be noted. First, in commercial matters the procedure whereby parties may submit a dispute for arbitration, on questions of both fact and law, has been approved by the courts (*Scott v Avery* (1855)), and legislation (Arbitration Acts 1950 and 1979). Secondly, a clause in an agreement arrived at on the separation of husband and wife under which the wife, in return for a promise of maintenance, agrees not to apply to the courts, is void to the extent that the wife is still free to apply, but is enforceable as regards the husband's promise to pay: Matrimonial Causes Act 1973, s 34.

Contracts 'in restraint of trade' are those which unfairly restrict competition, or unreasonably restrict people's ability to work. Such agreements are thought to be contrary to public policy, and therefore liable to be treated as unenforceable.

    Two aspects of this topic are not discussed in any detail: first, the provisions of Article 85 of the Treaty of Rome which applies to restraints which have an affect on cross-border trade within the European Community; secondly, the legislative regime (Restrictive Trade Practices Act 1976, Competition Act 1980) administered by the Restrictive Practices Court. Both of these areas are beyond the scope of this book, and are usually dealt with in courses on competition law, rather than contract law.

10.9 Contracts in restraint of trade: the general principles

Contractual provisions which attempt to restrict the ways in which one of the parties may do business, or earn a living, are *prima facie* void: *Nordenfelt v Maxim Nordenfelt* (1894). This rule is now well established, though at times the common law has treated such provisions as *prima facie* valid. The current presumption of unenforceability can, however, be rebutted, as is outlined in the following sections.

10.9.1 *Prima facie* void

Examples of the kind of restraint we are dealing with would be a restriction on a sales representative from soliciting the customers of a former employer, or a restriction on the vendor of a business from setting up in competition to the purchaser. For such restraints to be valid, there are three requirements which must be fulfilled:

10.10 Contracts relating to employment or the sale of a business

- there must be a valid interest to protect;

- the restraint must be no more extensive than is reasonable to protect that interest;

- the restraint must not be contrary to the public interest.

Looking at the first of these requirements, an employer will have a legitimate interest in restricting the activities of a departing employee, where that employee has either acquired trade secrets, or has gained influence over the employer's customers, either because they rely on the employee's skill and judgment, or because they have dealt exclusively with that employee. Examples from the cases include a hairdresser

10.10.1 Must have a valid interest

(*Marion White Ltd v Francis* (1972), a sales representative (*T Lucas & Co v Mitchell* (1974), and a tailor (*Attwood v Lamont* (1920)). Similarly, the purchaser of a business may well have paid a substantial amount for 'goodwill', that is, the existing trade which has been built up by the vendor. In that context, the purchaser has a legitimate interest in preventing the vendor from setting up a business which will attract all the old customers.

The courts have been prepared to recognise that the categories of interest are not closed. For example, in *Greig v Insole* (1978), which concerned restrictions placed on professional cricketers by the cricketing authorities, Slade J recognised that there might be a public interest that the game of cricket should be properly organised and administered. On the facts, however, the restraint was in any case unreasonable. In *Eastham v Newcastle United* (1964), however, Wilberforce J was unable to find a legitimate interest in relation to restrictions on freedom of transfer for professional footballers. It seems then that although in theory the categories of interest are open, the courts are likely to be very cautious in finding new interests.

10.10.2 Restraint must be reasonable

The reasonableness or otherwise of the restraint must be looked at in the context of the interest which is being protected. There are three main factors to consider:

- the geographical area covered;
- the length of time involved; and
- the scope of the activities covered.

For example, if a business is sold in one town, a restriction preventing the opening of a similar business anywhere in the country would be unlikely to be regarded as reasonable. In *Mason v Provident Clothing* (1913) a canvasser who had been employed to sell clothes in Islington, was restrained from entering into similar business within 25 miles of London. This was held to be too wide.

As regards time, this will again depend on the type of contract. In many employment cases a restraint of one or two years at most will be all that is reasonable. In *Fitch v Dewes* (1921), however, a lifelong restraint on a solicitor's managing clerk was upheld. The justification was that the business was one to which clients were likely to return over a long period.

The type of activity restrained must also be related to the interest being protected. A clause restraining someone who had been employed as a chiropodist from working as a hairdresser would be unlikely to be regarded as unreasonable.

At one time the approach of the courts was to take clauses literally in assessing their reasonableness. Thus, if no area were specified the restriction would be taken to be worldwide. The cases of *Littlewoods v Harris* (1978) and *Clarke v Newland* (1991), have suggested a different approach, requiring the restraint to be limited by the 'factual matrix' within which it was imposed. In *Littlewoods v Harris* (1978) an employee who had been employed solely in connection with the plaintiffs' mail-order business was made subject to a restraint which, on its face, covered all aspects of the plaintiffs' wide ranging business activities. The Court of Appeal, however, held that the relevant clause should be interpreted as being intended only to apply to the mail-order business in the UK. On that basis it was reasonable. Similarly in *Clarke v Newland* (1991) a broad agreement by a doctor 'not to practise' was held to mean 'practise as a medical practitioner' since that was the role in which the defendant had previously been employed.

There is some controversy as to whether the public interest part of the rules concerning enforceable restraints of trade does in fact exist. If it does, then it means that even if a restraint satisfies the other conditions (ie of legitimate interest, and reasonableness) it may still be struck down as being contrary to the public interest. This might be the case, for example, in relation to a restraint on the work of a leading artist, playwright, doctor or scientist, whose work might well be for the public benefit. The principle was stated in *Wyatt v Kreglinger and Fernau* (1933). The plaintiff's pension was made contingent upon his not taking any part in the wool trade. The Court of Appeal held that this stipulation was void, irrespective of whether it was reasonable as between the parties, because it was contrary to the public interest. This was followed in the similar case of *Bull v Pitney Bowes* (1967). It seems difficult, however, to find later authorities that have applied the principle, though Lord Denning supported it in relation to a solicitor in *Oswald Hickson Collier v Carter Ruck* (1984). In subsequent cases, such as *Deacons v Bridge* (1984) and *Kerr v Morris* (1986), the courts have refused to apply the principle to the circumstances before them, while not denying its existence.

10.10.3   Public interest

It was confirmed by the House of Lords in *Esso Petroleum v Harpers Garage* (1968) that a contract in which one party agrees to take all supplies of a particular product from one source (sometimes known as a 'solus agreement'), could amount to an unreasonable restraint on trade. The case in fact concerned two such agreements in relation to two garages run by the defendant. In respect of both there was an agreement to take

10.11   Contracts of exclusive dealing

all supplies of petrol from Esso, and to keep the garage open at all reasonable hours. In relation to garage A, the agreement was to last for four years, five months. In relation to garage B, the agreement was to last for 21 years, and was linked to a mortgage over the premises held by Esso, which was also irredeemable for 21 years. The defendants started to sell cut-price petrol of other brands. Esso sought an injunction to prevent them doing this. The defence was based on 'restraint of trade'.

The House of Lords held that contracts of this type could be regarded as being in restraint of trade. As with the categories looked at above, the question was then whether the restraint was reasonable as between the parties, and reasonable in the public interest. In relation to garage A, the five year restraint was reasonable. The 21 years in relation to garage B, however, was unreasonable, particularly as it was linked to a mortgage.

The *Esso* case gives no indication of what period greater than 5 years, but less than 21 years, might have been considered reasonable. In the later case of *Alec Lobb (Garages) Ltd v Total Oil (Great Britain) Ltd* (1985), however, a 21 year restraint was held to be reasonable because it was terminable after 7 or 14 years.

In *Shell v Lostock Garage* (1977) the Court of Appeal had to address the issue of the point in time at which a restraint should be judged. A 'solus' agreement which was probably, in the light of the *Esso* decision, reasonable when it was made, arguably became unreasonable when a price war in relation to petrol developed. The majority of the Court of Appeal took the view that the agreement had to be judged at the time it was made, and not in the context of subsequent developments.

10.11.1 Restraints on songwriters, and other entertainers

A particular area of difficulty has arisen in relation to contracts entered into by songwriters, or pop musicians, with music publishers or recording companies. These often require the artists to commit themselves to the one company for a lengthy period of time, with no necessary obligation on the company to promote, or even publish, the artists' work. The validity of this kind of 'exclusive dealing' agreement was considered in *Schroeder Music Publishing Co Ltd v Macaulay* (1974). The plaintiff was a young and unknown songwriter who entered into a standard form agreement with music publishers (the defendants). The copyright in all the plaintiff's compositions for the next five years was assigned to the defendants, with an automatic extension for a further five years if royalties exceeded £5,000. The defendants could terminate the agreement on one month's notice, but there was no similar power for the plaintiff.

The defendants were under no obligation to publish any of the plaintiff's work. The plaintiff sought a declaration that the agreement was in restraint of trade, and void. The House of Lords held that, where there was unequal bargaining power, a standard form agreement has to be looked at to see if, *inter alia*, the restrictions it contains only go so far as is reasonably necessary to protect legitimate interests. In this case the contract was in unreasonable restraint of trade, because, whereas the plaintiff was totally committed to the defendants, the defendants were not obliged to publish anything.

This decision was applied in the similar case of *Clifford Davis v WEA Records* (1975).

10.12   Trade associations

A group of manufacturers or producers may make an agreement between themselves to protect their interests. Such agreements may fall foul of legislative provisions relating to competition under domestic or European law, but they are also subject to the control of the common law and may be struck down as being in restraint of trade. The relevant principles were considered in *English Hop Growers v Dering* (1928). The defendant, in common with other hop-growers, had agreed to deliver all crops produced by him to a central selling agency. The object of the agreement was to protect the producers at a time when it was feared that there might be a glut of hops on the market. The defendant sought to escape from the agreement on the basis that it was in restraint of trade. Adopting a similar approach to the other areas which we have considered the majority of the Court of Appeal asked whether the restriction was reasonable to protect a legitimate interest. It was held that the restraint was not in this case an unreasonable one and the agreement was upheld. This perhaps reflects the fact that the agreement here had been reached between parties bargaining at arms length. If such an agreement affects third parties the court will be more likely to intervene, as in *Kores v Kolok* (1959). This concerned an agreement between two companies that neither would, without the consent of the other, employ any person who had been employed by the other company within the past five years. The agreement was intended to protect trade secrets, since they were both working on similar products involving chemical processes. In addition, at the time it was thought that their factories would be adjacent, though this turned out not to be the case. One of the companies brought an action to restrain the other from employing a particular former employee. It seems clear that there was in this case a legitimate interest to protect, but the Court of Appeal held that the restraint was too wide. It had the potential to cover an unskilled labourer, as much as the chief chemist. On that basis it was unreasonable.

Note that this type of agreement would now be regulated by the legislation on restrictive trade practices mentioned above, para 10.9.

10.13   Effects of illegality: enforcement

If a contract is found to be void for illegality, then this will, in general, mean that specific performance will be refused. If there is no contract the court cannot order it to be performed. They may, however, in some circumstances be prepared to award damages. This may be done by allowing the action to be framed in tort, as for example in *Saunders v Edwards* (1987) where the plaintiff who had been party to an illegal overvaluation of furniture (for the purpose of avoiding stamp duty) in a contract for the sale of a flat was nevertheless allowed to sue for deceit on the basis of the defendant's fraudulent misrepresentation that the flat included a roof garden. The court took account of the 'relative moral culpability' of the two parties, and this question of the 'guilt' or 'innocence' has always been relevant. During the 1980s it was transformed by a number of decisions (eg *Thackwell v Barclays Bank* (1987); *Howard v Shirlstar Container Transport* (1990)) into a rather vague test of whether enforcement would offend the 'public conscience'. The House of Lords in *Tinsley v Milligan* (1993) has rejected this, and reasserted a test based on whether the plaintiff needs to rely on the illegality to found the claim. In this case T and M had both supplied the money for the purchase of a house. It was, however, put into the name of T alone, in order to facilitate the making by M of false claims to social security payments. When the parties fell out, M claimed a share of the property on the basis of a resulting trust. It was argued for T that M could not succeed because the original arrangement had been entered into in order to further an illegal purpose. The trial judge and Court of Appeal found for M. The House of Lords also held by a majority of three to two, that M should succeed. In doing so the majority rejected the approach taken by the Court of Appeal that the issue should be decided by considering whether 'the public conscience would be affronted by recognising rights created by illegal transactions'. This was too 'imponderable'. The proper test to be applied was whether the plaintiff needed to rely on the illegality in order to support her claim. In this case, the presumption of a resulting trust was raised simply by the fact that M had contributed to the purchase price of the house. It was T who had to raise the illegality in order to try to rebut that presumption. Therefore M should succeed. (*Cf* the approach taken to the recovery of property in cases such as *Bowmakers v Barnet Instruments* (1945), below 10.15.4)

The general principle which applies in the area of recovery of money or property is expressed in the Latin maxim:

- *in pari delicto potior est conditio defendentis.*

This maxim, which is generally referred to in the abbreviated form '*in pari delicto*', roughly translates as:

- where there is equal fault the defendant is in the stronger position.

Thus, where money or other property has been transferred under an illegal contract, which is regarded as void, the court will not in general assist the plaintiff to recover it.

An example of the application of the rule of no recovery is to be found in the case of *Parkinson v College of Ambulance* (1925). Colonel Parkinson was approached by a third party who told him that if he made a contribution to the College (a charity), it would be able to obtain a knighthood for him. Parkinson made a contribution of £3,000, but no knighthood was forthcoming. He brought an action to recover his money. It was held that the contract was illegal, and that Parkinson could not sustain his action without disclosing this, and his own complicity. His donation would appear to be a gift, and therefore irrecoverable, until it was disclosed that it was given as part of a contract, the consideration being the promise of the knighthood. His action only made sense as being for breach of this illegal contract, but because the of the illegality the action had to fail.

The courts have developed and recognised a number of exceptions to this rule, and there are therefore several situations where recovery of money or property will be allowed despite the illegality.

If the contract is still executory the plaintiff should have the chance to have a change of mind or heart, resile from the contract, and recover property transferred. Thus in *Taylor v Bowers* (1876) the plaintiff had made a fictitious assignment of his goods to A as part of a scheme to defraud his creditors. Meetings of the creditors had been held, but no composition agreement had been reached. A had in the meantime parted with the goods to the defendant (who knew of the fraudulent scheme). The Court of Appeal held that because no creditors had actually been defrauded, the illegal purpose had not been carried out, and the plaintiff could recover his goods from the defendant.

10.14   Effects of illegality: recovery of money or property

10.14.1   General rule: no recovery

10.15   Exceptions to the general rule

10.15.1   Illegal purpose not yet carried out

This exception will not operate, however, where there has been substantial performance of the contract, as in *Kearley v Thomson* (1890). The plaintiff had paid money to the defendants, a firm of solicitors, in return for their agreement not to appear at the public examination of a bankrupt friend of the plaintiff, nor to oppose the order for his discharge. After the first part of the agreement had been carried out, the plaintiff changed his mind and tried to recover his money. The Court of Appeal refused to allow him to do so, because there had been 'a partial carrying into effect of an illegal purpose in a substantial manner'.

Note also that the withdrawal must be genuine. If the purpose of the contract is simply frustrated by the refusal of the other party to play his or her part, this exception will not apply: *Bigos v Bousted* (1951).

10.15.2 Oppression

In the case of oppression, if the plaintiff was in a weak bargaining position, so that there was virtually no choice about entering into the agreement, recovery may be possible. Thus in *Atkinson v Denby* (1862) a creditor refused to accept a composition agreement unless he was paid £50, so gaining an advantage over the other creditors. The debtor paid, but later brought an action to recover the money. It was held that the debtor could recover. Although the agreement was an illegal contract, the element of oppression meant that an exception to the general rule was justified.

The rationale of this exception is that the parties while both *in delicto* are not in fact *in pari delicto*, that is they are not *equally* at fault. As Cockburn CJ put it in *Atkinson v Denby*:

'It is true that both are in delicto, because the act is a fraud upon the other creditors, but it is not par delictum, because the one has the power to dictate, the other no alternative but to submit.'

10.15.3 Fraud

If one party entered into the contract as a result of the other's fraudulent misrepresentation that it was lawful, recovery will be allowed: *Hughes v Liverpool Victoria Legal Friendly Society* (1916). Again the parties are not regarded as being equally at fault.

10.15.4 No reliance on the illegal transaction

If the plaintiff can establish a right to possession of the property without relying on the illegal contract, then recovery will be allowed. In *Bowmakers v Barnet Instruments* (1945), for example, the defendant agreed to buy some machine tools on hire purchase terms from the plaintiffs. These agreements may well have been illegal, being in contravention of certain statutory regulations. There were three agreements. The defendants sold the machines which were the subject of two of the agreements, but kept the others. They refused to return them, or pay the hire. The plaintiffs' action to recover damages for conversion in relation to all the machines succeeded. The Court of Appeal held that they could establish their rights over the goods without needing to rely on the illegal contracts. The defendants' rights as bailees had been brought to an end by their actions, and so the plaintiffs could rely on their basic rights of ownership to found their action.

The decision in this case is not uncontroversial (see, for example, Cheshire & Fifoot, *Law of Contract*, 12th ed, pp 381-382; Treitel *Law of Contract*, 8th ed, pp 441-442), and is arguably inconsistent with *Taylor v Chester* (1869). Note, however, that the House of Lords adopted a similar line of argument in *Tinsley v Milligan* (1993), which is discussed above, at para 10.13. The principle thus seems to be well-established, though the basis of its application to the precise facts of *Bowmakers v Barnet Instruments* (1945) may be more difficult to justify, particularly in relation to the machines retained by the defendants.

10.15.5 Class-protecting statutes

In some situations, the purpose for which a statute makes an agreement illegal, is to protect a particular class. For example, the provisions forbidding the taking of illegal premiums under the Rent Acts, are designed to protect tenants. A member of that class may be able to recover property transferred under the agreement, notwithstanding the illegality. Many statutes of this kind now contain specific provisions for recovery (eg Rent Act 1977, s 125, Financial Services Act 1986, s 132). Where they do not, however, the courts will apply the common law rule, and allow recovery: *Kiriri Cotton Co Ltd v Dewani* (1960). The underlying principle again seems to be that in this situation the parties are not equally at fault.

10.16 Severance

It is likely to be the case in many illegal contracts that it is only part of the arrangement which is illegal. To what extent can the contract be split into its constituent parts, with the legal section being valid, and the illegal section unenforceable? There are two aspects to this, namely, severance of the consideration, and severance of promises. Suppose, for example, A agrees to pay B £1,000 if B will fraudulently obtain a valuable painting and frame it. The first part of this contract, involving the fraud, is illegal, but the second part, for the framing, is *prima facie* a perfectly legal arrangement. If B does what is required, and then sues for the £1,000, the issue of the severance of the consideration will arise. B's consideration for the promise to pay the £1,000 consists of both an illegal and a legal act. Can the two be separated? In other words, can B recover the £1,000 simply for framing the picture? If the action is by A, however, in relation to B's failure to frame the picture, the question concerns the separation of the promises. These two issues will now be considered in turn.

10.16.1   Severance of consideration

For severance of consideration to be allowed, the lawful part of the consideration must be more important than the unlawful part. For example, in a contract for employment, the employee's consideration for the payment of wages may be made up of performing the required work (legal), and a promise not to compete after leaving the employment (possibly illegal, see above, para 10.10). Nevertheless, even if the restraint on future employment is too wide, the employee will be allowed to sue for wages. The consideration can be severed here, because the performance of the work is the major part of the consideration, and the restraint is subsidiary.

Note that the approach will in general be 'all or nothing'. Thus in the example of the painting, given in the previous section, B would either be able to claim the full £1,000, or nothing at all (which would be the more likely outcome). This may not apply, however, if it is possible to assign a precise value to different parts of the contract. This occurred in *Ailion v Spiekermann* (1976) (above, para 10.2.3), where the contract to pay the illegal premium could be severed, because a precise amount could be assigned to the illegal part of the agreement. (*Cf* also *Carney v Herbert* (1985)).

10.16.2   Severance of promises

The attempt to sever promises occurs most frequently in relation to restraint of trade cases, where the wish is to 'edit out' from a list of restrictions those which make the restraint too wide, but to leave the rest in force. There have traditionally been two elements to the courts' approach, namely the 'Blue Pencil Test', and the requirement that the nature of the contract must be retained.

10.16.3   The Blue Pencil Test

The Blue Pencil Test means that severance must be possible simply by cutting out the offending words. The court will not become involved in re-drafting the contract. Thus in *Mason v Provident Clothing Co* (1913) (above, para 10.10.2) the court refused to substitute the phrase 'in Islington', for 'within 25 miles of London'. In *Goldsoll v Goldman* (1915) on the other hand, a covenant in the sale of a jewellery business contained a restriction on dealing in 'real or imitation jewellery' in any of a long list of countries. This was too wide both as regards scope (the business was only concerned with imitation jewellery) and geographical area (the business was limited to the UK). Both restrictions could be narrowed however by simple deletions, of the words 'real or', and the list of countries other than the UK, and this the court agreed to do.

Note that the strict application of this test requires that the clause as edited still makes sense, but see below, 10.16.5 'The current approach'.

The requirement that the nature of the contract must be retained seems to derive from *Attwood v Lamont* (1920), but is quite difficult to apply. In *Attwood v Lamont* the plaintiff owned a general outfitters. The defendant was employed in the tailoring department as a tailor and cutter. He found that his contract of employment bound him after leaving his employment not to be concerned in the trade or business of a tailor, dressmaker, general draper, milliner, hatter, haberdasher, gentlemen's, ladies, or children's outfitter. It was suggested that the clause could be made reasonable by cutting out all the trades except 'tailor'. The Court of Appeal refused to do this, treating the covenant as an entirety, intended to cover all aspects of the plaintiff's business. To sever it would be to affect its nature.

> 10.16.4   Nature of the contract must be retained

It is very difficult to reconcile this decision with the earlier decision in *Goldsoll v Goldman* (1915) (above), or the later decision in *Putsman v Taylor* (1927). In the latter case the employee worked as a tailor at one branch, but the restriction covered all three branches owned by his employer. The court agreed to sever the names of the branches where the employee had not worked.

Despite this difficulty, the principle stated in *Attwood v Lamont* has not been overturned, and we must still accept that there is, alongside the Blue Pencil Test, a further requirement that the nature of the contract is not altered. How this principle will be applied, however, is very unpredictable.

It may well be that the tests outlined in the previous two sections will not nowadays be applied so strictly by the courts. In *Lucas & Co Ltd v Mitchell* (1972), for example, the deletion left the phrase 'any such goods' in the contract. It was necessary to look at the deleted clause in order to see what 'such goods' meant, but the deletion was nevertheless allowed to stand. Moreover, the approach taken to the interpretation of restraint clauses in *Littlewoods v Harris* and *Clarke v Newland* (above, 10.10.2) may mean that the severance of provisions may not be so necessary. As we have seen, the courts in these cases rejected the view that widely phrased restrictions should be given their literal meaning. Instead, they had to be interpreted within the factual context in which they had been put forward. Such an interpretation is likely to lead to the restraint, as redefined, being regarded as reasonable, thus obviating the need to consider severance.

> 10.16.5   The current approach

Illegality

'Illegality' covers all contracts which are considered to be contrary to 'public policy'.

Introduction

Contracts which constitute a criminal offence may be conspiracies (eg agreement to murder), or statutory offences (eg Obscene Publications Act 1959).

Contracts which constitute a criminal offence

If the manner of performance is unlawful (*Re Mahmoud and Ispahani* (1921)), it is relevant whether the statute prohibits contracts as such: *St John Shipping Corp v Joseph Rank* (1957). Knowledge of the parties is also important: *Archbolds v Spanglett* (1961).

Performance contrary to statute

A contract to commit an intentional tort will be illegal.

Contract to commit a tort

Validity of an indemnity contract depends on the type of liability:

Contract to indemnify

- Criminal liability insurance is illegal, except as regards strict liability offences (*Osman v J Ralph Moss Ltd* (1970)).

- Civil liability indemnity is illegal with regard to intentional torts (*WH Smith & Sons v Clinton* (1909)), but possible as regards negligent or innocent liability (*Daily Mirror Newspapers Ltd v Exclusive News Agency* (1937)).

  Where civil liability arises out of a crime, indemnity will be illegal (*Gray v Barr* (1971)), except in relation to strict liability offences, and (non-deliberate) motor manslaughter (*Tinline v White Cross Insurance* (1921)).

'Public policy' covers a finite group of situations (outlined below), not involving crime or tort, which the courts have categorised as being contrary to public policy and therefore void.

Contracts contrary to public policy

Contracts which threaten the institution of marriage will be contrary to public policy. This includes:

Contracts concerning marriage

- Future separation: *Brodie v Brodie* (1917)

- Restraint of marriage: *Baker v White* (1690)

- Marriage brokage: *Hermann v Charlesworth* (1905)

Contracts promoting sexual immorality	Contracts promoting sexual immorality are unenforceable if related directly to immoral activities, or if goods or services are to be used for immoral purposes and both parties are aware of this: *Pearce v Brooks* (1866); *Appleton v Campbell* (1826).
Contracts to oust the jurisdiction of the court	Contracts made to oust the jurisdiction of the court cannot generally prevent the court's intervening (*Baker v Jones* (1954)), but there are exceptions with regard to arbitration, and separation agreements (Arbitration Acts 1950 and 1979, Matrimonial Causes Act 1973).
Contracts in restraint of trade	Contracts in restraint of trade are *prima facie* void (*Nordenfelt v Maxim Nordenfelt* (1894)), but the presumption may be rebutted in relation to:

Employment and sale of business - restraint must

- protect a valid interest (eg trade secrets, business 'goodwill');

- be reasonable in its extent - as to area, time, and scope (eg *Mason v Provident Clothing* (1913); *cf Littlewoods v Harris* (1978));

- not be contrary to the public interest (*Wyatt v Kreglinger and Fernau* (1933)).

With regard to exclusive dealing see *Esso Petroleum v Harpers Garage* (1968). Agreement must reasonable, judged at the time it was made (*Shell v Lostock Garage* (1977)). Exclusive contracts for entertainers may also be found to be illegal, if too one-sided (*Schroeder v Macaulay* (1974)).

With regard to trade associations agreements between producers may be reasonable (*English Hop Growers v Dering* (1928)), provided they do not act as a restriction on third parties (*Kores v Kolok* (1959)).

Effects of illegality

With regard to illegality enforcement will generally not be allowed, and compensation will only be recoverable if the plaintiff is morally innocent, and does not need to rely on the illegality (*Saunders v Edwards* (1987) - action based on tort; *Tinsley v Milligan* (1993) - property rights).

Recovery of money or property. Generally dealt with by the principle of *in pari delicto*, which means recovery (*Parkinson v College of Ambulance* (1925)). Exceptions include:

- illegal purpose which is not carried out: *Taylor v Bowers* (1876);

- oppression or fraud: *Atkinson v Denby* (1862); *Hughes v Liverpool Victoria Friendly Society* (1916);

- no reliance on illegal transaction: *Bowmakers v Barnet Instruments* (1945);

- class-protecting statutes.

Severance

Consideration may be severed if the illegality constitutes only a minor part of it, or it is possible to assign value to the legal and illegal aspects: *Ailion v Spiekermann* (1976).

Promises may be severed by applying:

- The Blue Pencil Test: *Goldsoll v Goldman* (1915);

- requirement that the nature of the contract is unchanged: *Attwood v Lamont* (1920).

But note the current more relaxed approach to interpretation: *Littlewoods v Harris* (1978); *Clarke v Newland* (1991).

Chapter 11

Frustration

The topic to be dealt with in this chapter, the doctrine of frustration, has links with preceding chapters, and with the one that follows. Frustration can, from one point of view, be looked at as something which vitiates a contract, in much the same way as mistake, or illegality. Whereas, however, these vitiating factors relate to things which happen, or states of affairs which exist, at or before the time when the contract is made, frustration deals with events which occur subsequent to the contract coming into existence. On the other hand, since frustration has the characteristics of an event which discharges parties from their obligations under a contract, it also has links with the topics of performance and breach (Chapter 12).

The situation that the doctrine of frustration is concerned with is where a contract, as a result of some event outside the control of the parties, becomes impossible to perform, at least in the way originally intended. What are the rights and liabilities of the parties?

In *Paradine v Jane* (1647) the court took the line that obligations were not discharged by a frustrating event, and that a party who failed to perform as a result of such an event would still be in breach of contract. The justification for this harsh approach was that the parties could, if they wished, have provided for the eventuality within the contract itself.

This approach, however, proved too strict, and potentially unjust, even for the 19th century courts, who were in many respects strong supporters of the concept of 'freedom of contract', taking the view that it was not for the court to interfere to remedy perceived injustice resulting from a freely negotiated bargain. The modern law has developed from the decision in *Taylor v Caldwell* (1863). This contract involved the letting of a music hall for the purposes of concerts, and other events. After the agreement, but before the first concert, the Hall was destroyed by fire. It was held that, since performance was impossible, this event excused the parties from any further obligations under the contract. Blackburn J justified this approach on the basis that, where the parties must have known from the beginning that the contract was dependent on the continued existence of a particular thing, the contract must be construed:

11.1 **The nature of the doctrine**

11.1.1 Original rule

11.1.2 Subsequent mitigation

'... as subject to an implied condition that the parties shall be excused in case, before breach, performance becomes impossible from the perishing of the thing without the fault of the contractor.'

The doctrine at this stage, then, is based on the existence of an implied term. This enabled the decision to be squared with the prevailing approach to freedom of contract, but it is in reality something of a fiction, and modern courts have preferred to base the doctrine simply on the need to avoid the injustice of imposing impossible obligations in the absence of fault.

11.2   Frustrating events

The types of event which will be regarded as frustrating a contract are those which render performance impossible, or at least, 'radically different' (Lord Radcliffe in *Davis Contractors Ltd v Fareham UDC* (1956)), from what had been contracted for. Although the categories can never be closed, it is possible to identify certain occurrences which have been recognised by the courts as amounting to frustration of the contract.

11.2.1   Destruction of the subject-matter

In the same way that the destruction of the subject-matter prior to the formation of a contract will render it void for mistake (above, para 8.6), destruction at a later stage will fall within the doctrine of frustration: *Taylor v Caldwell* (1863). If what is destroyed is fundamental to the performance of the obligations under the contract, then the doctrine will operate (*cf* Sale of Goods Act 1979, s 7, below para 11.5).

It seems that complete physical destruction may not be necessary, if the subject-matter has been affected in a way which renders it useless: *Asfar v Blundell* (1896) (cargo of dates impregnated with sewage).

11.2.2   Personal services – supervening incapacity

If a contract envisages performance by a particular individual, as in a contract to paint a portrait, and no substitute is likely to be satisfactory, then the contract will generally be frustrated by the incapacity of the person concerned. Thus in *Condor v Barron Knights* (1966) the drummer with a pop group was taken ill. Medical opinion was that he would only be fit to work three or four nights a week, whereas the group had engagements for seven nights a week. It was held that his contract of employment was discharged by frustration. The drummer was incapable of performing his contract in the way intended.

11.2.3   Non-occurrence of an event

If the parties reach an agreement which is dependent on a particular event taking place, then the cancellation of that event may well lead to the contract being frustrated. This situation arose in relation to a number of contracts surrounding the coronation of Edward VII, which was postponed owing to the King's illness.

In *Krell v Henry* (1903) the defendant had made a contract for the use of certain rooms owned by the plaintiff for the purpose of watching the coronation procession. It was held that the postponement of the procession frustrated the contract. Although literal performance was possible, in that the room could have been made available to the defendant at the appropriate time, and the defendant could have sat in it and looked out of the window, in the absence of the procession it had no point, and the whole purpose of the contract had vanished.

By contrast in another 'coronation case' *Herne Bay Steamboat Co v Hutton* (1903), the contract was not frustrated. Here the contract was that the plaintiff's boat should be 'at the disposal of' the defendant on the 25 June to take passengers from Herne Bay for the purpose of watching the naval review, which the King was to conduct, and for a day's cruise round the fleet. The King's illness led to the review being cancelled. In this case, however, the Court of Appeal held that the contract was not frustrated. The distinction from *Krell v Henry* must be that the contract was still regarded as having some purpose. The fleet was still in place (as Stirling LJ pointed out), and so the tour of it could go ahead, even if the review by the King had been cancelled. The effect on the contract was not sufficiently fundamental to lead to it being regarded as frustrated.

If a contract is made, and there is then a declaration of war, which turns one of the parties into an enemy alien, then the contract will be frustrated. Similarly, the requisitioning of property for use by the government can have a similar effect: *Metropolitan Water Board v Dick Kerr* (1918). In this case a contract for the construction of a reservoir was frustrated by an order by the Minister of Munitions, during the First World War, that the defendant should cease work, and disperse and sell the plant.	11.2.4 Government intervention

Here, as is the case in relation to the non-occurrence of an event, it must be clear that the interference radically or fundamentally alters the contract. In *FA Tamplin v Anglo-American Petroleum* (1916), a ship which was subject to a five-year charter was requisitioned for use as a troopship. It was held by the House of Lords that the charter was not frustrated, since judging it at the time of the requisition, the interference was not sufficiently serious. There might have been many months during which the ship would have been available for commercial purposes before the expiry of the contract.

Similarly, the fact that the contract has been rendered more difficult, or more expensive, does not frustrate it. The closure of the Suez Canal in 1956 forced the sellers of goods to ship them via the Cape of Good Hope, extending the time for delivery by about four weeks. The House of Lords in *Tsakiroglou & Co v Noblee and Thorl* (1962) held that this was not frustration. The route for shipment had not been specified in the contract, nor was any precise delivery date agreed. The fact that the re-routing would cost more was regarded as irrelevant.

An unsuccessful attempt was made in *Amalgamated Investment v John Walker* (1976) to base frustration on a different type of government interference, namely the 'listing' of a building as being of architectural and historic interest, and therefore subject to strict planning conditions. Despite the fact that this was estimated as reducing the market value of the building to £200,000 (the contract price was £1,700,000), the Court of Appeal held that the contract was not frustrated. It was not part of the contract that the building should not be listed, and the change in the market value of the property could not in itself amount to frustration. The decision presumably leaves open the possibility that if the non-listing of a building was a crucial element in the contract, then frustration could follow from a listing.

| 11.2.5 | Supervening illegality |

If, after a contract has been made, its purpose becomes illegal, then this will be regarded as a frustrating event. In *Denny, Mott & Dickson v James Fraser* (1944) there was an agreement for the sale of timber over a number of years. It provided that the buyer should let a timber-yard to the seller, and give him an option to purchase it. In 1939 further dealings in timber were made illegal. The House of Lords held that not only the trading contract, but also the option on the timber-yard, was frustrated. The main object of the contract was trading in timber, and once this was frustrated, the whole agreement was radically altered.

| 11.2.6 | Other frustrating events |

Other types of event which have been held to lead to frustration are strikes (*The Nema* (1981) - time charter affected so that only two out of the anticipated six or seven would be able to be made); and the effects of war (*Finelvet AG v Vinava Shipping Co Ltd* (1983) - ship trapped by continuing Gulf War between Iran and Iraq). Note that in the former case it was the extent of the effect of the strike that was important, and in the latter that it was made clear that the outbreak of war did not necessarily frustrate a contract on which it had a bearing. This again emphasises the point that, whatever the frustrating event (and the categories are never likely to be closed), it is the *effect* of that event on the contract, and what the parties have agreed, that is the most important consideration, and not the nature of the event itself. Only if it vitally and fundamentally changes the conditions of the contract, and makes performance radically different from what the parties had agreed, will frustration take place.

The general limitations on the availability of a plea of frustration, in terms of the seriousness of the event, and its effect on what the parties have agreed, have been discussed above. In this section, three more specific limitations are noted.

If it is the behaviour of one of the parties which, while not amounting to a breach of contract, has brought about the circumstances which are alleged to frustrate the contract, this will be regarded as 'self-induced frustration', and will not discharge the contract. This is an obvious restriction, but it may not always be easy to determine what type of behaviour should fall within its scope. An example of the application of this restriction is *Maritime National Fish v Ocean Trawlers* (1935). The appellants chartered a trawler from the respondents. The trawler was fitted with an 'otter' trawl, which it was illegal to use without a licence, as both parties were aware. The appellants applied for five licences to operate otter trawls, but were only granted three. They decided to use these for boats other than the one chartered from the respondents. They claimed that this contract was therefore frustrated, since the trawler could not legally be used. The Privy Council held that the appellants were not discharged. It was their own election to use the licences with the other boats which had led to the illegality of using the appellants' trawler.

This decision seems fair where it is the case, as it was here, that the party exercising the choice could have done so without breaking any contract (since the trawlers to which the licences were assigned all belonged to the appellants). It may not be so fair, however, as Treitel has pointed out, if a person is put in a position where there is no choice but to break one of two contracts. Nevertheless, when this situation arose in *The Super Servant Two* (1990), the Court of Appeal applied the concept of self-induced frustration strictly. The parties had made a contract for the transportation of a drilling rig, which, as they both knew, could only be carried out by one of two vessels owned by the defendants, namely *Super Servant One* and *Super Servant Two*. The defendants, intending to use *Super Servant Two*, allocated *Super Servant One* to other contracts. *Super Servant Two* then sank. The defendants claimed that the contract was frustrated, but the plaintiffs alleged that the impossibility of performance arose from the defendants' own acts, and that they should not therefore be discharged from performance. The Court of Appeal agreed that, even though

11.3 Limitations on the doctrine

11.3.1 Self-induced frustration

the defendants were neither negligent, nor in breach of contract, in the way in which they had allocated the vessels, they were still liable under the contract with the plaintiffs.

It seems then that any exercise of choice by one of the parties, which contributes to a situation where the contract becomes impossible, or radically different, will prevent the doctrine of frustration from applying.

| 11.3.2 | Events foreseen and provided for |

One way in which the parties can avoid the situation discussed in the previous section, and its perceived unfairness, is by including specific provision in the contract to deal with that situation. Indeed, in *Super Servant Two* (1990) it was held that the defendants could take advantage of a specific force majeure clause, even though the contract was not frustrated as far as the common law was concerned. A *force majeure* clause is one which the parties have inserted to cover various eventualities outside their control, which may effect the contract. It will provide the way in which losses are to be distributed in such circumstances. The existence of such a clause, covering the facts that have arisen, will generally prevent the contract from being frustrated. It will not inevitably do so, however, as is shown by *Jackson v Union Marine Insurance Co Ltd* (1874). A ship was chartered in November 1871, to proceed with all possible dispatch, 'damages and accidents of navigation excepted' from Liverpool to Newport and there to load a cargo for carriage to San Francisco. She sailed on 2 January, but before reaching Newport, ran aground off the Welsh coast. On 15 February the charterers abandoned the charter and found another ship. On 18 February the ship got off, but repairs were not finished until August. The shipowner brought an action against the charterers for failure to load. It was held by the Exchequer Chamber that the exception in the contract absolved the shipowner from liability in the event of delay, but did not give him the right to sue if the delay was bad enough to frustrate the contract. This was the situation here, and so the shipowner's action failed.

A similar conclusion was reached in *Metropolitan Water Board v Dick Kerr* (1918) (above, para 11.2.4) where the contract contained a provision for extension of the time for performance in the event of delays 'howsoever caused'. It was held by the House of Lords that this provision was only meant to deal with temporary delays, and did not:

'... cover the case in which the interruption is of such a character and duration that it vitally and fundamentally changes the conditions of the contract, and could not possibly have been in the contemplation of the parties to the contract when it was made.'

A contract for the sale of land can apparently be frustrated. This must have been assumed to be the case *Amalgamated Investment v John Walker* (above, para 11.2.4), since otherwise there would have been no need to consider whether the listing of a building could have such an effect. In practice the purchaser of land will virtually always insure it from the point of exchange of contracts, and so the issue of frustration will be unlikely to arise.

11.3.3   Land

In relation to leases, at one time it seemed as though frustration was not possible. Although it is clear that the doctrine of frustration can apply to contracts to use property on the basis of a licence, as in *Taylor v Caldwell* and *Krell v Henry* (above paras 11.1.2 and 11.2.3), this was not necessarily the case with a lease, which involves the tenant taking an interest in the land itself. The issue was raised in *Cricklewood Property Investment Trust v Leighton's Investment Trusts Ltd* (1945). This concerned a building lease, which was expressed to last for 99 years, from May 1936. Following the outbreak of the Second World War, in 1939, legislation was passed prohibiting building. The tenant claimed that the lease was frustrated. Two members of the House of Lords expressed the view that a lease could never be frustrated, while two others thought that it could if, for example, the land was washed into the sea, or became subject to a permanent ban on building. The fifth member of the panel refused to express a view on this issue, but agreed with the decision that on the facts there was in any case no frustration, because there were still 90 years left on the lease once the wartime restrictions were lifted.

The matter did not arise for decision again until 1981, and the case of *National Carriers Ltd v Panalpina (Northern) Ltd* (1981). This contract concerned a 10 year lease of a warehouse. After five years the local authority closed the street, preventing access, because of problems with another (listed) building in the street. The closure was likely to last for about 18 months. There would, therefore, have been some three years of the lease to run after the street re-opened. The tenants, however, stopped paying rent, on the basis that the contract had been frustrated. The House of Lords took the view (Lord Russell dissenting) that there was no reason in logic or law why a lease should not be frustrated in a situation where no substantial use of a kind permitted by the lease and contemplated by the parties, remained possible for the lessee. Thus even where the land itself remained available, rather than slipping into the sea, or being covered by sand, the lease could be frustrated, if its purpose had been frustrated. On the facts of the case, however, the interruption to the availability of the premises was not sufficient to amount to frustration, and the landlords' action for the rent therefore succeeded.

11.4	**Effects of the doctrine: common law**	The effects of a frustrating event are dealt with both by common law rules, and the provisions of the Law Reform (Frustrated Contracts) Act 1943. This section deals with the common law, and the next one (para 11.5) with the Act.

11.4.1   Automatic termination

The first point to note is that the common law regards the frustrating event as automatically bringing the contract to an end. It is not a situation such as that which arises in relation to mistake, misrepresentation, or breach of contract, where one party can decide, notwithstanding what has happened, that the contract should continue. The application of this rule can be seen in *Hirji Mulji v Cheong Yeong Steamship* (1926). By a charterparty entered into in November 1916, shipowners agreed that their ship, the *Singaporean*, should be placed at the charterers' disposal on 17 March 1917, for 10 months. Shortly before this date the ship was requisitioned by the government. The shipowners thought the ship would soon be released, and asked the charterers if they would still be willing to take up the charter when this happened. The charterers said that they would. In fact the ship was not released until February 1919, at which point the charterers refused to accept it. The shipowners argued that the charterers had affirmed the contract after the frustrating event, and were therefore still bound. The House of Lords held that affirmation was not possible. The frustrating event automatically brought the contract to an end, and discharged both the shipowners and the charterers from their obligations.

11.4.2   Future obligations only discharged

It is important to note that frustration, unlike an operative common law mistake, does not render a contract void *ab initio*. Its effect is to bring the contract to an end prematurely, but all existing obligations at the time of the contract remain unaffected, as far as the common law is concerned. If money has been paid, or property transferred, then it cannot generally be recovered, and if valuable services have been provided, compensation cannot be claimed.

Thus in *Krell v Henry* (1903) (above, para 11.2.3) the hirer of the room had paid a deposit, which was irrecoverable. On the other hand, the obligation to pay the balance did not, under the terms of the contract, arise until after the date on which the coronation procession was cancelled. This, therefore, was also irrecoverable. By contrast, in *Chandler v Webster* (1904) another case on the hiring of a room to view the coronation, under the terms of the contract the obligation to pay arose before the frustrating event occurred. In this case it was held that not only could money paid not be recovered, but the obligation to pay money due before the event was cancelled remained.

Because frustration only discharged the contract from the point when the event occurred, the court refused to regard this as a case where there was a total failure of consideration, which might have justified recovery in quasi-contract (for which see Chapter 14).

This aspect of *Chandler v Webster* was, however, overruled by the House of Lords in *Fibrosa Spolka Akcyjna v Fairbairn Lawson Combe Barbour Ltd* (1942), where it was held that a frustrated contract could in some situations lead to a claim for recovery of money paid, on the basis of a total failure of consideration. An English company (the respondents) had made a contract to supply machinery to a Polish company (the appellants). The appellants had paid £1,000 towards this contract. It was then frustrated by the German invasion of Poland in 1939. The appellants sought to recover the £1,000. The House of Lords held that, since they had received nothing at all under the contract, there had been a total failure of consideration, and recovery was therefore possible.

11.4.3   Total failure of consideration

This decision is probably an improvement on *Chandler v Webster*, but it still leaves two areas of difficulty, and potential injustice. First, it can only apply where the failure of consideration is total. If the other party has provided something, no matter how little, no recovery will be possible. Secondly, it takes no account of the fact that the party who has received the money may well have incurred expenses in relation to the contract, and so will end up out of pocket if the entire sum has to be refunded. Both of these difficulties are addressed by the Law Reform (Frustrated Contracts) Act 1943 (below, para 11.5).

This Act also attempts to tackle another limitation of the common law, which is exemplified by *Appleby v Myers* (1867). In this case the contract was for the erection of machinery on the defendant's premises. Payment was to be made on completion of the work. When the work was nearly finished, the whole premises, including the machinery, were destroyed by fire. The contract was undoubtedly frustrated, but the question was whether the plaintiffs could recover any compensation for the work that they had done. The answer was no. The obligation to pay had not arisen at the time the contract was frustrated, and therefore the plaintiffs were entitled to nothing.

The injustices caused by the application of these common law rules led to the reform contained in the Law Reform (Frustrated Contracts) Act 1943.

| 11.5 | **Effects of frustration: the 1943 Act** |

Before considering the provisions of s 1(2) and s 1(3), which contain the most significant provisions of the Act, it must be noted that not all contracts are within its scope. Section 2(5) indicates that the Act does not apply to, for example, charterparties, contracts of insurance, or contracts for the sale of specific goods. Note that some, but not all, contracts in the latter category are governed by s 7 of the Sale of Goods Act 1979, which provides that:

> '... where there is an agreement to sell specific goods, and subsequently the goods, without any fault on the part of the seller or buyer, perish before the risk passes to the buyer, the agreement is thereby avoided.'

An 'agreement to sell' is a contract under which ownership (described as 'property') has not yet passed to the buyer. This concept, and the rules relating to passing of 'risk', are discussed further in Chapter 16 (para 16.2).

In relation to these contracts, the common law rules on the effects of frustration will apply.

Section 2(3) also makes it clear that the parties may reach their own agreement as to what the effects of frustration are going to be. In this situation, again, the Act will have no application.

| 11.5.1 | **Section 1(2): Money paid or payable prior to frustration** |

Section 1(2) of the Act deals with the *Chandler v Webster*, or *Fibrosa*, type of situation, that is where money has been paid, or is owed under the contract, before the frustrating event takes place. The section provides that in such a situation, money paid is recoverable, and money owed ceases to be payable. To that extent the section adopts and extends the *Fibrosa* decision, in that the rule now applies even where there is not a total failure of consideration. Subject to the provisions of s 1(3) (below, para 11.6.2) concerning the conferring of valuable benefits, there can be recovery of sums paid even where there has been partial performance by the other side.

There is, however, a proviso to s 1(2) which is designed to limit the injustice in the *Fibrosa* decision noted above (para 11.6.1), that is, that, even where there is a total failure of consideration, the other party may have incurred expenses in getting ready to perform. The section accordingly provides that if the party to whom sums were paid or payable:

> '... incurred expenses before the time of discharge in, or for the purposes of, the performance of the contract, the court may, if it considers it just to do so having regard to all the circumstances of the case, allow him to retain or, as the case may be, recover the whole of the sums paid or payable, not being an amount in excess of the expenses so incurred.'

It is important to note two limitations on this attempt to spread the losses of frustration between the parties. First, the recovery of expenses can only take place where there was an obligation to pay some money prior to the frustrating event. If the contract provided for the entire payment to become due only on completion of the contract, then there will be no scope for the recovery of expenses under s 1(2). Secondly, even if some money was paid or payable, it is possible that the expenses will exceed this amount, and so will not be fully recoverable. For example, if on a contract worth £5,000 a deposit of £500 has been paid, but the other party has incurred expenses of £750, the maximum that can be recovered is £500. The remaining £250 is irrecoverable, unless s 1(3) (below, para 11.6.2) can be brought into play.

Finally, even if expenses have been occurred which could be compensated by money paid or payable, this cannot be claimed as of right. It is entirely at the court's discretion to decide whether or not there should be any recovery of expenses, depending on its view as to whether this would be just in all the circumstances.

Section 1(3) of the 1943 Act provides that where a party to a contract has obtained a 'valuable benefit' (other than money) before the time of discharge, the other party can obtain compensation for having provided this. Suppose, then, that A has contracted to hire B's hall for a series of 10 concerts, with the fee to be payable at the end of the contract. If after one concert, the hall is destroyed by fire, B would be entitled to seek compensation from A in relation to the use of the hall for that concert. As with section 1(2), recovery is not available as of right, but is in the discretion of the court, which can award what it considers just in all the circumstances, up to the value of the benefit to the party obtaining it. In particular the court is directed to take into account any expenses incurred by the party obtaining the benefit, and the effect, in relation to the benefit, of the circumstances which frustrated the contract.

11.5.2   Section 1(3): compensation for a 'valuable benefit'

This provision would seem at first sight to provide a more satisfactory outcome to the case of *Appleby v Myers* (1867) (above, para 11.4.3), in that it might allow the supplier of the machinery to recover compensation for the work that had been done. This depends, however, on whether the 'valuable benefit' has to be judged before or after the frustrating event has occurred. If it is the former, then some compensation may be possible; if it is the latter, then the other party may well argue that no benefit has in the end been received, since the machinery was not completed, and was in any case destroyed by the fire.

These issues were considered in some detail by Goff J, as he then was, in the only reported case on the 1943 Act, *BP Exploration v Hunt* (1982). The case concerned oil concessions which had been frustrated by expropriation by the Libyan government. Goff J started by stating that the underlying principle of the Act was not the apportionment of losses, but the prevention of the 'unjust enrichment' of one party to a frustrated contract at the expense of the other. Applying this approach to s 1(3) he came to the conclusion that 'benefit' means the 'end product' of what the plaintiff has provided, not the value of the work that has been done. Thus, he concluded:

> '... where a contract is frustrated by a fire which destroys a building on which work has been done, the award will be nil.'

In other words, he adopted the second of the approaches outlined in the previous paragraph as regards the assessment of the benefit. This is not accepted as the correct analysis by all commentators. Treitel, for example, argues that although the Act makes reference to the relevance of the effect of the frustrating circumstances, this should be interpreted as applying to the assessment of the 'just sum' to be awarded, rather than the valuation of the benefit itself (*Law of Contract*, 8th ed, p 813). Goff J's judgment, however, was approved by the Court of Appeal and the House of Lords, and must be taken to represent the current law on this issue. As a result, it is clear that in a case such as *Appleby v Myers* (1867), the answer given by the Act is the same as that under the common law, and that no compensation will be recoverable for the work that has been done, because, once the frustrating event has occurred, it is of no value to the other party.

Frustration

A frustrating event is one which, without any fault on either party, prevents performance of the contract. It was originally not thought to discharge obligations (*Paradine v Jane* (1647)), but since *Taylor v Caldwell* (1863) it has been accepted that this is its effect.

Nature of the doctrine

Anything which renders performance impossible, or at least 'radically different' (*Davis Contractors Ltd v Fareham UDC* (1956)), can be a frustrating event. Thus it includes destruction of the subject-matter (*Taylor v Caldwell* (1863)); personal incapacity (*Condor v Barron Knights* (1966)); non-occurrence of an event (*Krell v Henry* (1903)); government intervention (*Metropolitan Water Board v Dick Kerr* (1918)); supervening illegality (*Denny Mott & Dickson v James Fraser* (1944)); industrial action (*The Nema* (1981)) or the effects of war (*Finelvet AG v Vinava Shipping Co Ltd* (1983)).

Frustrating events

The contract must not still have some surviving purpose: *Herne Bay Steam Boat Co v Hutton* (1903). Nor is it enough that the contract is made more difficult or more expensive to perform: *Tsakiroglou & Co v Noblee and Thorl* (1962).

Limitations on the doctrine

- Self-induced frustration

    If the impossiblity results from a choice exercised by one party, then the contract will not be frustrated: *Maritime National Fish v Ocean Trawlers* (1935). This is so even if the party had in the end no choice but fail to perform one contract or another: *The Super Servant Two* (1990).

- Events foreseen and provided for

    Parties may include a clause dealing with the consequences of frustration. The courts will generally give effect to this, provided that the clause was truly intended to cover the circumstances which have occurred: *Jackson v Union Marine Insurance Co Ltd* (1874).

It seems that contracts for the sale of land can be frustrated (*Amalgamated Investment v John Walker* (1976)). It is also possible, though unlikely, for a lease to be frustrated: *National Carriers Ltd v Panalpina (Northern) Ltd* (1981).

Land

Effect of frustration: common law

The contract is automatically terminated: *Hirji Mulij v Cheong Yeong Steamship* (1926). Only future obligations are discharged, those which arose prior to the event still survive: *Chandler v Webster* (1904). Recovery of money paid will be allowed, however, if there has been a total failure of consideration: *Fibrosa Spolka Akcyjna v Fairbairn Lawson Combe Barbour Ltd* (1942). There can be no recovery, however, for work done before the frustrating event but for which payment was not yet due: *Appleby v Myers* (1867).

Effects of frustration: Law Reform (Frustrated Contracts) Act 1943

Note that the Act does not apply to all contracts, eg charterparties, insurance, or the sale of specific goods. Nor does it apply where the parties have included their own provision for the consequences of frustration.

- Section 1(2): money paid or payable prior to frustration

  This will be recoverable, cease to be payable, subject to a deduction for expenses incurred by the other party. This is subject to the courts' view as to what is just in all the circumstances.

- Section 1(3): compensation for a valuable benefit

  If a party has obtained a valuable benefit, the other party can obtain compensation, to the extent that the court considers just in all the circumstances. The benefit must survive the frustrating event, however, otherwise there can be no recovery: *BP Exploration v Hunt* (1982).

Chapter 12

Performance and Breach

This chapter is concerned with ways in which a contract may be discharged, so that the parties no longer have any obligations under it. We have already discussed one way in which this can happen in the previous chapter, under the doctrine of frustration. Contracts may also be discharged by express agreement. If both parties decide that neither of them wishes to carry on with a contract which contains continuing obligations, or in relation to which some parts are still executory, they may agree to bring it to an end early. The only problems which arise here are where the executory obligations are all on one side, so that the party who has completed performance receives no consideration for promising not to enforce the other party's obligations. This issue has already been dealt with in Chapter 3, in connection with the doctrine of consideration, and in particular the concept of promissory estoppel (above, para 3.8), and so is not discussed further here. The focus in this chapter is on discharge by performance, or by breach: discharge in this context meaning that all further obligations of either or both of the parties are at an end.

Once the parties have done all that they are bound to do under a contract, all 'primary' obligations will cease. (There may, of course, be some continuing 'seondary' obligations, such as the obligation to pay compensation if goods turn out to be defective at some point after sale and delivery). The problem that concerns us here is what constitutes satisfactory performance. If there is some minor defect, does this negative discharge by performance?

The general rule is that performance must be precise and exact, and the courts have at times applied this very strictly. Consider, for example, two cases under the Sale of Goods Act. In *Re Moore and Landauer* (1921) the defendants agreed to buy from the plaintiffs 3,000 tins of canned fruit. The fruit was to be packed in cases of 30 tins. When the goods were delivered a substantial part of the consignment was packed in cases of 24 tins. It was held that this did not constitute satisfactory performance, and the defendants were entitled to reject the whole consignment. Similarly, in *Arcos Ltd v Ronaasen* (1933) the buyer had ordered timber staves for the

12.1   Introduction

12.2   Discharge by performance

12.2.1   Performance must be precise and exact

purpose of making barrels. The contract description said that they should be 1/2" thick. Most of the consignment consisted of staves which were in fact 9/16" thick. They were still perfectly usable for making barrels. Nevertheless, it was held that this did not constitute satisfactory performance, and the buyer was entitled to reject all the staves. In other words, in both these cases the seller had not performed satisfactorily, and so had not discharged his obligations under the contract.

Both of these cases turned in part on the interpretation of s 13 of the Sale of Goods Act, which implies an obligation to supply goods which match their contract description. In recent years the courts have been a little more flexible in the application of this section (see below, para 16.5.2), but the principle that each party is entitled to expect the other to perform to the letter of their agreement remains.

| 12.2.2 | Partial provision of services |

In the sale of goods cases, a failure to meet the terms of the contract prevented the seller from claiming any compensation, even in relation to the supply of goods which did match the contract description. The same approach is applied to the provision of services. Here a person may have done a certain amount of work towards a contract, and the question is whether there is any right to claim payment under the contract for what has been done, if it does not amount to complete performance. The starting point for the consideration of this issue is *Cutter v Powell* (1795). The defendant agreed to pay Cutter 30 guineas provided that he served as second mate on a voyage from Jamaica to Liverpool. The voyage began on 2 August. Cutter died on 20 September, when the ship was 19 days short of Liverpool. Cutter's widow brought an action to recover a proportion of the 30 guineas. This failed. The contract was interpreted as being an 'entire' contract for a lump sum, and nothing was payable until it was completed. Thus, even though the defendant had had the benefit of Cutter's labour for a substantial part of the voyage, no compensation for this was recoverable. One reason for this rather harsh decision seems to have been that the 30 guineas was about four times the normal wage for such a voyage. The court therefore looked on it as something of a gamble. Cutter had agreed to take the chance of a larger lump sum at the end of the voyage, rather than to take wages paid on a weekly basis. This element of the decision was not picked up in later cases, however, and *Cutter v Powell* was taken to lay down a general rule that in 'entire' contracts (ie where various obligations are to be performed in return for a lump sum) nothing is payable until the contract has been fully completed.

One way to mitigate this rule, which has the potential to operate very harshly, is to find that the contract is not entire, but divisible into sections, with the completion of each section giving rise to a right to some payment. Thus, if Cutter had been engaged at a certain rate per week, instead of for a lump sum for the whole voyage, his widow would probably have been able to recover for the time he had actually served.

This will also apply if there are concurrent but independent obligations. In *Bolton v Mahadeva* (1972), there was a contract to (a) install a central heating system, and (b) supply a bathroom suite. The central heating system turned out to be defective, and there was no obligation to pay for this, but the supply of the bathroom suite was severable, and an appropriate proportion of the contract price was recoverable in relation to this obligation.

If a promisee prevents the promisor from completing the obligations under an entire contract, the promisor will be able to recover on a *quantum meruit* basis for the work already done, and may in addition be able to obtain damages for breach of contract: *Planché v Colburn* (1831).

If the promisee accepts partial performance, this may be sufficient in certain circumstances to discharge the promisor's further obligations under the contract, and moreover allow the promisor to sue on a *quantum meruit* for the work already done. For example, suppose that goods are to be transported from London to Hull, and the van breaks down en route. If the recipient of the goods agrees to take delivery at Doncaster, the carrier will be able to sue for a proportion of the carriage. In *Christy v Row* (1808) this rule was said to be based on a fresh agreement involving an implied promise to pay for the benefit received.

This exception will not apply, however, if the party effectively has no option but to accept the performance. In *Sumpter v Hedges* (1898) the plaintiff, a builder, contracted to build 2 houses and stables on the defendant's land, for £565. The plaintiff did work to the value of £333, and then abandoned the contract, because he had no money. The defendant finished the buildings himself, using building materials left by the plaintiff. The plaintiff brought an action to the recover for the value of the work he had done on the buildings. Although it might appear that the defendant had accepted the performance, the Court of Appeal held that the plaintiff could not recover. As Collins LJ pointed out, although in some circumstances an agreement to pay might be inferred from the acceptance of a benefit, nevertheless:

12.2.3   Divisible contracts or obligations

12.2.4   Non-performance due to promisee

12.2.5   Acceptance of partial performance

'... in order that that may be done, the circumstances must be such as to give an option to the defendant to take or not take the benefit of the work done.'

It would not be reasonable to expect the defendant to keep on his land a building which was in an incomplete state, and would constitute a nuisance.

| 12.2.6 | Substantial performance |

This has the possibility of constituting a more general exception. The principle of 'substantial performance' is based on the idea that where there is only a minor variation from the terms of the contract, the other party cannot claim to be discharged, but must rely on an action for damages for breach. The origins of it can be traced to *Boone v Eyre* (1779), but it was stated most clearly in *Dakin v Lee* (1916), and *Hoenig v Isaacs* (1952).

In *Dakin v Lee* the contract was for the repair of a house. The work was not done in accordance with the contract. In particular, the concrete underpinning was only half the contract depth; the columns to support a bay window were of 4" diameter solid iron, instead of 5" diameter hollow; and the joists over the bay window were not cleated at the angles or bolted to caps and to each other. The official referee found that the plaintiffs had not performed the contract, and therefore could not claim for any payment in respect of it. The Court of Appeal noted that there was a distinction between failing to complete (as in *Sumpter v Hedges* (1898), above para 12.2.5), and completing badly. Here the contract had been performed, though badly performed, and the plaintiff could recover for the work done, less deductions for the fact that it did not conform to the contract requirements.

Similarly, in *Hoenig v Isaacs* (1952) there were found to be defects (which would cost £55 to repair) in work done in redecorating a flat. The total contract price was £750. It was held that there was substantial performance, and that the plaintiff could recover the contract price, less the cost of repairs.

The Court of Appeal refused to apply this, however, in *Bolton v Mahadeva* (1972), as regards the obligation to install a central heating system. The system as fitted gave out much less heat than it should have done, and caused fumes in one of the rooms. Although the complete system had been fitted, it did not fulfil its primary function of heating the house, and so the installer was not allowed to recover.

The doctrine of substantial performance has been little used in subsequent cases, and it may be that it has no great practical significance. Indeed, Treitel, *Law of Contract*, 8th ed, p 688, regards it as resulting from using the terminology of entire contracts, rather than entire obligations, and therefore doubts whether it exists at all.

Being ready to perform a contract ('tender of performance') is generally treated as equivalent to performance, in the sense that if it is rejected, then it will lead to a discharge of the tenderer's liabilities. Thus, as s 27 of the Sale of Goods Act 1979 puts it, where the expectation is that goods will be paid for on delivery:

> '... the seller must be ready and willing to give possession of the goods to the buyer in exchange for the price and the buyer must be ready and willing to pay the price in exchange for the possession of the goods.'

12.3   Tender of performance

What amounts to satisfactory 'tender', so as to bring the above principle into play? This will largely depend on the terms of the contract, but something of the approach of the courts can be seen from *Startup v Macdonald* (1843). The plaintiff agreed to sell 10 tons of oil to the defendant. Delivery was to be 'within the last fourteen days of March'. Delivery was in fact tendered at 8.30 pm on the 31 March, which was a Saturday. The defendant refused to accept or pay for the goods. It was held that provided that the seller had actually found the other party, and that there was time to examine the goods to check compliance with the contract, this was a satisfactory tender.

From this it will be seen that the requirements are that the tender should meet the strict terms of the contract, and that it should be brought to the attention of the other party in time for any rights which might arise on tender to be exercised.

12.3.1   Definition of tender

If a debtor tenders payment, and this is not accepted, this does not cancel the obligation to pay. The debtor, however, is not obliged to attempt to pay again, but can wait until the creditor calls for payment.

The exact amount must be tendered. There is no legal obligation to give change, though of course in the majority of situations the creditor will be quite happy to do so.

There are particular statutory rules as to the maximum amounts of particular types of coin which will constitute 'legal tender': Coinage Act 1971.

12.3.2   Tender of money

Is the time for performance important? Is time, as the courts put it, 'of the essence'? The common law said that it was, unless the parties had expressed a contrary intention. Equity took the opposite view, so that time was not of the essence unless the parties had specifically made it so. The equitable rule was given precedence in s 41 of the Law of Property Act 1925, so that where under equity time is not of the essence, contractual provisions dealing with time should be interpreted in the same way at common law. Note also that s 10(1) of the Sale of Goods Act 1979 states that:

12.3.3   Time

'Unless a different intention appears from the terms of the contract, stipulations as to time of payment are not of the essence of a contract of sale.'

The reference to the intention of the parties which appears in this section is of general application, as was confirmed by the House of Lords in *United Scientific Holdings Ltd v Burnley Borough Council* (1978). Refusing to be bound by the position as regards the common law and equitable rules prior to 1873, the House preferred to look at the nature of the contract itself. The dispute concerned the operation of a rent review close within a 99 year lease. The House held that time was not of the essence as far as the activation of the review machinery was concerned, so that the landlord was able to put it in motion even though he had just missed the ten-year deadline specified in the lease itself.

Where time is not initially of the essence, it seems that it may become so by one party giving notice. This is what happened in *Rickards v Oppenheim* (1950), the facts of which are given in Chapter 3 (para 3.7.2). This possibility appears to arise as soon as the contractual date for performance has passed: *Behzadi v Shaftesbury Hotels Ltd* (1991) (but *cf British and Commonwealth Holdings plc v Quadrex Holdings Inc* (1989) which seemed to suggest that there must be an unreasonable delay before the right to give notice making time of the essence arises. Since both these cases are Court of Appeal decisions, the latter one, ie *Behzadi v Shaftesbury*, must be taken to prevail, pending a ruling by the House of Lords).

12.4   Discharge by breach

A breach of contract will have a range of consequences. It may entitle the innocent party to seek an order for performance of the contract, to claim damages, or to repudiate the contract. It is the last of these consequences that we are concerned with in this chapter (the other two are discussed in Chapter 13), since repudiation of the contract will also entail the discharge of future obligations.

12.4.1   Effect of repudiatory breach

There have at various times been suggestions that a breach of contract, if sufficiently serious, might bring a contract to an end automatically, irrespective of the wishes of the parties. See, for example, Lord Denning's judgment in *Harbutt's Plasticine v Wayne Tank and Pump* (1970), or, in the employment law context, *Hill v CA Parsons* (1972), and *Sanders v Neale* (1974). The current view, however, is that a breach only ever has the effect of allowing the innocent party the choice of whether to terminate the agreement, or allow it to continue. This was confirmed in the employment area by the Court of Appeal in *Gunton v London Borough of Richmond upon Thames*

(1980). In all cases, therefore, the innocent party will have the possibility of electing to either treat the contract as repudiated, or to affirm it (and possibly claim damages).

Repudiation is not the same thing as 'rescission', though the courts do not always distinguish between them, and in certain circumstances the effects are the same. In a simple sale of goods transaction, for example, if there is a repudiatory breach in relation to the quality of the goods, the effect will be that the buyer will return the goods, and can reclaim the price. This is exactly the same as if there had been rescission for misrepresentation. There are differences, however. First, there will always be a right to claim damages for a repudiatory breach, whereas rescission (for example in relation to a totally innocent misrepresentation) may be a remedy in itself. Secondly, although in a simple transaction the effects may be the same, in a complex, or continuing contract, whereas rescission requires the whole transaction to be undone, repudiation may leave certain obligations which have arisen prior to the breach in tact: *Johnson v Agnew* (1980).

What types of breach of contract will give rise to the right to treat the agreement as repudiated? There are a number of ways of approaching this issue. It could be said that this is a matter for the parties to determine, and that they should agree in their contract whether a particular type of breach is to be repudiatory or not. Secondly, it could be argued that the issue can only be determined when the consequences of an actual breach are known. Thirdly, it might be thought best to have specific legal rules which state that particular contractual obligations fall into one category or the other. English law, as we shall see, uses a mixture of all three approaches. It will be convenient, however, to start with the third, and look at a situation where a statute determines the consequences of particular breaches.

12.4.2   Nature of repudiatory breach

The implied terms under the Sale of Goods Act 1979 are labelled as being either 'conditions' or 'warranties'. The consequences of this are spelt out in s 11(3), which indicates that a 'condition' is a stipulation the breach of which may give rise to a right to treat the contract as repudiated, whereas a breach of 'warranty' may give rise to a claim for damages, but not to a right to reject the goods.

12.4.3   Sale of Goods Act 1979: implied conditions and warranties

The Sale of Goods Act thus uses the terminology of condition and warranty to distinguish between repudiatory and other breaches. Only if the term broken is a condition will the breach be repudiatory. The question then arises as to which terms are conditions and which are warranties? As far as the implied terms under the Sale of Goods Act 1979 are concerned, the Act itself provides the answer, by labelling them as one or the other. In relation to other provisions in a Sale of Goods contract, however, the question is, as s 11(3) makes clear, one of the 'construction of the contract'. This is the position in relation to most other contracts, as well, and so we need to consider this next.

Before doing so, however, it is important to note that both 'condition' and 'warranty' are at times used in other senses than the ones under consideration here. 'Condition' is used for example in relation to a 'condition precedent' or 'condition subsequent', or generally to mean the provisions of a contract, as in 'terms and conditions'. 'Warranty' on the other hand can mean simply a 'promise' or a 'guarantee'. Care is needed, therefore, in looking at discussions of contractual terms, particularly by judges, in order to be sure that the meaning which is being attached to a particular word is clear.

12.4.4	**Categorisation of terms: the courts' approach**

Where a term is not labelled by statute, the courts themselves have to decide whether it is a condition, breach of which will be repudiatory, or a warranty, breach of which will only give rise to a right to damages. The main factor will be the importance of the term in the context of the contract. Is it of major significance in relation to the purpose of the contract, or is its role only minor?

The approach of the courts can be seen in the contrasting cases of *Bettini v Gye* (1876) and *Poussard v Spiers* (1876). Both cases concerned singers. In *Poussard v Spiers* (1876) the singer was contracted to play a part in an operetta. She was unable, as a result of illness, to be present at the start of the run, and arrived a week late. By this time a substitute had been employed, and her failure to appear was treated as a repudiatory breach. In *Bettini v Gye* (1876) the singer was required to be present for rehearsals six days before the start of the performance. Again as a result of illness he was delayed, and arrived three days late. On this occasion the court treated the failure to appear for the rehearsals as a breach which was not repudiatory. As Blackburn J said, the classification of terms 'depends on the true construction of the contract as a whole'. In *Poussard v Spiers* the failure to meet the obligation to be present for a performance was treated as much more serious than Bettini's failure to meet the obligation to be present for a rehearsal. The former breach had a much more significant impact on the main purpose of the contract than the latter.

In some cases the courts will not look so much to the interpretation of the individual contract, but to the expectations of parties who regularly include clauses of a particular type in their agreements. In *Bunge Corporation v*

Tradax Export SA (1981), it was stated that time clauses in mercantile contracts should usually be treated as conditions.

One way in which the courts may be able to determine the parties' intentions as regards the effect of breaking particular terms, is where these have been labelled. If they have gone through the contract and referred to certain terms as conditions, and the rest as warranties, then it may be presumed that this was intended to have the same significance as the labels used in the Sale of Goods Act 1979. The use of labels will not be conclusive, however, as is shown by *Schuler AG v Wickman Tools Sales Ltd* (1973). The defendants were under an obligation to make weekly visits to six named firms, over a period of four and a half years, in connection with a contract under which they were given the sole selling rights of the plaintiffs' panel presses. This obligation was referred to as a 'condition', and none of the other 19 clauses in the contract was described in this way. This would seem to suggest that the parties intended that any breach of it would be repudiatory. The majority of the House of Lords refused to interpret it in this way, however. Noting that the contract required in total some 1,400 visits to be made, and that it was likely that in a few cases a visit would be impossible, Lord Reid pointed out that:

12.4.5 Categorisation of terms: labelling by the parties

> '[I]f Schuler's contention is right failure to make even one visit entitles them to terminate the contract, however blameless Wickman might be. This is so unreasonable that it must make me search for some other possible meaning of the contract.'

This the House found by treating a breach of the visits clause as being a 'material breach' sufficient to bring into play other termination procedures under another clause.

The decision in *Schuler v Wickman* does not mean that the parties' own labelling of terms is to be ignored, simply that it is not conclusive of the issue. In subsequent cases the courts have shown themselves to be willing to give effect to clearly stated provisions as to the consequences of a breach. In *Awilco A/S v Fulvia spA di Navigazione, The Chikuma* (1981), for example, in discussing a clause giving a right to withdraw a ship for late payment of hire, Lord Bridge said that where parties bargaining at arm's length use 'common form' clauses, it is very important that their meaning and legal effect should be certain:

> 'The ideal at which the courts should aim, in construing such clauses, is to produce a result such that in any given situation both parties seeking legal advice as to their rights and obligations can expect the same clear and confident answer from their advisers and neither will be tempted to embark on long and expensive litigation in the belief that victory depends on winning the sympathy of the court.'

Similarly in *Lombard North Central plc v Butterworth* (1987) the Court of Appeal upheld the parties own express provisions as to the consequences of breach of terms as to payment in a contract of hire, even though they were not happy about the justice of the overall result.

| 12.4.6 | Consequences of categorisation |

The categorisation of terms as either conditions or warranties, implies that the actual consequences of a particular breach is not a relevant factor. Once a term is a 'condition', any breach of it will be repudiatory, no matter that it can be easily remedied, or has on this occasion caused no substantial loss to the other party. Similarly, whatever the consequences of a breach of warranty, and however great the losses it causes, it will never give rise to the right to treat the contract as repudiated. This approach is therefore rigid, and may appear to cause injustice in some cases, but it has the merit of certainty, in that the parties can be aware in advance what the legal consequences of any particular breach will be (*cf* the comments of Lord Bridge in *The Chikuma*, quoted above, para 12.4.5).

| 12.4.7 | Intermediate terms |

There are times when the categorisation of terms in the way outlined in the previous sections does not work, and at least since 1962, the courts have recognised that it is necessary to have an intermediate category. The leading case is *Hong Kong Fir Shipping Co v Kawasaki Kisen Kaisha* (1962), though some would argue that earlier decisions were in fact based on the same considerations (see, eg, Smith & Thomas, *A Casebook on Contract*, 9th ed, p 421). The term that was under consideration in *Hong Kong Fir* was that of 'seaworthiness', which appeared in a time charter of a ship. Diplock LJ admitted that some terms may be classifiable as conditions or warranties, but felt that there are many contractual undertakings of a more complex nature which cannot be classified in that way. The obligation as to seaworthiness, for example, could be broken in any number of ways. For example, the failure to have the correct number of lifejackets on board could render a ship 'unseaworthy' just as much as a major defect in the hull. In such a case it was not possible to determine beforehand the consequences of a breach, in terms of whether it would be repudiatory or not. Rather, what a judge had to do was to:

> '... look at the events which had occurred as a result of the breach at the time when the charterers purported to rescind the charterparty and to decide whether the occurrence of those events deprived the charterers of substantially the whole benefit which it was the intention of the parties as expressed in the charterparty that the charterers should obtain from the further performance of their own contractual undertakings.'

So, on this analysis, the focus is not on the parties' intentions at the time of the contract, but on the effect of the actual breach which has occurred: ie the second of the approaches outlined at the start of this section (above, para 12.4.2). If the breach is so serious as to strike fundamentally at the purpose of the contract, then it will be treated as repudiatory, in the same way as if it was a breach of condition; if it is less serious it will give rise only to a remedy in damages, like a warranty.

It has never been doubted since the decision in *Hong Kong Fir* that there are three categories of term, namely conditions, warranties, and 'innominate' or intermediate terms. An approach based on the consequences of breach has even been adopted, perhaps somewhat surprisingly, in relation to sale of goods contracts: *Cehave NV v Bremer Handelsgesellschaft* mbH, *The Hansa Nord* (1975). The attraction of the flexibility of Diplock LJ's analysis has frequently bowed, however, to considerations of the desirability of commercial certainty, spelt out in the quotation from Lord Bridge in *The Chikuma* (above, para 12.4.5). Thus in *The Mihalis Angelos* (1970) the obligation of being 'expected ready to load' at a particular time, a clause which clearly could be broken with varying degrees of seriousness, was treated as a condition, irrespective of the consequences of the particular breach. And as we have seen (above para 12.4.4) a similar view was taken of time clauses in mercantile contracts in *Bunge Corporation v Tradax SA* (1981). It will continue to be important, therefore, to ask the question 'is this a condition or a warranty', before considering the consequences of the breach of contract. The answer to that question may render such consideration unnecessary.

12.4.8   Effects of
Hong Kong Fir

There are two particular situations which call for some special consideration. The first is where the contract is to be performed in instalments, and the breach relates to only a small proportion of those instalments. The second is where the consequences of the breach do not affect the possibilities of the physical performance of the contract, but its commercial viability.

**12.5   Some special types
of breach**

In a contract which is to be performed by instalments, will the breach of one of them ever amount to a repudiatory breach? If so, then the contract can been brought to an end as soon as that one breach has occurred, and there will be no further obligations as regards the rest of the instalments. On the other hand, if the innocent party allows the contract to continue, that may well amount to affirmation of the contract, so that the breach could not subsequently be relied on as being repudiatory.

12.5.1   Instalment contracts

The resolution of these issues may, of course, be determined by what the parties have themselves agreed in the contract. This is confirmed by s 31(2) of the Sale of Goods Act 1979, which states that in cases of defective delivery, or a refusal to accept delivery:

> '... it is a question in each case depending on the terms of the contract and the circumstances of the case whether the breach of contract is a repudiation of the whole contract or whether it is a severable breach giving rise to a claim in compensation but not to a right to treat the whole contract as repudiated.'

An example of the application of this is to be seen in *Maple Flock Co Ltd v Universal Furniture Products (Wembley) Ltd* (1934). The sellers had contracted to sell 100 tons of rag flock to the buyers. Out of the first 20 loads delivered, one, the sixteenth, was defective. The Court of Appeal held that this was not a repudiatory breach, since it related only to one instalment, and therefore only one and a half tons out of the whole contract. In contrast, in *RA Munro & Co Ltd v Meyer* (1930), 1500 tons of meat and bone meal were to be delivered in 12 instalments of 125 tons. After 768 tons had been delivered it was discovered that all were adulterated, and did not match the contract description. It was held that this was sufficient to amount to a repudiatory breach.

The proportion of the instalments involved in the breach is not the only issue, however, as is shown by the House of Lords decision in *Mersey Steel and Iron Co v Naylor, Benzon & Co* (1884). The contract was for the sale of 5,000 tons of steel, to be delivered at the rate of 1,000 tons per month, with payment within three days of receipt of the shipping documents. The sellers delivered only part of the first instalment, but delivered the second complete. Shortly before payment was due the sellers were the subject of petition for winding-up, and as a result the buyers (acting on inaccurate legal advice) withheld payment. The sellers sought to treat this as repudiatory breach. The House of Lords noted that the buyers had indicated a continuing willingness to pay as soon as any legal difficulties had been resolved, and therefore held that this was not a repudiatory breach. The context was important in determining the effect of a breach in relation to one instalment.

As well as illustrating the courts' approach to instalment contracts, this case shows that the intention of the party in breach, and the reasons for the breach, may be important factors in determining whether it is repudiatory. The fact that the buyers had no intention to repudiate, but were acting under a bona fide mistake of law, was a very relevant consideration.

In most cases of repudiatory breach there is some act or omission which means that the obligations under the contract have only partially been fulfilled. Goods do not match their description, or are supplied in insufficient quality; services are not supplied, or do not meet contractual standards; money owed is paid late or not at all. In all these situations the innocent party is being deprived of the benefit of the contract. It is possible, however, for a party to complete his or her major obligations, but for the consequences of some minor breach to be such that, although it does not affect the practical possibility of continuing with the contract, commercially it would be unreasonable to do so. This is exemplified by *Aerial Advertising Co v Batchelors Peas* (1938). The contract was for the towing of an advertising banner on daily flights by an aeroplane. The pilot was supposed to clear his flight plan each day, but on one occasion he failed to do so. He flew over Salford, and saw a large crowd assembled in the main square. He flew close to it displaying the sign 'Eat Batchelors' Peas'. Unfortunately the date was 11 November, and the crowd had assembled to keep the traditional two minutes silence on Armistice Day. The actions of the pilot led to much criticism of Batchelors. The judge held that it was 'commercially wholly unreasonable to carry on with the contract', and that in the circumstances the consequences of the breach (ie the failure to clear the flight plan) meant that Batchelors were entitled to treat the contract as repudiated.

12.5.2 Commercial destruction

While there are obligations still to be performed one party may indicate in advance that he or she intends to break the contract. This is known as an 'anticipatory breach', and will generally give the other party the right to treat the contract as repudiated, and to sue at once for damages. For example, in *Hochster v De La Tour* (1853) the defendant engaged the plaintiff on 12 April to enter his service as a courier, and accompany him on foreign tour. This employment was to start on 1 June. On 11 May the defendant wrote to the plaintiff to inform him that his services would no longer be required. It was held that the plaintiff was entitled to bring an action for damages immediately, without waiting for the 1 June.

12.6 Anticipatory breach

The reason for allowing this type of action, rather than making the plaintiff wait until performance is due, was given by Cockburn CJ in *Frost v Knight* (1872). He held that it involves a breach of a right to have the contract kept open as a subsisting and effective contract. It, of course, also has the practical benefit of enabling the innocent party to obtain compensation for any damage speedily.

As will be seen in the next section, however, the innocent party does not have to accept the anticipatory breach as repudiating the contract. He or she may wait until performance is due, and then seek damages for non-performance at that stage. It has even been held in one case that the innocent party can legitimately incur expenses towards his or her own performance even after a clear indication of an intention to break the contract has been given by the other side. These may then be claimed as damages once the contract date for performance has passed: *White & Carter (Councils) v McGregor* (1961).

12.7 Effect of breach: right of election

In relation to all repudiatory breaches the innocent party has the right to elect to treat the contract as discharged, and claim for damages, or to affirm the contract, notwithstanding the breach. The latter course will prevent the contract from being discharged, but damages may still be recovered.

12.7.1 Need for communication

Where the innocent party elects to treat the breach as repudiatory, this decision should normally be communicated to the other party, but this is not apparently essential, as is shown by *Vitol SA v Norelf Ltd, The Times*, 20 May 1993. V and N had entered into a contract on 11 February 1991 for the purchase of a cargo of propane. On 8 March, V sent a telex to N repudiating the contract. This was subsequently agreed to amount to an anticipatory breach which, if accepted by N would bring the contract to an end immediately. N did not communicate with V, but, on 12 March started to try to find an alternative buyer, and on 15 March sold the cargo to X. V challenged the arbitrator's decision that these actions by N amounted to an acceptance of the anticipatory breach. Phillips J upheld the decision of the arbitrator. He stated that there was an analogy to be drawn with offer and acceptance in the formation of contracts, but it was not one which could be applied precisely. Acceptance of repudiation could be effected by acts as well as words, and it did not matter that the acts would (if they were not a response to a repudiation) themselves amount to a breach. V had argued that such acts would always be equivocal, in that it would not be apparent that the act was a response to the repudiation. Where, however:

> '... the innocent party did not respond to a repudiation by affirmation but proceeded to take action which was incompatible with his own continued performance of the contract, it might be quite clear that he was responding to the repudiation by treating the contract as at an end.'

Moreover, it was quite possible for mere failure to perform contractual obligations in itself to constitute acceptance of an anticipatory breach.

There are, of course, dangers in treating an action by the other party as repudiatory, if it turns out to be viewed otherwise by the court. The party purporting to accept a repudiatory breach may well take action (as was the case in *Vitol v Norelf*) which itself involves a breach of obligations under the contract. If this turns out not to be justified by what the other party has done, then the party who thought they were acting in response to a repudiatory breach, may find the tables turned, and that they themselves are now liable to damages for their own breach of the contract (eg *Federal Commerce and Navigation v Molena Alpha* (1979)). In *Woodar v Wimpey* (1980) the majority of the House of Lords seemed to take the view that this consequence would not necessarily follow if the party purporting to accept the repudiation was acting as a result of a mistake made in good faith as to his or her rights. Most commentators regard this as aspect of the *Woodar v Wimpey* decision as dubious, and prefer to follow the bulk of authorities which suggest that an unjustified failure to meet contractual obligations is itself a repudiatory breach, even if it is a response to action from the other party which is mistakenly thought to be repudiatory.

An election to affirm the contract carries risks as well, as is shown by *Avery v Bowden* (1855). The plaintiff chartered his ship to the defendant. The ship was to sail to Odessa, and there to take a cargo from the defendant's agent, which was to be loaded within a certain number of days. The vessel reached Odessa, but the agent was unable to supply a cargo. The ship remained at Odessa, with the master continuing to demand a cargo. Before the period specified in the contract had elapsed war broke out between England and Russia, and the performance of the contract became legally impossible. The plaintiff sued for breach. It was held, however, that even if the original action of the agent constituted a repudiatory breach, the contract had been affirmed by the fact that the ship remained at Odessa awaiting a cargo. The contract was then frustrated, and it was too late at that stage for the plaintiff to claim for breach.

Similarly in *Fercometal Sarl v Mediterranean Shipping Co SA* (1988) it was held that a party which had affirmed a contract following an anticipatory breach could not subsequently rely on that breach to justify its own failure to fulfil its obligations under the contract.

12.7.2   Risks of acceptance

12.7.3   Risks of affirmation

Summary of Chapter 12

Performance and Breach

Parties will be released from primary obligations once they have completed all that they were bound to do by the contract.

Discharge by performance

- Performance must generally be precise and exact:

  Re Moore & Landauer (1921); *Arcos v Ronaasen* (1933).

- Partial provision of services

  If the contract or obligation is 'entire', performance must be complete to discharge: *Cutter v Powell* (1795).

- Divisible contracts or obligations

  Compensation can be recovered for partial performance.

- Non-performance due to promisee

  Promisor will be able to claim *quantum meruit*: *Planché v Colburn* (1831).

- Acceptance of partial performance

  May have the effect of discharging further obligations, and allow recovery on a *quantum meruit*: *Christy v Row* (1808). This will not apply where the acceptor has no real choice: *Sumpter v Hedges* (1898).

- Substantial performance

  Minor defects in performance will not necessarily prevent discharge: *Dakin v Lee* (1916); *Hoenig v Isaacs* (1952). The distinction is made between failure to complete, and completing badly.

Generally this is treated as equivalent to performance (*cf* Sale of Goods Act 1979, s 27). Satisfactory tender will depend on the terms of the contract, and the overall context: *Startup v Macdonald* (1843). Note: there are special rules regarding the tender of money.

Tender of performance

- Time of performance

  Time is not generally 'of the essence' unless the contract makes it so (*cf* Law of Property Act 1925, s 41; Sale of Goods Act 1979, s 10). Time may become of the essence by giving notice: *Rickards v Oppenheim* (1950).

Only 'repudiatory' breaches will lead to discharge. The effect is not automatic, but depends on the acceptance of the breach as repudiatory by the innocent party: *Gunton v London Borough*

Discharge by breach

of Richmond upon Thames (1980). Whether breach is repudiatory depends on either the classification of terms, or the effects of the breach.

- Classification of terms

  Sale of Goods Act 1979 classifies implied terms into 'conditions' and 'warranties'. Breach of condition is repudiatory; breach of warranty allows only damages to be recovered. This classification is also used by the courts, based largely on the significance of the term: *cf Bettini v Gye* (1876) with *Poussard v Spiers* (1876).

- Labelling of terms by the parties

  This may be indicative of their intentions, but is not conclusive: *Schuler AG v Wickman Tools Sales Ltd* (1973). Parties bargaining on equal terms, however, should normally be taken to have intended the consequences of what they have stated in the contract: *The Chikuma* (1981); *Lombard North Central plc v Butterworth* (1987).

- Intermediate terms

  This category recognised in *Hong Kong Fir Shipping Co v Kawasaki Kisen Kaisha* (1962). Whether breach is repudiatory will depend on its consequences - does it deprive the other party of 'substantially the whole benefit' of the contract. The approach has the advantage of flexibility, but reduces certainty.

- Instalment contracts

  The effect of breach will largely depend on its extent - *cf Maple Flock Co Ltd v Universal Furniture Products (Wembley) Ltd* (1934) with *RA Munro & Co Ltd v Meyer* (1930).

Anticipatory breach

An advance indication of an intention to break a contract may in itself be treated as a repudiatory breach: *Hochster v De La Tour* (1853). It does not have to be accepted as such, however: *White & Carter (Councils) v McGregor* (1961).

Right of election

An innocent party may accept a repudiatory breach, or affirm the contract, *cf Vitol SA v Norelf Ltd* (1993). Treatment of the breach as repudiatory, if not justified, may itself be a breach of contract: *FCN v Molena Alpha* (1979). Affirmation will prevent future reliance on the breach if, for example, the contract is frustrated (*Avery v Bowden* (1855)), or as a justification for the other party's failure to perform (*Fercometal Sarl v Mediterranean Shipping Co SA* (1988)).

Chapter 13

Remedies

At various points during the earlier chapters remedies of one kind or another have been considered. Rescission for mistake, and damages for misrepresentation were discussed in Chapter 8, for example, and repudiation as a result of breach was dealt with in Chapter 12. Here we are considering more generally the award of damages for breach of contract, and the order of specific performance to compel a party to go through with an agreement. Some reference to injunctions will also be necessary. The primary common law remedy for breach of contract is, however, damages, and it is with this area that we start.

13.1   Introduction

The basic principle of contractual damages is that of *restitutio in integrum*, or full restitution. In other words the innocent party is to be put into the position he or she would have been in had the contract been performed satisfactorily (*Robinson v Harman* (1848)). The main objective of contract damages is therefore compensation, not punishment. Although, of course, in some situations, a party thinking about breaking an agreement may be deterred by the prospect of having to pay damages, or a party who has broken an agreement may suffer considerably from having to pay compensation, nevertheless these consequences are not the purpose of the award. This is shown by the fact that if the party not in breach has suffered no quantifiable loss, only nominal damages will be awarded. If, for example, there is a failure to deliver goods, and the buyer is able to obtain an alternative supply without problem, and at a price which is the same or lower than the contract price, no substantial damages will be recoverable (see, Sale of Goods Act 1979, s 51(3)).

13.2   Damages: purpose

Within the general principle of compensation, there are three basic methods by which damages may be calculated. These are conveniently labelled as 'expectation', 'reliance', and 'restitution'. Some consideration also needs to be given to consequential losses, and non-pecuniary losses.

13.3   Damages: measure

This is the approach which most clearly relates to putting the innocent party into the position he or she would have been in had the contract been performed. It is concerned with fulfilling the expectations of that party as to the benefits that would

13.3.1   Expectation interest

have flowed from the successful completion of the contract. In particular, where the innocent party, as will commonly be the case, was expecting to make a profit as a result of the contract, that will generally be recoverable (subject to the rules of remoteness, mitigation, etc dealt with below, para 13.4), as well as any other consequential losses flowing from the breach. Suppose, for example, A has a piece of machinery that needs repair, and he engages B to carry out the work. A tells B that the work must be done on 1 November, because A has an order for which he needs the machine on 2 November, and which he will lose if it is unavailable. If B, in breach of contract, fails to carry out the work, A will probably be able to claim the lost profit on the 2 November contract. If B had performed the contract properly, A would have made the profit, and therefore it should be recoverable.

Even if the profit was not certain to be made, there may be a partial recovery, on the basis that the plaintiff has lost the chance to make it. In *Chaplin v Hicks* (1911), for example, the breach of contract prevented the plaintiff from taking part in a beauty contest. She was allowed to recover a proportion of what she might have won. Similarly, in *Simpson v London and North Western Ry Co* (1876) the defendant failed to deliver some specimens to a trade fair by the specified date. The plaintiff was allowed to recover compensation for the loss of sales he might have made had the specimens arrived on time. In these cases it should be noted that the plaintiff may do better than would have been the case if the contract had not been broken. Ms Chaplin might not have won any prize in the beauty contest, and Mr Simpson might not have made any sales. The court may be said in fact to be placing a monetary value on what is essentially a non-pecuniary loss - ie the loss of a chance. Alternatively, it might be said that in this situation the compensatory aspects of contract damages are tinged with a punitive element, in that the defendant is made to pay in order to show that his or her behaviour fell below an acceptable level.

13.3.2   Reliance interest

In some situations it may not be easy for the plaintiff to estimate the profits that would have been made. Here it may prove more sensible to abandon the attempt, and instead to seek recovery of the expenditure which has been incurred in anticipation of the contract. An example of this type of situation is *Anglia Television v Reed* (1971). Reed was an actor who was under contract to play a leading role in a television film. At a late stage Reed withdrew, and the project was unable to go ahead. In suing Reed for breach of contract, Anglia did not seek their lost profits. It would have been very difficult to estimate exactly what these would have been, given the uncertainties of the entertainment industry. Instead, they sought, and were awarded, compensation for all the expenses incurred towards setting up the film. This included expenditure incurred *before* the contract with Reed was entered into, provided that these fell within the rule of remoteness (below, para 13.4).

The decision as to whether to seek expectation or reliance damages will generally lie with the plaintiff (as was made clear in *Anglia v Reed*). There have been examples, however, of the court deciding that reliance is the appropriate measure. This was the case in *McRae v Commonwealth Disposals Commission* (1951) (see Chapter 8, para 8.6.1), in relation to the contract to salvage a non-existent ship. In some situations, on the other hand, the court may say that the reliance measure should not be available. This will be the case, for instance, where the difficulty in identifying profits results primarily from the fact that the plaintiff has made a bad bargain. Thus in *C&P Haulage v Middleton* (1983), some of the plaintiff's costs were in fact reduced as a result of the breach, and the plaintiff's loss of equipment (which had to be handed over to the defendant) was an integral part of the original contract. In that situation the plaintiff was only allowed to sue for the expectation interest. The burden of proving that the bargain was 'bad' in this sense falls, however, on the defendant: *CCC Films v Impact Quadrant Films* (1984). The plaintiff does not have to prove that sufficient would have been made on the contract to cover the expenses incurred.

Restitutionary damages are largely a corollary of repudiatory breach. If such a breach has been accepted, and the plaintiff has returned any benefits received, or is willing to do so, then he or she will also be entitled to claim the restitution of anything which has been given to the defendant. The easiest example is the situation of defective goods. The buyer returns the goods, and expects the refund of the price. In many situations, and in particular in relation to consumer contracts, that may be all that can be recovered by way of damages. The buyer may not have been expecting to make a profit out of the use or resale of the goods, and there may be no other losses resulting from the breach.

13.3.3   Restitution

Restitution also has a more general role to play in relation to contracts which are void, or rescinded (eg for mistake or misrepresentation), or where no contract has ever come into existence (see Chapter 14). These situations are not ones which arise on breach, and so are not discussed further here.

13.3.4	Consequential losses	There are some losses which flow from the breach, but which cannot be put into the category of 'expenses' (ie reliance) or thwarted expectations. Provided the causal link can be established, and they are not too remote (see below, para 13.4), then they will be recoverable. If there is a contract for the purchase of a piece of machinery, for example, and it is defective then the expectation interest may allow the recovery of lost profits that would have been gained by using the machine. If, however, the defect causes the machine to explode, which results in damage to the buyer's premises, this consequential loss can also be recovered. In general the court will allow the recovery of the 'cost of cure' - ie the expense of repairs and refurbishment to put the premises back into the position they were in prior to the explosion. This is subject to the limitation that if the cost of cure is significantly greater than the reduction in value of the property concerned, then the court may refuse to allow it (*Watts v Morrow* (1991) - cost of repairing house £34,000; diminution in value £15,000). This limitation does not, however, apply to the situation where the 'cure' relates to the plaintiff providing something which was specifically promised in the contract. Thus in *Radford v De Froberville* (1978) the plaintiff was allowed to recover for the cost of building a brick wall, because this is what had been contracted for, even though a cheaper fence would have served the purpose (which was simply to mark a boundary).
13.3.5	Non-pecuniary losses	Contract damages are primarily concerned with economic losses of one kind or another, which are more or less quantifiable in money terms. In some situations, however, non-pecuniary losses will be caused. If, for example, a defective product results in personal injury to the purchaser, there seems no reason why damages should not be recovered in relation to the pain and suffering so caused. Of course, third parties who are injured will have to rely on tortious remedies at common law or under the Consumer Protection Act 1987.

A more difficult question arises in relation to mental distress, anguish, or annoyance caused by a breach of contract. The courts have tended to be wary of awarding compensation under this heading. In *Addis v Gramophone Company Ltd* (1909) the House of Lords refused to uphold an award which had been made in relation to the 'harsh and humiliating' way in which the plaintiff had been dismissed from his job in breach of contract. This line was followed in a more recent dismissal case, *Bliss v South East Thames RHA* (1988). On the other hand, it has been held that where one of the purposes of the contract is to provide pleasure and enjoyment, damages for distress and disappointment caused by a breach may be recovered.

Thus in *Jarvis v Swan's Tours* (1973), such damages were awarded in relation to breach of contract in the provision of a holiday which had promised to provide 'a great time'. A similar approach can be seen in *Jackson v Horizon Holidays* (1975) (see Chapter 4, para 4.4). Where, however, the contract is a purely commercial one, damages for anguish and vexation will not be allowed: *Hayes v James & Charles Dodd* (1990). The decision in *Cox v Phillips Industries Ltd* (1976), in which damages for distress and anxiety resulting from a demotion were recovered, now looks anomalous, and the current trend is for a strictly limited approach to the award of damages in this area.

There are two main limitations on the amount of damages which can be recovered for a breach of contract, namely the rule of remoteness, and the requirement of mitigation. The issue of contributory negligence will also be considered in this section.

13.4   Limitations on recovery

At various points in this chapter it has been mentioned that the award of damages under a particular head will be subject to the rule of remoteness. This is a rule which basically prevents consequential losses extending too far, and placing unreasonable burdens on the defendant. It should also be recalled that in Chapter 8 it was noted that in relation to the tort of deceit, and the remedy for negligent misrepresentation under s 2(1) of the Misrepresentation Act 1967, all consequential losses are recoverable, without limitation. This is exceptional, however, and in general, in both tort and contract, damages are only recoverable in relation to losses which are not too remote.

13.4.1   The rule of remoteness

The type of recovery the rule is designed to prevent is as follows. Suppose that a contract for the hire of a car is broken, because the one supplied is unfit for its purpose and breaks down. The hirer may as a result fail to arrive at a sale where she would have been able to buy a valuable painting which she could have resold for a £100,000 profit. Should the hire company be liable for the £100,000? English law will normally regard this loss as too remote from the breach to be recoverable.

In contract, the starting point for the rule of remoteness is *Hadley v Baxendale* (1854). In this case there was delay in the transport of a broken mill-shaft which resulted in considerable losses for the mill-owner, because no spare shaft was available. The court stated the rule as being that the defendant will only be liable for losses:

13.4.2   The rule in *Hadley v Baxendale*

'either arising naturally, that is, according to the usual course of things, from such breach of contract itself, or such as may reasonably be supposed to have been in the contemplation of both parties at the time they made the contract as the probable result of the breach of it.'

Applying this to the facts of the case, the court held that in most cases of a breach of this kind, no such losses would have followed, so that it could not be said that the losses followed naturally from the breach. Nor were the defendants aware, at the time of the contract, of the circumstances which meant that the mill would not be able to function at all without this particular shaft. Therefore, the losses were not recoverable.

13.4.3	Relevance of knowledge

There are two aspects of this test which should be noted. First, it is clear that remoteness rule has to be assessed on the basis of the parties' knowledge at the time the contract is made. The reason for this is that awareness of a particular risk may affect the terms of the contract. If, to use the example given above, the firm hiring a car is aware that the customer is using it to attend a sale in order to buy a rare painting, the firm may want to:

(a) increase the price;

(b) insert an exclusion clause;

(c) seek insurance of the risk; or

(d) refuse to enter into the contract at all.

Knowledge which the defendant acquired after the formation of the contract is therefore irrelevant to the rule of remoteness.

13.4.4	'Reasonable contemplation' test

Secondly, the rule as stated in *Hadley v Baxendale* appears to have two parts, the first relating to the natural consequences of breach, and the second to the contemplation of the parties. As interpreted in the later cases of *Victoria Laundry (Windsor) Ltd v Newman Industries* (1949), and *The Heron II* (1969), however, the two limbs are really just aspects of one general principle. The situation must be looked at through the eyes of the reasonable defendant, who will be presumed to have in contemplation the normal types of loss which would follow from the breach. As regards anything more unusual, it will have to be established that the defendant had sufficient actual knowledge to be aware of the risk. The test is thus simply, what can this defendant, bearing in mind his or her state of knowledge, be reasonably presumed to have expected to be the consequence of the breach of contract which occurred.

In *Victoria Laundry (Windsor) v Newman* the breach of contract was a lengthy delay in the delivery of a boiler which the plaintiffs (as the defendants were aware) wished to use in their laundry and dyeing business. The Court of Appeal held that the plaintiffs could recover from lost profits at a level reasonably to be anticipated from a business of this type. They could not recover, however, in relation to some particularly lucrative dyeing contracts with the Ministry of Defence, of which the defendants were unaware.

In *The Heron II* the House of Lords had to consider the degree of risk that had to be contemplated before a loss was not too remote. It is a difficult concept to pin down, and there is no clear, single phrase, which is used to express it. The House agreed, however, that the test in contract was distinguishable from that in tort, which is based on 'reasonable foreseeability'. The contract test is stricter than that, and depends on the loss being contemplated as a 'not unlikely', or 'liable to result'.

It seems that it is the *type* of loss, rather than the precise way in which it occurs, or its extent, which must be contemplated. In *Parsons (Livestock) Ltd v Uttley Ingham & Co Ltd* (1978), the defective installation of a hopper used for storing pig food led to the death of a large number of the plaintiff's pigs, as a result of the food going mouldy. The defendants were held liable for this loss, because some harm to the pigs was within the reasonable contemplation of the parties as something which would result from a defective installation, even though the particular disease was not. As Lord Scarman put it:

> 'While, on [the judge's] finding, nobody at the time of contract could have expected E coli to ensue from eating mouldy nuts, he is clearly, and as a matter of common sense, rightly, saying that people would contemplate ... the serious possibility of injury and even death among the pigs.'

Once a breach of contract has occurred, the plaintiff is not entitled to sit back and do nothing while losses accumulate. There is an obligation to take reasonable steps to mitigate losses, which was laid down by the House of Lords in *British Westinghouse Electric and Manufacturing Company v Underground Electric Railways Co of London* (1912). The plaintiff will be debarred from claiming any part of the damage which is due to a failure to take such steps. So, if the seller fails to deliver in a sale of goods contract, the buyer will be expected to go into the market and attempt to obtain equivalent goods. If such are available at, or below, the market price, then only nominal

13.4.5   Mitigation

damages will be recoverable. If the buyer fails to enter the market until the price has risen, or pays over the odds, these increased losses will not be recoverable. Similarly, a reasonable offer of performance following a breach should not be spurned. In *Payzu Ltd v Saunders* (1919) the plaintiffs had failed to make prompt payment for an instalment of goods. The defendants had, in breach of contract, then refused to deliver unless the plaintiffs agreed to pay cash with each order. It was held that the plaintiffs should have accepted this offer, which would have reduced their loss (since the market value of the goods in question was rising above the contract price).

Mitigation only requires the plaintiff to act 'reasonably' in all the circumstances. In *Wroth v Tyler* (1974), the plaintiff's lack of resources was considered a reasonable ground for a failure to go into the market and make an alternative purchase.

The principle of mitigation raises particular problems in cases of anticipatory breach. If the plaintiff accepts the breach, and the contract terminates immediately, then the normal rules will apply. If, however, the plaintiff does not accept the breach, but elects to wait for the other party to perform, it seems that there is not at that stage any duty to reduce losses. In *White & Carter (Councils) v McGregor* (1962) the defendants had contracted to buy advertising space on litter bins owned by the plaintiffs. This contract was wrongfully cancelled by the defendants before any work had been done. The plaintiffs refused to accept this anticipatory breach, and went ahead with the production and display of the advertisements. They then sued for the full sum due under the contract. The House of Lords held that there was no obligation on the plaintiff in such a situation to mitigate the losses, and full recovery is possible. The decision has been regarded as harsh on the defendant, and has been widely criticised, but it still stands as the leading authority on this issue.

13.4.6   Contributory negligence

In tort it is well-established that the damages recoverable may be reduced by the plaintiff's own, contributory, negligence: Law Reform (Contributory Negligence) Act 1945. Does the same principle apply in contract? The issue was considered by the Court of Appeal in *Forsikingsaktieseslkapet Vesta v Butcher* (1988), which stated, *obiter*, that the 1945 Act did apply where there was concurrent liability in tort and contract (ie where the breach of contract consisted of negligent performance, in a situation where there was also a tortious duty of care). It is not clear whether the Act can operate in other situations. It seems that it will not do so where the liability for the breach is not dependent on negligence. Where, however, the contractual liability is based on 'negligence', but there is no concurrent tortious duty, there is no clear authority. There is some suggestion from the case of *De Meza and Stuart v Apple Van Straten* (1974) that the Act does apply in such a case, but this was not supported by *dicta* in *Vesta v Butcher*. And although losses were apportioned in *Tenant Radiant Heat Ltd v Warrington Development Corporation* (1988), this was on the basis of one side having broken the contract, and the other being independently liable in tort. The area is thus in some confusion, and a clear ruling from the House of Lords would be helpful.

The parties to a contract may decide to include provision as to the compensation which is to be paid in the event of a breach. This is known as a 'liquidated damages' clause, and is generally a perfectly acceptable arrangement, to which the courts will happily give effect. The limitation on this is that the sum specified in the contract must be a 'genuine pre-estimate' of the plaintiff's loss, and not a 'penalty'. If it is the latter, then it will be unenforceable. This distinction was insisted upon by the House of Lords in *Dunlop Pneumatic Tyre Co Ltd v New Garage and Motor Co Ltd* (1915). In this case a sum of £5 was stated to be payable 'by way of liquidated damages and not as a penalty' in relation to a wide range of breaches of contract. The House of Lords held that, despite the parties' own statement, a sum payable could constitute a penalty not only if it was excessive in comparison to the loss, but also if it was payable on the occurrence of a range of events, which would be likely to produce a range of different losses. That was the case here, but nevertheless the House felt that on balance the £5 should not be regarded as a penalty.

13.5   Liquidated damages and penalty clauses

The principles in this area are clear enough. The difficulty comes in applying them to particular provisions. The area was reconsidered by the Privy Council in *Philips Hong Kong Ltd v Attorney General of Hong Kong, The Times*, 15 February 1993. The case concerned a claim by Philips that they were not liable to pay the Hong Kong government liquidated damages for delay to completion of contract works, because these amounted to a penalty. The Court of Appeal of Hong Kong allowed an appeal from a first instance decision upholding Philips' claim. Philips appealed to the Privy Council. The Privy Council stated that in deciding whether a clause was a penalty clause, or a genuine pre-estimate of damages, the court was not helped by the use in argument of unlikely hypothetical examples of situations where the sums payable under the liquidated damages clause would be wholly out of proportion to any loss. Although the clause must be judged objectively, at the date the contract was made, what happened subsequently could provide valuable

13.5.1   Application of the principles

evidence of what could reasonably be expected to be the loss at the time the contract was made. The appeal was dismissed. In reaching its conclusions the Privy Council accepted Lord Dunedin's statement in *Dunlop Pneumatic Tyre Co Ltd v New Garage & Motor Co* (1915) that:

> 'The question whether a sum stipulated is penalty or liquidated damages is a question of construction to be decided upon the terms and inherent circumstances of each particular contract, judged of as at the time of the contract not at the time of the breach ...'

Nevertheless, it was felt that what had actually happened might provide a better guide than hypothetical examples thought up by counsel. Furthermore, where the range of possible losses was broad, the better approach might be simply to say that the clause was not intended to apply to breaches where the liquidated damages would be totally out of proportion to the loss, rather than to strike the clause down in its entirety. The court was clearly influenced by the fact that this was a commercial contract where 'what the parties had agreed should normally be upheld'. The decision suggests a flexible, but to some extent unpredictable, approach, of a kind which has been advocated, for example, by Treitel - see *Law of Contract*, 8th ed p 885.

13.6   Specific performance

The remedy of specific performance involves the court in issuing an order directing one of the parties to a contract to carry out his or her obligations. The sanction for a failure to comply is that the person concerned will be in contempt of court, and liable to fines and imprisonment as a consequence. The remedy is, of course, an equitable one, developed by the chancery courts. As a result, unlike damages, it is discretionary. This means that a plaintiff is not entitled to the order simply as a result of proving that the other party is in breach of his or her obligations. Once this has been established the court will then decide whether it is appropriate in this particular case that the order should be made. For example, as we saw in Chapter 8, one way in which the courts will allow a party to escape the consequences of a mistake concerning the terms of the contract is by refusing to order specific performance (see para 8.10.1). Similarly, the order may not be granted if the plaintiff has taken advantage of the defendant, for example because he or she was drunk: *Malins v Freeman* (1837).

Although this discretionary element inevitably attaches a degree of uncertainty to the remedy, in fact the courts have developed a number of rules about its use, which mean that in many cases it will be fairly easy to determine whether or not the order is likely to be granted. The rest of this section looks at these.

One of the reasons why the remedy of specific performance developed is that in certain situations damages will be an inadequate remedy. If no pecuniary loss can be established, or it is impossible to quantify, this would mean that there would be no effective sanction for a breach of contract, in the absence of the order for specific performance. In *Harnett v Yielding* (1805), for example, Lord Redesdale said:

> 'Unquestionably the original foundation of these decrees was simply this, that damages would not give the party the compensation to which he was entitled; that is it would not put him in a situation as beneficial to him as if the agreement were specifically performed.'

Thus, as Kindersley VC explains in *Falcke v Gray* (1859), the Courts of Equity would not allow an injustice to stand, but intervened to order performance of the obligations. Now, of course, the remedy is available in all courts, and the question to be asked is, when will damages not be regarded as an adequate remedy?

If there is a contract for the sale of goods in which there is an active market, then it is very unlikely that an order for specific performance will be granted. The party not in breach can buy or sell in the market, and be compensated by way of damages for any financial loss resulting from a difference between the contract and market prices. If, on the other hand, what is being sold is a valuable antique, or some other item which is not generally available, specific performance may well be the appropriate remedy. This distinction is supported by s 52 of the Sale of Goods Act 1979, which allows for specific performance in relation to 'specific' or 'ascertained' goods, but not 'generic' goods (see Chapter 16 for discussion of these categories).

Similarly, it is normally the case that the order will be available to enforce contracts for the sale of land, since every piece of land is regarded as unique. In *Behnke v Bede Shipping Co Ltd* (1927) a 'unique' ship was held to be capable of being subject to an order for specific performance, but in *The Stena Nautica* (1982) the decision went the other way.

In some cases it seems that if damages would only be nominal then the order may be made. Thus in *Beswick v Beswick* (1968) (above, para 4.2.1) the fact that the deceased's estate suffered no direct loss from the failure of the nephew to pay his aunt meant that only nominal damages would be recoverable in an action by the estate. Justice clearly

13.6.1   Adequacy of damages

demanded, however, that the contract should be enforced, and so the order was granted. It will not always be the case that the fact that damages would be nominal will allow specific performance to be ordered. If that were so it would include all the cases of sale of goods where there is an available market offering a price more attractive than the contract one. There must be some other factor which will persuade the court to make the order, but it is difficult to predict what this will be, or to make a list of the appropriate circumstances.

| 13.6.2 | Need for supervision |

The court will be reluctant to order specific performance where it would have to supervise the parties over a period of time to ensure compliance. In *Ryan v Mutual Tontine Westminster Chambers Association* (1893), for example, the court refused to grant specific performance of a landlord's obligation to have a resident porter 'constantly in attendance'. It appears, however, to be only where the supervision would need to concern the detail of performance that this limitation applies . In *Wolverhampton Corporation v Emmons* (1901), for example, the contract concerned a building contract for some new houses, which would obviously take time to complete. The court was prepared to order specific performance because the obligations of the defendant were clearly defined by the building plans, and so there would be no need for detailed supervision while the work was being done.

| 13.6.3 | Personal services |

The courts will be reluctant to grant an order for specific performance in relation to employment, or other contracts for personal services. The fact that the matter has come to court almost certainly shows that relations between the parties have broken down, and it would be undesirable to try to force them to work together. Where, however, it can be demonstrated that mutual trust and respect does still exist, then the order may be available. In *Hill v Parsons* (1972), for example, a dismissal had resulted from union pressure, rather than a dispute between employer and employee. This limitation on the general rule as regards personal services was also recognised in *Powell v Brent London Borough Council* (1987), where an injunction was granted. The problem in this case had arisen simply because the employer had appointed the employee after a procedure which did not comply with the requirements of its equal opportunities procedures, rather than being the result of any dissatisfaction with the employee's work. Of course, most disputes about employment will nowadays fall to be considered under the employment protection legislation, which specifically provides for 're-instatement' as one of the remedies for unfair dismissal.

A court will not order specific performance unless it would also be available against the party seeking it. Thus a minor trying to enforce a contract for non-necessary goods would be likely to fail on the basis of this lack of mutuality. If, however, unenforceable obligations have in fact already been performed, the court may order the other side to go through with the contract. The time to assess the issue is as at the date of trial, rather than the date of contract: *Price v Strange* (1978).

13.6.4   Need for mutuality

If the granting of an order, which on other grounds would seem to be available, will cause disproportionate hardship to the defendant, the court will refuse it. This is an aspect of the general 'equitable' nature of the remedy, which requires the court always to have in mind the need to achieve justice between the parties. In *Denne v Light* (1857), for example, specific performance of a contract for the sale of land would have left the defendant with a plot surrounded by land owned by others, and with no point of access. The order was not granted. Even straightforward financial hardship, if sufficiently severe, may be enough, particularly if it was unforeseeable at the time of contract. In *Patel v Ali* (1984) the defendant had become disabled, and relied greatly on a network of support from neighbours. This network would have been lost if she had been forced to move, and it would have been very expensive to have to pay for equivalent help. The order for specific performance was not granted.

13.6.5   Hardship

Since specific performance is an equitable remedy the courts will apply the general equitable maxims that 'he who seeks equity must do equity', and 'he who comes to equity must come with clean hands'. In other words, the plaintiff will not be granted the remedy unless he or she, in the eyes of the court, has also acted equitably (*Walters v Morgan* (1861) - plaintiff taking advantage of defendant's ignorance as to the true value of property over which a mining lease had been granted). Thus in *Shell v Lostock Garage* (1977) (above, para 10.11) the Court of Appeal refused to grant an injunction which would have in effect compelled the defendants to go through with a contract. The plaintiff's discriminatory pricing policy was regarded as unfair, and a basis for refusing the order.

13.6.6   Plaintiff must have
acted equitably

In some situations the courts will be prepared to grant an injunction restraining a person from acting in a way which will amount to a breach of contract. The injunction may be 'interlocutory', that is, temporary, pending a full trial, or permanent. One example of a situation where this may be a valuable remedy is in relation to restrictive covenants relating

13.7   Injunctions

to the sale of a business, or competing employment (see Chapter 10, para 10.10). In any contract in which a party promises *not* to do something, then there will be potential scope for the use of an injunction. An injunction, however, like the order for specific performance, is an equitable remedy, and thus subject to the discretion of the court

The courts will not allow an injunction to be used as an indirect means of specifically enforcing a contract for which a direct order to perform would not be granted. Thus in *Page One Records v Britton* (1968) the court refused an injunction which would have restrained a pop group from employing anyone as their manager other than the plaintiff, with whom they had fallen out. This was regarded as effectively forcing the group to employ the manager, and would amount to an indirect enforcement of a contract for personal services . Earlier decisions, however, had shown the courts being more willing to act in this area. In *Lumley v Wagner* (1852), for example, a singer had been restrained from singing in other theatres (*cf Lumley v Gye* (1853), above para 4.9), and in *Warner Bros v Nelson* (1937) the actress Bette Davis had been restrained from working in films or theatre for any other company. The court in this case felt that she was not being compelled to work for Warner Bros because she could have found employment other than as an actress, a conclusion which was technically correct, but practically very unrealistic! It may be that the *Page One* decision represents the more likely approach of a modern court to these issues.

Remedies

The purpose of damages is *restitutio in integrum*, not punishment. The plaintiff should be put in the position he or she would have been in had the contract been performed satisfactorily: *Robinson v Harman* (1848).

- Expectation interest

    This is the normal measure of damages. It can take into account lost profits. It will also cover the 'loss of a chance': *Chaplin v Hicks* (1911).

- Reliance interest

    This allows the plaintiff to recover lost expenses, instead of the expectation interest: *Anglia Television v Reed* (1971). The choice of which remedy to seek normally lies with the plaintiff.

- Restitution

    This will be available if a repudiatory breach leads to the return, for example, of the goods and money exchanged under a sale of goods contract.

- Consequential losses

    Losses which flow from the breach may be recovered, as long as they are not too remote. The 'cost of cure' will generally be allowed, in place of 'diminution in value', unless the difference is significant: *Watts v Morrow* (1991).

- Non-pecuniary losses

    Damages may be recovered for physical injuries, but not usually for injury to feelings: *Addis v Gramophone Company Ltd* (1909). An exception exists, however, for contracts which have the provision of enjoyment as one of their purposes: *Jarvis v Swans Tours* (1975).

The rule of remoteness derives from *Hadley v Baxendale* (1854). As interpreted by *Victoria Laundry (Windsor) Ltd v Newman Industries* (1949) and *The Heron II* (1969), it limits recovery to those losses which were within the reasonable contemplation of the parties as not unlikely to result from the breach.

The plaintiff has an obligation to take reasonable steps to mitigate losses: *British Westinghouse Electric and Manufacturing Company v Underground Electric Railways Co of London* (1912). Lack of resources may make it unreasonable to mitigate: *Wroth v Tyler* (1974). Where there is an anticipatory breach which is not accepted, there is no obligation to mitigate prior to the date of performance: *White & Carter (Councils) v McGregor* (1962).

The Law Reform (Contributory Negligence) Act 1945 probably applies where there is concurrent liability in tort and contract: *Forsikingsaktieseslkapet Vesta v Butcher* (1988).

<table>
<tr><td>Liquidated damages and penalty clauses</td><td>Genuine pre-estimates of loss will be enforced; penalty clauses will not: Dunlop Pneumatic Tyre Co Ltd v New Garage and Motor Co Ltd (1915). The clauses must be judged objectively as at the time the contract was made (Philips Hong Kong Ltd v Attorney General of Hong Kong (1993)), but subsequent events may provide valuable evidence or what could reasonably have been expected at that time.</td></tr>
</table>

Liquidated damages and penalty clauses

Genuine pre-estimates of loss will be enforced; penalty clauses will not: *Dunlop Pneumatic Tyre Co Ltd v New Garage and Motor Co Ltd* (1915). The clauses must be judged objectively as at the time the contract was made (*Philips Hong Kong Ltd v Attorney General of Hong Kong* (1993)), but subsequent events may provide valuable evidence or what could reasonably have been expected at that time.

Specific performance

Specific performance is an equitable remedy, available at the court's discretion. It may be awarded where damages provide an inadequate remedy: *Harnett v Yielding* (1805). This will generally be the case in relation to land.

- Need for supervision

  The order will not generally be made if it would require detailed supervision to enforce: *Ryan v Mutual Tontine Westminster Chambers Association* (1893).

- Personal services

  The courts are reluctant to enforce contracts of service, unless it is clear that mutual trust and respect still exists between the parties: *Hill v Parsons* (1972).

- Need for mutuality

  The order will not be available, unless the plaintiff would also be liable to it. Thus a minor may have difficulty in obtaining the order in relation to a contract for non-necessary goods.

- Hardship

  If the order will cause disproportionate hardship, it will not be granted: *Denne v Light* (1857); *Patel v Ali* (1984).

- Plaintiff must have acted equitably

  Walters v Morgan (1861).

Injunctions

These may be awarded where a party has promised not to do something. They must not, however, become an indirect method of enforcing a contract for which specific performance would not be available: *Page One Records v Britton* (1968) (but *cf Lumley v Wagner* (1852), and *Warner Bros v Nelson* (1937).

Chapter 14

Quasi-Contract and Restitution

The topics to be covered in this chapter have close links with those dealt with Chapter 13. We are concerned again with ways in which a person can seek compensation for losses, or, perhaps more accurately, avoid suffering a loss. In this case, however, we are dealing with situations where the standard contract remedies are unavailable because the parties are not in a contractual relationship. This will either be because their attempt to make a binding agreement has failed in some way (eg it is void for mistake), or their negotiations have never succeeded in reaching the stage of a mutually acceptable contract. We are therefore concerned with situations which have some relationship to contract (hence the label 'quasi-contract') but which strictly speaking fall outside its remit. This area can be regarded as part of a more general area of law, which has come to be known as 'Restitution'. Its basis and limits have been most fully expounded by Goff and Jones in their book *The Law of Restitution*, 3rd ed 1988. Central to this concept is the idea of 'unjust enrichment'. Restitution comprises a body of rules for recovery of money or property in order to prevent a person becoming 'unjustly enriched'. As Lord Wright put it in *Fibrosa Spolka Akcynja v Fairbairn Lawson Combe Barbour* (1943):

> 'It is clear that any civilised system of law is bound to provide remedies for what has been called unjust enrichment, or unjust benefit, that is, to prevent a man from retaining the money of, or some benefit derived from, another which it is against his conscience he should keep.'

It is English law's response to this requirement that we are concerned with in the rest of this chapter. There are two main topics to consider: the recovery of money, and the payment for work which has been done.

14.1 The nature of the concepts

The transfer of money outside a contractual relationship raises particular problems. Whereas if I give you possession of my car in connection with a contract which turns out to be void I can maintain an action for the recovery of it relying on my continuing rights of ownership, with money the position is more complicated. There will not be any possibility of identifying the particular notes or coins which have been transferred, or of 'unmixing' funds from a bank account into

14.2 Recovery of money

which they have been paid. In other words, the money itself has become the property of the person to whom it has been transferred, and the most that is left is the obligation to repay an equivalent sum. There are three situations where the possibility of such recovery is clearly recognised: first, where there is a total failure of consideration; secondly, where the money was transferred under a mistake of fact; and thirdly, where money has been paid to a third party for the benefit of the defendant.

14.2.1   **Total failure of consideration**

One example of this situation has already been discussed in Chapter 11, in relation to the doctrine of frustration. As we saw there, the House of Lords in the *Fibrosa* case (above, para 11.4.3) accepted that if a party who had paid money under a frustrated contract had received nothing in return, the money could be recovered. The rule is thus that the plaintiff must have received nothing of what had been contracted for. If there has been partial performance of any kind, then this remedy will not be available.

As we saw in the *Fibrosa* case itself, this rule has the potential to cause a certain amount of injustice, in that the defendant who has used the money to prepare for performance may lose out. It was in part for this reason that the procedure for a rather more equitable distribution of losses was introduced in the frustration area by the Law Reform (Frustrated Contracts) Act 1943 (above, para 11.5).

The action based on a total failure of consideration has also been used, not without controversy, in the sale of goods area. In *Rowland v Divall* (1923) the plaintiff car dealer had bought a car from the defendant. The car had previously been stolen, but neither party was aware of this at the time. The plaintiff resold the car to a third party, from whom it was reclaimed, some months later, by the true owner's insurance company. The plaintiff had to repay the purchase price to the third party, and then sought to recover what he had paid to the defendant. Despite the fact of the lapse of time, and the consequent reduction in the value of the car, which was demonstrated by the fact that the insurance company had in fact sold it back to the plaintiff at much less than the original contract price, the plaintiff was allowed to recover what he had paid to the defendant in full, on the basis of a total failure of consideration. The use that the plaintiff had made of the car was irrelevant. The essence of a sale of goods contract is not the use of the goods, but the transfer of ownership. Since this had never been transferred, because the car was stolen, the plaintiff was entitled to recover all his money.

In *Rowland v Divall* the plaintiff as a dealer was primarily interested in the ability to resell the car. The same principle, however, applies to a private purchaser. In *Butterworth v Kingsway Motors* (1954) the plaintiff had bought a car which, unknown to him, was subject to a hire purchase agreement, and was reclaimed by the finance company nearly a year later. The plaintiff was allowed to recover the full purchase price from the defendant, notwithstanding the fact that the defendant was equally ignorant of the defect in title. The plaintiff thus had almost a year's free use of the car. This decision has been the subject of considerable criticism, but has not as yet been overruled.

In cases outside the sale of goods area, the fact that property has been used by the plaintiff, for example by his or her going into residence under a tenancy, may well prevent a claim based on a total failure of consideration: *Hunt v Silk* (1804).

Money paid under a mistake of fact will be recoverable, provided that the mistake is as to a fact which, if true, would have legally (*Aiken v Short* (1856)), or morally (*Larner v LCC* (1949)), obliged the plaintiff to pay the money , or, at least, is sufficiently serious to justify the requirement of repayment (Cheshire, Fifoot & Furmston, *Law of Contract*, 12th ed p 660) . Where a contract is void as a result of being based on a common mistake of fact (such as a false belief in the existence of the subject-matter), then recovery will certainly be possible. Other situations where recovery has been held to be possible include mistaken payments under insurance policies. Thus in *Norwich Union Fire Insurance Society Ltd v Price Ltd* (1934) payment was made on the basis that cargo of fruit had been destroyed, whereas in fact it had been resold because it was becoming overripe. Recovery of the payment was allowed. Similarly, in *Kelly v Solari* (1841) payment was made on a life insurance policy as a result of the company failing to realise that the final premium had not been paid. Although it might be argued that this was something of which the company should have been aware, recovery of the payment was allowed.

Lord Goff has suggested (in *Barclays Bank Ltd v Simms & Cooke (Southern) Ltd* (1980)) that recovery under this head will not be possible if the payer intended the payee to benefit in any event; or there is good consideration from the payee (such as the discharge of a debt); or the payee has changed his or her position in good faith as a result of the payment.

14.2.2   Mistake of fact

| 14.2.3 | Payment to a third party | We are here concerned with money which has been paid by the plaintiff to a third party, but which benefits the defendant. Can the plaintiff recover this money from the defendant? One major limitation on this is that the plaintiff must not have been acting purely as a volunteer, but under some constraint. A mother who decides, out of the goodness of her heart, to settle her son's debts, cannot then claim restitution from the son. This rule was applied in a commercial context in *Macclesfield Corporation v Great Central Railway* (1911), where the plaintiffs carried out repairs on a bridge which the defendants were legally obliged (but had refused) to maintain. The plaintiffs were regarded as acting purely as volunteers, and so could not recover from the defendants the money spent on the work. An example of a situation where recovery was allowed is *Exall v Partridge* (1799). The plaintiff in this case paid off arrears of rent owed by the defendant. The reason for doing this was to avoid the seizure by bailiffs of a carriage belonging to the plaintiff which had been left on the defendant's premises. The plaintiff was thus acting under a constraint, and not simply as a volunteer, and could recover his money. |

A second limitation is that the *defendant* must have been under a legal obligation to pay the money. In *Exall v Partridge* for example, the obligation on the defendant was to pay his rent. In *Metropolitan Police District Receiver v Croydon Corporation* (1956), however, the plaintiff failed to satisfy this requirement. A policeman had been injured and could not work, but the plaintiffs, the police authority, were obliged to continue to pay his wages. The policeman sued the defendants for negligence, and recovered compensation. This did not, however, contain any element for loss of wages, since the policeman was still being paid by the plaintiffs. The plaintiffs sought to recover the cost of the policeman's wages from the defendants. Their argument was that they had made payments to the policemen which were the responsibility of the defendants, since it was their negligence which had caused the policeman to be off work. The court, however, took the view that the defendants had no legal obligation to pay the policeman's wages. Their only obligation was to compensate him for his losses. Since he had lost no wages, there was no legal obligation in this respect, and therefore the plaintiffs could not recover.

| **14.3** | **Recovery of compensation for a benefit** | The plaintiff, rather than paying money to the defendant, may have done work, or provided some other benefit. Since, by definition, any compensation for such a benefit is not defined by any agreement between the parties, the plaintiff will be |

seeking compensation on a *quantum meruit* basis. This means, the payment of an amount equivalent to the value of the benefit conferred. An analogy may be drawn with the remedy under s 1(3) of the Law Reform (Frustrated Contracts) Act 1943, which empowers the court to award a sum that is just and reasonable in all the circumstances on the basis of the benefit received by the other party (see above, para 11.5.2). There are three situations to consider, namely where a contract has been broken; where it is void; and where agreement is never reached.

A broken contract will not usually give rise to consideration of a *quantum meruit* remedy, but an example of how it can be appropriate can be seen in *Planché v Colburn* (1831) (see also para 12.2.4). The plaintiff had been engaged to write a book on Costume and Ancient Armour. He carried out research, and did some of the writing. The defendants then abandoned the project. There were some further negotiations to try to renew the contract, but these failed, and the plaintiff then sued for breach of contract, and for a *quantum meruit*. The action for breach of contract would have been unlikely to succeed, because it appears that the original contract was 'entire' (see above, para 12.2.2), with a specific sum payable on completion of the book. The court held that, nevertheless, the plaintiff could recover on a *quantum meruit* basis, and awarded him 50 guineas.

14.3.1   Contract broken

This type of action is likely to be unusual, but is clearly available in appropriate circumstances where a contract has come to an end, and the plaintiff would otherwise be without a remedy. It is difficult to see, however, that the defendant had received any benefit from the plaintiff's work, since a half-finished book was of no use to them. This makes it difficult to fit this case within the general principle of 'unjust enrichment', since the defendants had not in fact been 'enriched'.

We have seen that money paid under a void contract is recoverable. Equally work which has been done may be compensated on a *quantum meruit* basis. In *Craven-Ellis v Canons Ltd* (1936), for example, the proper procedures were not followed in appointing the plaintiff as managing director. As a result his appointment was a nullity. Before this was discovered, however, the plaintiff rendered services for the company in accordance with the agreement which he thought had been entered into. Since the company had benefited from this work he was allowed to recover on a *quantum meruit* claim. This enabled him to claim reasonable remuneration for the work which he had done.

14.3.2   Contract void

14.3.3	Agreement never reached	It is not uncommon in relation to complex contracts, such as those entered into in the building or engineering industries, for work to be done on a project prior to the formalisation of a contract. Although an 'agreement to agree' will not be enforced (*Courtney & Fairbairn v Tolaini Bros (Hotels) Ltd* (1975)), no particular problem arises with this as long a contract does materialise at some point. The Court of Appeal's decision in *Percy Trentham Ltd v Archital Luxfer Ltd* (1993) (discussed above, para 2.6.5) confirms that in such a situation the courts will be happy to allow the eventual contract to act retrospectively, and govern the work that has been done. Moreover, that decision has also relaxed to some extent the rules concerning formation, making it more likely that a binding contract will be found. Nevertheless, there will still be situations where no contract exists, and it becomes necessary to decide whether, and if so on what basis, compensation can be recovered for work that has been done. (The position as regards money paid will be governed by the rules discussed above, para 14.2).
14.3.4	Principles governing recovery	Two principles seem to govern this area. First, recovery will be allowed where the work has been requested by the defendant. Secondly, if the work has been done without a request, but has been 'freely accepted', it seems likely that the defendant will be expected to pay something for it. In *William Lacey (Hounslow) Ltd v Davis* (1957) the plaintiffs had submitted the lowest tender for a building contract, and had been led to believe that they would be awarded it. At the defendant's request they then prepared various plans and estimates. The defendants then decided not to proceed. The court argued by analogy from *Craven-Ellis v Canons* (1936) (above, para 14.3.2). If it was possible to recover in relation to work done on a void contract, Barry J thought that the same should be true of:

> '... work done which was to be paid for out of the proceeds of a contract which both parties erroneously believed was about to be made. In neither case was the work done gratuitously, and in both cases the party from whom the payment was sought requested the work and obtained the benefit of it.'

The plaintiffs were therefore allowed to recover a reasonable sum for the work done.

This line was followed in *British Steel Corp v Cleveland Bridge and Engineering Co Ltd* (1984). The project in this case was for the construction and delivery of a set of cast-steel nodes. A 'letter of intent' was issued by the defendants, indicating that they intended to enter into the contract with the plaintiffs. The defendants then requested the plaintiffs to start work on the construction of the nodes. It proved impossible to reach agreement, however, on a number of major terms, including the price. Despite this, all the nodes were eventually constructed and delivered, though some were delivered late. The plaintiffs claimed for the value of the nodes. It was clear that there was no contract. On the other hand, the defendants had requested the work to be done, and had freely accepted the nodes when they were delivered. As a result the plaintiffs were able to succeed in a restitutionary claim for the value of what had been supplied. It should be noted, however, that the defendants' counterclaim for compensation for late delivery failed. Since there was no contract there could be no obligations concerning the date for delivery, and therefore there was no basis on which such a claim could succeed. This indicates that although the remedy of restitution does allow the courts to avoid unjust enrichment, it is not sufficiently flexible as yet to allow the courts to take into consideration all the circumstances, and distribute losses and benefits between the parties accordingly.

Quasi-Contract and Restitution

Quasi-contract and restitution provide remedies where money or property has changed hands, or benefits have been provided, but a contract has failed to come into existence, or has been avoided (eg for mistake). It is based on principle that the law should provide remedies against 'unjust enrichment': Lord Wright *Fibrosa Spolka Akcynja v Fairbairn Lawson Combe Barbour* (1943).

Nature of the concepts

There are three bases for the recovery of money:

Recovery of money

- Total failure of consideration

  This ground for recovery was recognised in the *Fibrosa* case. It has been applied in the sale of goods act area, with controversial results: *Rowland v Divall* (1923); *Butterworth v Kingsway Motors* (1954). Any partial performance will prevent a claim on this basis: *Hunt v Silk* (1804).

- Mistake of fact

  There must be a mistake as to a fact which if true would have involved a legal or moral obligation to pay (*Aiken v Short* (1856); *Larner v LCC* (1949)), or at least is very serious. Contracts void for common mistake will fall within this. Note also its use in relation to insurance contracts - eg *Kelly v Solari* (1841).

- Payment to a third party for the defendant's benefit

  The payment must be made under some constraint: *Macclesfield Corporation v Great Central Railway* (1911) (no constraint, therefore no recovery); *Exall v Partridge* (1799) (payment to protect plaintiff's property; recovery allowed). The *defendant* must have been legally bound to pay the money: *Metropolitan Police District Receiver v Croydon Corporation* (1956).

This will involve a *quantum meruit* claim for work done.

Recovery of compensation for a benefit

- Contract broken

  A restitutionary remedy may be appropriate where there has been a breach of an entire contract towards which work has been done: *Planché v Colburn* (1831).

- Contract void

  Work done on a contract which is void can be compensated for: *Craven-Ellis v Canons Ltd* (1936).

- Agreement never reached

  The courts will not enforce an 'agreement to agree': *Courtney & Fairbairn v Tolaini Bros (Hotels) Ltd* (1975). Some recovery will be allowed, however, for work which has been done at the request of the defendant, or which has been freely accepted by the defendant: *William Lacey (Hounslow) Ltd v Davis* (1957). See also *British Steel Corp v Cleveland Bridge and Engineering Co Ltd* (1984) where work was done on the strength of a 'letter of intent' from the defendant.

Chapter 15

Agency

The concept of the agent is a useful one in the law of contract, but not all that easy to define. For our purposes we may take it as referring to the situation where one person (the agent) has the power to bring another person (the principal) into a contractual relationship with a third party. (Throughout this chapter the 'third party' will be used to refer to a person who deals with an agent.)

It is important to remember that to describe someone as an agent is to identify a *relationship* and not a *job*. Thus, although many agents will be appointed and described as such, many other 'agents' have this status simply from the responsibilities which arise out of their employment. The shop assistant who deals with customers is in that situation acting as agent for the owner of the shop. The company director who makes a contract on behalf of an incorporated company is equally acting as an agent. The company has a separate legal personality, but of course cannot itself physically make contracts. It has to act through human agents.

It quickly becomes apparent that the concept of agency is of vital importance in all areas of commercial activity. Without it, dealings would become cumbersome, expensive, and impractical.

Because the central core of agency is the relationship that it denotes, the labels used by the parties are of only minor significance. If a person is described as an 'agent' this many well indicate that he or she has authority to bind his or her principal, but it does not necessarily do so. The point was considered in *Lamb & Sons v Goring Brick Company* (1932). The GBC were manufacturers of bricks and other building materials. Lamb & Sons were builders' merchants. An agreement was made under which Lamb were appointed 'sole selling agents' of GBC's bricks and other materials. Following a change of ownership of GBC it became important to establish the exact effect of this agreement. The Court of Appeal held that it did not create a relationship of agency. The arrangement was that GBC sold its bricks to Lamb, and that Lamb then sold them on to others. In a true agency relationship Lamb, as agent, would simply have brought GBC into a contractual relationship with the purchasers, and would not themselves have bought and sold the bricks.

15.1 The concept of 'agency'

15.1.1   Relevance of labels

15.1.2	Relationship to doctrine of privity	In some situations agency operates as an exception to the doctrine of privity. This is particularly so where the agent contracts on behalf of an undisclosed principal. In other words, the third party thinks that he or she is contracting with the agent in person, whereas in fact there is a principal standing behind the agent, who will step in and take over the contract. This, as far as the third party is concerned, is an exception to the general principle that only those who are parties to a contract can have rights and liabilities under it. Moreover, the concept of agency can be used to circumvent the restrictions of privity. In *New Zealand Shipping Co v Satterthwaite* (1974), for example (above, para 4.10.2), the carriers were deemed to be the agents of the stevedores in order to create a contract between the stevedores and the owners, and thus give the stevedores the protection of an exclusion clause set out in the contract between the owners and the carriers.

15.2   Creation of agency

Agency can be created in a variety of ways. The three principal ones are express agreement; implied agreement; and operation of law. The agent may be appointed generally, to make contracts on behalf of the principal in a range of situations, or simply to act in connection with one particular project.

15.2.1	Express agreement	Subject to the limitations indicated by *Lamb v Goring Brick Company*, there are no particular problems with this way of creating agency. No special formalities are required, and the agreement does not even need to constitute a contract. Even where the agent has the power to make agreements which have to be in writing (such as contracts for the sale of land), the appointment does not have to be in writing.

The one exception to this is where the agent is to have power to execute a deed, for example a conveyance of land. In that situation the agency itself must be created by deed, generally known as a power of attorney.

15.2.2	Implied agreement	The courts here profess to be looking for the intentions of the parties, and if they think that they intended to create an agency relationship, then that will be given effect. As is usual in contract law, the intention will be determined by an objective consideration of what the parties have said or done. We have already noted one situation where the courts implied agency, that is, in *New Zealand Shipping Co v Satterthwaite* (1974). It may well be thought, however, that although the parties probably did intend that the stevedores should be able to take the benefit of the exclusion clause, it is much more dubious whether they intended to achieve this by means of the concept of agency. A similar pragmatic approach to the

implication of agency may perhaps also be seen in *Heatons Transport (St Helens) Ltd v Transport and General Workers Union* (1972) where shop stewards were deemed to be agents of the union, and thus rendered the union responsible for their unlawful continuance of industrial action.

Agency can be imposed by law, irrespective of the intentions of the parties in three ways, that is, by statute, by necessity, or from cohabitation

15.2.3   Operation of law

An example of agency created by statute is to be found in s 56(2) of the Consumer Credit Act 1974, which has the effect of making a dealer who negotiates with a customer to arrange a credit transaction, such as a hire purchase arrangement, the agent of the finance company for the purpose of such negotiations. (This reversed the common law position as stated in *Branwhite v Worcester Works Finance* (1969), which made the dealer the agent of the *customer*.)

Agency of necessity arises chiefly in relation to shipping contracts. Thus if a cargo is in danger of perishing, the master of the ship will have the power to sell it, or even jettison it (*The Gratitudine* (1801)). Similarly, if the ship itself is in urgent need of repairs, the master may incur expenses towards this, or even sell the ship to raise the money to carry out the work (*Gunn v Roberts* (1874)). The Court of Appeal's decision in *The Choko Star* (1990) emphasised the exceptional nature of agency of necessity, and the fact that it would only arise where the 'agent' was unable to receive instructions from the 'principal'. Modern communications make it rare that such instructions will be unobtainable, and thus the scope for this type of agency seems greatly reduced.

Agency from cohabitation is presumed wherever a man and woman are living together in a household (not a hotel - *Debenham v Mellon* (1880)), whether or not they are married. It will entitle the woman to pledge the man's credit in order to purchase 'necessaries'(*cf* the position in relation to minors' contracts, above, para 5.2.1). In *Miss Gray Ltd v Earl Cathcart* (1922) the presumption was said to be rebuttable by the issue of an express warning to traders; by the fact that the woman was already adequately supplied, or had a sufficient allowance, or had been specifically forbidden to pledge the man's credit; or if the order was extravagant. Given these limitations, the practical application of this type of agency seems very limited.

The power that an agent has to bind the principal depends on the agent's authority. There are three types of authority to be considered: express, implied, and ostensible.

15.3   **The powers of an agent**

15.3.1	Express authority

The limits of the agent's authority may well be expressly established by the agreement between the principal and agent. This may occur when the relationship is first established, or may change over time. The principal will generally be entitled at any time to alter the agent's authority, provided that this does not conflict with any contractual agreement between them. The third party will be bound by the limits of the agent's express authority, as long as he or she is aware of them. If the third party does not know of certain limitations, and contracts outside them, then issues of implied or ostensible authority, or ratification, may arise. This will also be the case if the agreement between principal and agent is silent, or unclear, as to the extent of the agent's authority.

15.3.2	Implied authority

Implied authority derives either from the type of work which the agent is doing, or the place where the agent is working. The first category will be referred to here as 'usual authority', that is the authority 'usually' attaching to a particular job. The second category will be labelled 'customary' authority, in that it will arise out of the customs of a particular place of business.

A classic, though not unproblematic, example of usual authority is to be found in *Watteau v Fenwick* (1893). The defendant owned a beerhouse and employed a manager, who had authority to buy goods for the business. The manager was under express instructions, however, not to buy cigars, as these would be supplied by the defendant. The manager bought cigars on credit from the plaintiff. The plaintiff sued the defendant for the price of the cigars. It was held that, since the plaintiff was unaware of the express limitation, and since it was within the usual authority of a manager of a beerhouse to order goods of this type, the defendant was liable.

The decision may be contrasted with *Daun v Simmins* (1879) where it was held that the manager of a 'tied' public house would normally only have authority to buy spirits from a particular source. The supplier in this case could not rely on an implied usual authority in order to sue the principal.

The main issue here is therefore one of fact. What exactly is the usual authority of this particular type of agent, and was the third party aware of any express limits on it?

The controversial aspect of *Watteau v Fenwick* is that the third party was unaware that he was dealing with an agent, and it is not at all clear that the usual authority should be allowed to operate in the situation of an undisclosed principal - see *Rhodian River Shipping Co SA v Halla Maritime Corpn* (1984).

Customary authority operates to authorise the agent to act according to the usages or customs of a particular place or market. Thus in *Scott v Godfrey* (1901) a custom of the Stock Exchange allowed a stockbroker to act as agent for several principals at once in buying shares from one seller, thus bringing each principal into a separate contractual relationship with the seller.

Ostensible authority involves the principal having, by words or action, led the third party to believe that the agent has authority, when in fact the agent does not. It is also sometimes referred to as 'apparent authority' or 'agency by estoppel'.

15.3.3   Ostensible authority

The requirements for its existence were set out in *Rama Corporation Ltd v Proved Tin and General Investments Ltd* (1952). Slade J said that ostensible authority was a kind of estoppel, and that therefore what was needed was:

'(i)   a representation,

(ii) a reliance on the representation, and

(iii) an alteration of your position resulting from such reliance.'

The precise nature of the representation required was expanded on by Diplock LJ in *Freeman & Lockyer v Buckhurst Properties (Mangal) Ltd* (1964) in the following passage:

'... "ostensible" authority ... is a legal relationship between the principal and the contractor created by a representation, *made by the principal to the contractor*, intended to be and in fact acted upon by the contractor, that the agent has authority to enter on behalf of the principal into a contract of a kind within the scope of the "apparent" authority so as to render the principal liable to perform any obligations imposed upon him by such a contract.' (Emphasis added.)

Moreover, the agent 'must not purport to make the agreement as principal himself'.

The 'representation' may come from conduct rather than a statement. In *Summers v Solomon* (1857), for example, it came from the conduct of the principal in allowing the agent to buy goods for his jewellery business. When the agent was dismissed, the ostensible authority created by this conduct survived, and a third party who was unaware of the termination of the agency was allowed to recover from the principal the price of jewellery with which the agent had absconded. Similarly in *Lloyd v Grace, Smith & Co* (1912), the representation came from the fact that a firm of solicitors had allowed a clerk to carry out conveyancing work without supervision. The firm was liable when the clerk acted fraudulently in relation to the third party.

As the quotation by Diplock given above makes clear, the representation must emanate from the principal, not the agent. This was confirmed in *Armagas v Mundogas* (1986), where the agent, a chartering manager, falsely represented that he had authority for a particular transaction involving the sale and lease-back of a ship. The third party could not enforce the transaction against the principal, since the principal had not made any representation of authority.

The other two requirements for ostensible authority noted by Slade J are more easily dealt with. That of reliance simply means that the third party will not be able to plead ostensible authority if he or she was not aware of the representation, or did not actually believe that the agent had authority, or ought to have known that the agent's authority was limited: *Overbrooke Estates Ltd v Glencombe Properties* (1974). The requirement of an 'alteration of position' will be satisfied in the context in which we are discussing agency by the fact that the third party has entered into a contract.

15.4   Ratification

Where an agent enters into an authorised contract, the principal may be happy to adopt it. This can be done by the process of ratification. For ratification to be available, however, the agent must purport to act on behalf of a principal, the principal must be in existence at the time of the contract, and the principal must have capacity.

15.4.1   Agent must purport to act for a principal

Ratification is not available where the principal is undisclosed. The third party must know that there is, or is supposed to be, a principal in the background. If the third party thinks that the agent is acting on his or her own account, no later ratification will be possible: *Keighley Maxted & Co v Durant* (1901). In this case the agent had made a contract at a higher price than that which his principal had authorised. The principal later purported to ratify this unauthorised act. The House of Lords held that he could not, because the agent had not disclosed to the third party that he was acting on behalf of someone else.

Provided, however, that the agent mentions the principal, it does not matter that the agent is in fact intending to act independently. In *Re Tiedemann and Ledermann Freres* (1899), the agent acted in the principal's name in relation to a sale which he in fact intended to be for his own benefit. The third party then tried to rescind the contract on the basis of the misrepresentation as to whom he was contracting with. The principal, however, ratified the contract, and this prevented the third party from rescinding it.

This issue arises mainly in relation to contracts made on behalf of new companies which are being formed. In *Kelner v Baxter* (1866) it was held that if the company was not in existence, that is, it had not been incorporated, at the time of the contract, it could not later ratify the agreement. The purported 'agents', the promoters of the company, were therefore personally liable. Such personal liability is now imposed by statute, by virtue of s 36C of the Companies Act 1985.

15.4.2   Principal must have been in existence

There are in theory two aspects to this rule. The first is that the principal must have capacity to make the transaction at the time of the contract. This has most obvious relevance to minors, who might want to ratify after reaching majority. It could also apply to contracts made outside the powers of a company. Both these situations have now been affected by statutory provisions, however, namely the Minors Contracts Act 1987 (above, para 5.3.1), and the Companies Act 1985, s 36, which means that this aspect of the rule is of little practical significance.

15.4.3   Principal must have capacity

The second aspect is that the principal must have capacity at the time of ratification. This was applied in *Grover & Grover v Matthews* (1910). A contract of fire insurance was purported to be ratified after a fire had destroyed the property which was the subject of the insurance. It was held that this was ineffective, because at the time of the purported ratification the principal could not have made the contract himself (because the property no longer existed). 'Capacity' is thus being given a rather broader meaning than usual, to cover the issue as to whether the principal would have in practice been able to make the contract in question.

Ratification is retrospective in its effect, and the original contract must be treated as if it had been authorised from the start. The implications of this are clear from the decision in *Bolton Partners v Lambert* (1889). Bolton Partners owned a factory, which Lambert offered to buy. This offer was accepted by the managing director, though in fact he had no authority to do this. On 13 January there was a disagreement, and Lambert withdrew his offer. On 17 January Bolton Partners started proceedings for breach of contract. On 28 January, the Board of Directors of Bolton Partners ratified the actions of the managing director. Lambert argued that this ratification came too late, but the Court of Appeal held that it had retrospectively validated the original contract, and that Lambert's attempt to withdraw was therefore ineffective.

15.4.4   Effect of ratification

Despite the considerable leeway granted by this decision it has subsequently been held that the ratification must take place within a reasonable time of the acceptance, and certainly before the contract has been performed: *Metropolitan Asylums Board Managers v Kingham & Sons* (1890). Moreover, if the contract has been specifically stated to be 'subject to ratification' a withdrawal prior to ratification will be effective: *Watson v Davies* (1931).

15.5   Duties of the agent

An agent has a duty to carry out instructions, to act with due care and skill, and to act personally rather than through another. In addition the agent has various fiduciary duties.

15.5.1   Carry out instructions

An agent is obliged to do anything which the agreement creating the agency binds him or her to do. In *Fraser v Furman* (1967) an agent failed to take out an insurance policy on behalf of some employers, who, as a result were liable to compensate an injured employee. The agent was held liable to re-imburse the employer.

An agent is also under a duty not to exceed the authority granted by the principal. We have already considered the issue of authority as it effects the third party. At this point we are looking at the express and implied authority as between principal and agent. Express authority needs no discussion. Implied authority will arise from the relationship, and will include authority to take all actions necessarily incidental to the purposes for which the agent has been engaged. The authority as between principal and agent may not be identical with that between agent and third party, as is shown by the following quotation from *Waugh v Clifford* (1982). Note that 'implied authority' is here used to refer to the authority as between principal and agent . Brightman J said that if in a defamation action, the defendant's solicitor offered £100,000 in settlement:

> 'It would in my view be officious on the part of the plaintiff's solicitor to demand to be satisfied as to the authority of the defendant's solicitor to make the offer. It is perfectly clear that the defendant's solicitor has *ostensible* authority to compromise the action on behalf of his client, notwithstanding the large sum involved ... But it does not follow that the defendant's solicitor would have *implied* authority to agree to damages on that scale without the agreement of his client. In the light of the solicitor's knowledge of his client's cash position it might be quite unreasonable and indeed grossly negligent for the solicitor to commit his client to such a burden without first inquiring if it were acceptable ... It follows in my view that a solicitor (or counsel) may in a particular case have ostensible authority vis-à-vis the opposing litigant where he has no implied authority vis-à-vis his client.'

Thus an agent may be able to bind the principal to a contract with the third party, but at the same time be in breach of the duty to carry out instructions.

The degree of care and skill required of an agent will depend on the circumstances. The agent must act with the skill which an agent in his or her position would normally possess. Thus a solicitor or accountant must act with the skill to be expected of someone qualified in that profession. The standard is one of 'reasonable care' in that context.

15.5.2   Must act with due care and skill

If the agent is not acting for reward, then this duty will be applied less strictly.

The agent is normally expected to act personally on behalf of the principal. Delegation of the agent's responsibilities will only be permissible where this has been authorised, expressly or impliedly, by the principal: *De Bussche v Alt* (1878). Where there is authority to delegate, then the sub-agent will take over the agent's duties, and will be directly liable to the principal for any breach of them. Thus in *De Bussche v Alt* the sub-agent made a secret profit (see below, para 15.5.5) from dealing with the principal's property, and had to account for this to the principal.

15.5.3   Non-delegation

The agent must not put him or herself into a position where there is a conflict between the duties owed to the principal and the agent's own interests. In *Armstrong v Jackson* (1917) a stockbroker sold his own shares to a client. This was held to involve a conflict of interest:

15.5.4   Fiduciary duties: conflict of interest

> 'As vendor it is to his interest to sell his own shares at the highest price. As broker it is his clear duty to the principal to buy at the lowest price and to give unbiased and independent advice ... as to the time when and the price at which shares shall be bought.'

As a result the principal was entitled to rescind the contract, and this was available irrespective of any of the normal bars to rescission for misrepresentation (see Chapter 8, para 8.3.1).

The agent will not be liable, however, if the principal is fully aware of the position. In *Harrods v Lemon* (1931) one department of the plaintiffs was acting as estate agents for the defendant, Mrs Lemon, and another department as surveyors for a person who was seeking to buy her house. There was a clear conflict of interest, but Mrs Lemon continued with the contract with full knowledge of the facts. Harrods were entitled to their commission.

15.5.5	Fiduciary duties: secret profits and bribes	An agent who makes a secret profit out of his or her position will be liable to account for this (ie hand it over) to the principal (as in *De Bussche v Alt* (1878)).

Equally the agent must not take a 'bribe', which was defined in *Industries & General Mortgage v Lewis* (1949) as involving:

(a) a payment made, or to be made, to the agent by the third party;

(b) knowledge by the third party that the agent is acting as an agent;

(c) failure by the third party to disclose the payment to the agent to the principal.

If these three conditions are satisfied the payment will be treated as a bribe. There is no need to show any fraudulent intent on the part of anyone involved.

The effects of a bribe being given are that the agent may be dismissed, and the principal may sue the agent and the third party in tort for any loss caused by the bribe. Alternatively, the principal may recover the amount of the bribe from the agent, or from the third party, if not yet paid: *Mahesan v Malaysia Government Officers' Co-operative Housing Society Ltd* (1979). If the bribe is paid over, the principal is still entitled to set aside the transaction to which it related: *Logicrose Ltd v Southend United Football Club Ltd* (1988).

15.6 Duties of the principal

The main duty of the principal is to pay the agent for the work that has been done. The agent's right to be paid will exist wherever this can be either expressly or impliedly taken to arise from their agreement. Where there is a written agreement the courts will look at this very carefully in deciding whether the agent is entitled to payment. Thus in *Taylor v Brewer* (1813) the agreement referred to the principal paying 'such remuneration ... as shall be deemed right'. It was held that this did not entitle the agent to reasonable remuneration, or indeed to any payment at all. It was entirely at the discretion of the principal. Similarly, in *John Meacock v Abrahams* (1956) the fact that the contract provided for payment in certain circumstances (which had not arisen) precluded the agent from claiming on a *quantum meruit* basis.

15.6.1 When is payment earnt?

If it is decided that the agreement does allow for payment, when will it be earnt? As would be expected, this will be when the agent has done what he or she has been employed to do. The difficulty arises, however, in deciding in some cases whether this has occurred. In one of the leading cases, for example, *Luxor (Eastbourne) Ltd v Cooper* (1941), a company wished to sell some cinemas, and Cooper agreed to try to provide a purchaser. He was to be paid 'on completion of the sale'. Cooper provided a willing purchaser, but the company withdrew from the sale. The House of Lords refused to imply a term that the principal would not unreasonably prevent the completion of the transaction. The clause referred to payment 'on completion'; since that had not occurred the agent was not entitled to his commission. The way around this is for the agent to insist that the commission should be earnt by providing someone 'ready, willing and able' to purchase. This was held to be effective to entitle the agent to his commission in *Christie Owen & Davies v Rapacioli* (1974).

Here again, the approach is to look very carefully at the wording of the agreement, and to apply it strictly.

Where the principal is 'disclosed', ie the third party knows who the principal is, or at least is aware that the agent is acting for a principal, the basic rule is that the agent will drop out of the transaction. The third party will be able to sue the principal, and vice versa. Where the principal is undisclosed, however, the position is more complex.	**15.7 Position of third party vis-à-vis principal**

As has been noted above, the fact that an undisclosed principal is allowed to take over a contract from an agent runs counter to the general doctrine of privity. It means that the third party will find that he or she has rights against, and liabilities towards, a person with whom there was not intention to contract, and of whom the third party had no knowledge at the time of the contract. This rather unusual concept has been limited by two requirements: first, that the terms of the contract should be consistent with an agency relationship; secondly, that no personal considerations should militate against allowing the principal to take over the contract.

15.7.1 Undisclosed principal

If an undisclosed principal is going to step in, this must be consistent with the terms of the contract. In *Humble v Hunter* (1848), for example, the alleged 'agent' who had entered into a charter of a boat, was described in the documentation as 'owner'. It was held that this designation was inconsistent with his acting as an agent, and so the court refused to allow an alleged undisclosed principal to take over the contract. In *Fred Drughorn Ltd v Rederiaktiebolaget Transatlantic* (1919), however, the description of a party as 'charterer' rather than 'owner' was held not to preclude an undisclosed principal from stepping into the agent's place.

15.7.2 Consistency with contract

15.7.3	Personal considerations

If the character of the person with whom he or she is contracting is an important consideration for the third party, an undisclosed principal may be prevented from suing on the contract. For example, in *Collins v Associated Greyhound Racecourses* (1930) the Court of Appeal held that the identity of the underwriters of shares in a new company was crucial, because the company needed to be sure that they were 'responsible persons'. If the underwriters failed then the company would be in financial difficulties. There was no scope in this situation for an undisclosed principal.

The concerns need not relate to financial solvency. In *Said v Butt* (1920) a person had arranged for someone else to buy him a ticket for the first night of a play, when he knew that the manager would not have sold him one. It was held that since at first nights the manager traditionally exercises control over the audience, the 'principal' should not be allowed to use the ticket acquired by his 'agent'. On the other hand, if the contract is not of a type to which personal considerations are relevant, the fact that there is personal animosity between the principal and third party will not be a bar to their being brought together by an agent, without the third party's knowledge. This was the case in *Dyster v Randall* (1926) which concerned the sale of a piece of land. The personal considerations were held to be immaterial to this contract.

15.7.4	Liability of principal

The third party will, of course, have rights against the principal (whether disclosed or undisclosed) in the same way as any other contracting party. Problems may arise, however, where payment to the third party is to be made via the agent. If the principal pays the agent, but the agent fails to pass this on, can the third party still sue the principal? In *Armstrong v Stokes* (1872) it was held that if the third party was unaware that the other party was dealing as agent, and the principal paid the agent in good faith while the third party was still giving credit to the agent, the third party could not then recover from the principal. This case suggests, then that the third party cannot recover from the principal if the principal has paid the agent. The court, however, clearly limited its views to the facts before it, and did not express an opinion as to what the situation would be if:

(a) the principal was disclosed; or

(b) if the principal had a set-off against the agent.

The first situation was considered by the Court of Appeal in *Irvine v Watson* (1880) where it was held that even though a disclosed principal had paid the agent, the third party could still recover from the principal. The only exception would be where the third party had acted in such a way as to lead the principal to believe that the agent had paid the third party.

The second situation (ie that of set-off by the principal against the agent) does not seem to have been judicially considered. The reverse situation, ie a set-off between agent and third party was considered in *Cooke v Eshelby* (1887). The House of Lords held that the third party could not plead a set-off against the agent in an action by the principal, unless the principal had acted so as to induce the third party to believe that the agent was contracting as principal. By analogy it would seem to follow that in an action by the third party against the principal, the principal would not be able to rely on a set-off against the agent.

The general rule, as has been stated above, is that the agent drops out, and has no liability under, or power to enforce, the contract between the principal and third party. In some situations, however, the third party may be able to sue the agent. The dominant issue is the intention of the parties. According to Brandon J in *The Swan* (1968) this is to be determined from

15.8 Position of third party vis-à-vis the agent

(a) the nature of the contract;

(b) its terms;

(c) the surrounding circumstances.

The test is objective, based on:

'what two reasonable businessmen making a contract of that nature, in those terms, and in those surrounding circumstances, must be taken to have intended.'

Relevant factors may include the way in which the agent has signed the contract. If the signature indicates that it is signed on behalf of someone else, then this will suggest the agent is not liable. Custom or trade usage may also suggest that the agent may have some liability or rights under the contract.

In *The Swan* itself the relevant surrounding circumstances included the fact that the agent was also the owner of the boat, which was chartered to a company of which the agent was the major shareholder. The company, via the agent, ordered repair work to be done by the third party. It was held that since the repairers knew that the agent was also the owner, it was natural for them to assume that he would accept personal liability for the repairs.

15.8.1   Position where there is no principal

There are two situations to consider here. First, it may be that the agent is in fact the principal, and is just pretending to be an agent. In this situation the agent will certainly be liable on any contract, and will also be able to enforce, unless the third party would thereby be prejudiced (eg if there were personal considerations involved (*cf* above, para 15.7.3)).

Secondly, the principal may not be in existence, eg because it is a company which has not yet been formed. The position is now largely governed by statute, ie Companies Act 1985, s 36C(1). This states that:

> 'A contract which purports to be made by or on behalf of a company at a time when the company has not been formed has effect, subject to any agreement to the contrary, as one made with the person purporting to act for the company or as agent for it, and he is personally liable on the contract accordingly.'

This is very clear as regards the agent's *liability*. It is not specific as to whether the agent would also be able to enforce against the third party. The Court of Appeal (in *Phonogram v Lane* (1981)) has, however, indicated a willingness to interpret the section broadly, in line with its purpose, and this suggests that the agent would be allowed to sue the third party in such a situation. Earlier authorities, such as *Newborne v Sensolid* (1954) which turned on narrow interpretations of the precise form of signature used, must now be regarded as of dubious authority.

15.8.2   Right of election

If the third party can sue either the principal or the agent, at what stage does a choice have to be made as to who to pursue? Judgment cannot be enforced against both, but what if, for example, the principal is sued, but turns out to be unable to pay. Can the third party at that stage act against the agent?

The rules are not very clear, but the Civil Liability (Contribution) Act 1978, s 3, has established that (contrary to the previous position) obtaining judgment against one party is not an automatic bar to suing the other. The test in all cases now seems to be whether the third party has 'elected' to sue one party or the other. The case of *Clarkson Booker Ltd v Andjel* (1964) said that this was a question of fact not law. What was required was a 'truly unequivocal act' taken with 'full knowledge of all the facts'. Clearly a choice exercised at a time when the third party was unaware that the selected defendant was insolvent would not be taken with 'full knowledge'. Otherwise, however, the court seemed to feel that the institution of proceedings would raise a *prima facie* case of election. It is not an area, however, about which it is possible to state any propositions with any degree of certainty.

It may be possible for the third party to take action against the agent on the basis of a collateral contract. This will be particularly appropriate as regards pre-contractual statements or promises which the agent may have made. An example is *Andrews v Hopkinson* (1957) where a dealer told the plaintiff that a car being bought on hire-purchase terms was 'a good little bus. I would stake my life on it.' When the car later turned out to be seriously defective, the plaintiff was allowed to recover on the basis of a collateral contract.

15.8.3   Collateral contract

The final way in which the agent may be liable to a third party is for breach of the implied warranty of authority. Any agent who purports to act as such impliedly warrants that he or she has the required authority to enter into the contract. If this turns out to be untrue, the third party may sue. The remedy is less satisfactory than in an action for breach of contract, however, in that recovery will be limited to whatever the third party would have been able to obtain from the principal. If the principal is insolvent this may be very little.

15.8.4   Implied warranty
of authority

The remedy exists, however, irrespective of whether the warranty is fraudulent, negligent, or innocent: *Collen v Wright* (1857). It has even been held to be available where, unknown to the agent, the principal had become a certified lunatic, and therefore the agent's authority automatically terminated: *Yonge v Toynbee* (1910).

Agency may be brought to an end either by the act of the parties, or by operation of law.

15.9   Termination of
agency

Where the agency was created by agreement it will be determinable in the same way. A continuing agency may also be determined by the giving such period of notice as is specified in any agreement, or failing that, reasonable notice. Finally, if either party acts in a way which is inconsistent with the continuation of the agency then it will be terminated - though of course this may well give rise to rights of action for breach of contract.

15.9.1   Act of the parties

If an agency is for a particular transaction, the relationship will terminate when that transaction is completed. If it is for a specified period, it will cease at the end of that period.

15.9.2   Operation of law

Agency may also be terminated by subsequent events. These may be physical, as where, for example, the subject-matter is destroyed, or the principal or agent dies, or becomes insane. Alternatively they may be legal, as where the principal or agent becomes bankrupt, or the relationship becomes illegal (if the principal becomes an enemy alien, for example).

15.10   Effects of termination

As far as principal and agent are concerned, rights vested at the time of the termination will subsist, but no new rights can be created, at least once the agent has notice of the termination.

In relation to the third party, again rights accrued against either principal or agent will remain. New rights against the principal will only arise on the basis of ostensible authority. Otherwise, the agent will be liable, either directly on the contract, or for breach of the implied warranty of authority.

Agency

Concept of agency

Agency depends on the type of relationship, not on labels: *Lamb & Sons v Goring Brick Co* (1932). It can operate as an exception to, or a way around, the doctrine of privity: *New Zealand Shipping Co v Satterthwaite* (1974).

Creation of agency

Creation of agency can be by express or implied agreement. No special formalities are required, unless the agent is to have power to execute a deed.

Agency can be created by operation of law as a result of a statutory provision (eg s 56 Consumer Credit Act 1974), necessity (eg *The Gratitudine* (1801); *The Choko Star* (1990)), or cohabitation. The presumption of agency from cohabitation is rebuttable: *Miss Gray Ltd v Earl Cathcart* (1922).

The powers of an agent

The powers of an agent may be defined by express, implied, or ostensible authority.

Implied authority can be divided into 'usual' authority, based on the type of job (eg *Watteau v Fenwick* (1893), and 'customary' authority, based on the place of business (eg *Scott v Godfrey* (1901)).

Ostensible authority requires a representation, reliance, and alteration of position: *Rama Corporation Ltd v Proved Tin and General Investment Ltd* (1952). The representation may be by conduct (eg *Summers v Solomon* (1857); *Lloyd v Grace, Smith & Co* (1912)), but must come from the principal, not the agent: *Armagas v Mundogas* (1986).

Ratification

For ratification to be possible, the agent must purport to be acting for a principal (*Keighley Maxted & Co v Durant* (1901)), the principal must have been in existence (*Kelner v Baxter* (1866)), and the principal must have capacity both at the time of contract and at the time of ratification (*Grover & Grover v Matthews* (1910)).

Ratification is retrospective: *Bolton Partners v Lambert* (1889). It must take place within a reasonable time, and before the contract has been performed: *Metropolitan Asylums Board Managers v Kingham & Sons* (1890).

Duties of the agent

The agent must carry out instructions: *Fraser v Furman* (1967). This will include things which are implied by, or incidental to, the main purpose of the agency: *Waugh v Clifford* (1982). The agent must also act with due care and skill, and not delegate without authorisation (*De Bussche v Alt* (1878)).

The agent must not get into a position where the agent's interests conflict with those of the principal: *Armstrong v Jackson* (1917). Nor must the agent take a secret profit, or bribe. The principal may recover either the bribe, or any loss suffered: *Mahesan v Malaysian Government Officers' Co-operative Housing Society Ltd* (1979).

Duties of the principal

The main duty of the principal is to pay the agent. The existence of the right to payment *(Taylor v Brewer* (1813)), and the question when payment is earnt *(Luxor (Eastbourne) Ltd v Cooper* (1941)), both depend on the terms of the agreement.

Position of third party vis-à-vis principal

Where the principal is disclosed the third party can sue, and be sued. Where undisclosed, the third party will only be liable if the terms of the contract are consistent with its being made by an agent *(Humble v Hunter* (1848)), and personal considerations are not important *(Collins v Associated Greyhound Racecourses* (1930); *Said v Butt* (1920)).

Where the principal has paid the agent, but this has not been passed on, an undisclosed principal may not be liable *(Armstrong v Stokes* (1872)), but a disclosed principal generally will be *(Irvine v Watson* (1880)).

Position of third party vis-à-vis agent

Normally the agent drops out, but sometimes there may be personal liability. This depends on an objective view of whether in all the circumstances a reasonable businessman would have expected the agent to be liable: *The Swan* (1968).

If the agent is in fact the principal, he or she will be fully liable. If the principal is an unincorporated company, then the agent will again be liable by virtue of s 36C(1) Companies Act 1985, and will probably be able to sue as well: *Phonogram v Lane* (1981).

If third party can sue either principal or agent, an election to sue one will preclude action against the other: *Clarkson Booker Ltd v Andjel* (1964).

The agent may also be liable on a collateral contract *(Andrews v Hopkinson* (1957)), or for breach of the implied warranty of authority *(Collen v Wright* (1857); *Yonge v Toynbee* (1910)).

Termination of agency

Agency may be brought to an end by the agreement of the parties, notice, or by breach of the original agreement. It may also be terminated by operation of law, or the destruction of the subject-matter, or the death or bankruptcy of either party.

Effects of termination are that rights vested at the time will subsist. No new rights can be created, other than by ostensible authority.

Chapter 16

Sale of Goods

16.1   Definition

Every contract for the sale of goods, be it for a packet of tea in a supermarket, or for goods worth many thousands of pounds between two large companies, is governed by the Sale of Goods Act 1979. (Note however, that international sales may be subject to different rules). Throughout this chapter, unless otherwise stated, section numbers refer to the 1979 Act.

Section 2(1) of the 1979 Act defines a contract for the sale of goods as a:

> '... contract by which the seller transfers or agrees to transfer the property in goods to the buyer for a money consideration, called the price.'

Note that there must be at least partial money consideration. An exchange of goods is not within the scope of the Act. Nor does the Act cover other similar contracts which may transfer the possession or ownership of goods, such as hire, hire purchase, or contracts for work and materials. These types of contract are controlled by other statutes, principally the Consumer Credit Act 1974, and the Supply of Goods and Services Act 1982. If A engages B to build a wall, for example, the bricks which make up the wall will become A's property. The contract is for work and materials, however, and so is not governed by the Sale of Goods Act. It will, however, be to some extent controlled by the Supply and of Goods and Services Act 1982, for example as regards implied terms as to the quality of the bricks.

16.1.1   Agreements to sell

Section 2(5) distinguishes 'sales' from 'agreements to sell'. Whereas under a sale the property in the goods is transferred at the time of the contract, if this is to take place at some point in the future the contract is an agreement to sell.

16.2   Passing of property

The Act uses the phrase 'passing of property' to refer to what would in common parlance be called 'transfer of ownership'. It defines the moment when the buyer becomes the owner of the goods, and is very important to determine. If one party has been fraudulent, or the goods are destroyed, or the goods cause damage to a third party, it will be vital in the determining of rights and liabilities to know whether property has passed.

Before looking at the rules relating to this, it is important to emphasise that 'property' and physical 'possession' are entirely distinct as far as the law is concerned. It is quite possible for goods to become the property of the seller while still remaining in the possession of the buyer, and vice versa. Equally, the question of payment does not determine the passing of property. A person may become the owner of goods before paying for them, or may pay, yet only become the owner at some later point.

The rules relating to the passing of property are to be found in ss 16-18 of the Act.

16.2.2	Goods must be ascertained	Section 16 requires that goods must be 'ascertained' before property can pass. If there is an order for 5,000 grade 3 widgets, for example, no property will be able to pass until the particular widgets which are to comprise the order are identified or 'ascertained.'
16.2.3	Intention of the parties	Subject to s 16, the parties themselves are entirely free to decide when property is to pass. This is made clear by s.17. They are not, therefore automatically bound by any of the following rules, set out in s 18. These apply only where the intention of the parties cannot be determined from the contract itself, the parties conduct, or the surrounding circumstances. If the parties wish to express their own intention as to when property should pass, however, this must be done before or in the contract. In *Dennant v Skinner* (1948) the plaintiff sold a car by auction. The buyer wanted to pay by cheque and take the car. The plaintiff was only prepared to agree if the buyer signed a document stating that property would not pass until the cheque was cleared. The buyer signed the document, took the car, and sold it to the defendant. The cheque was not met. It was held that the expression of intention came too late, and the rules in s 18 applied, which meant that property had passed to the buyer, and then to the defendant. The plaintiff could not recover his car, but was left with his remedy against the buyer.
16.2.4	Specific goods: deliverable state	Section 18 rule 1 states that where there is an unconditional contract for the sale of specific goods in a deliverable state then property passes when the contract is made. Many shop sales will be of this kind, though it can also apply in other situations. 'Specific goods' are defined in s 61(1) as 'goods identified and agreed on at the time' of the contract. 'Deliverable state' is defined in s 61(5) as meaning that the goods 'are in such a state that the buyer would under the contract be bound to take delivery of them.'

Section 18 rule 2 says that if specific goods are not in a deliverable state at the time of the contract, then property does not pass until the seller has put them into such a state, and the buyer has notice that this has been done. If goods are loose in a warehouse, for example, and need to be packaged for delivery, then this will delay the passing of property.

16.2.5 Specific goods: not deliverable

Section 18 rule 3 deals with specific goods in a deliverable state, but which need to be weighed, measured, etc by the seller to determine the price. It may be, for example, that the contract is for an entire stock of grain which is sitting in bags in the sellers warehouse. The price may have been fixed at so much per bag, but the parties may not know precisely how many bags there are. Property will not pass until the seller has counted them, and has given the buyer notice that this has been done.

16.2.6 Specific goods: price not ascertained

Where goods are provided 'on approval', or on a 'sale or return' basis, s 18 rule 4 governs the passing of property. This states that property will pass either when the buyer signifies approval or acceptance to the seller, or when the buyer does some other act 'adopting the transaction'. Using, or reselling, the goods, would clearly come into this category. Failing any action on the part of the buyer, property will pass on the expiry of any term fixed for the return of the goods, or else at the expiry of a reasonable time.

16.2.7 Approval, or sale or return

Where the contract is for the sale of unascertained or future goods by description, s 18 rule 5 states that property will not pass until goods are 'unconditionally appropriated' to the contract. The meaning of 'ascertained' has been indicated above. Future goods are defined in s 61(1) as 'goods to be manufactured or acquired by the seller' after the making of the contract. The 'appropriation' may be done by either the seller or the buyer, but must be with the express or implied 'assent' of the other party, which can be given either before or after the appropriation. The appropriation must be unconditional. The fact that the seller has set aside goods in his or her warehouse, and has it in mind that these will be the ones to be supplied to the buyer, may well not satisfy rule 5. Although there has clearly been an appropriation, it is not 'unconditional', in that the seller could later decide to send different goods matching the contract description to the buyer. Giving the goods to a carrier will often amount to unconditional appropriation, as is recognised by rule 5(2), but will not necessarily do so. In *Healey v Howlett* (1917) the contract was for 20 boxes of mackerel. The seller handed over 170 boxes to the carrier, with instructions that 20 were to be delivered to the buyer, and the rest to other

16.2.8 Unascertained or future goods

contractors. The mackerel deteriorated in transit, and was rejected by the buyer. It was held that property had not passed to the buyer on delivery to the carrier. There was no unconditional appropriation because no specific 20 boxes had been assigned to the buyer's contract until the point where the carrier was about to deliver.

| 16.2.9 | Passing of risk |

The risk of loss or damage to the goods will generally pass at the same time as the property in the goods, according to the rules just discussed: s 20. The parties may, however, agree to a different arrangement, if they so wish.

16.3   Transfer of title

The rules we have just been considering are concerned with the point in time at which property passes, and the buyer becomes the owner. This section is concerned with the question of who may pass a good title to the buyer, and in what circumstances. The basic rule is set out in s 21(1), and states that where the goods are sold by someone who is not the true owner, then the buyer will obtain no better title than the seller. This is often referred to as the 'nemo dat' rule, this being shorthand for the Latin phrase 'nemo dat quod non habet' - no one may give what they do not have. It means, for example, that if goods are stolen, and then sold by the thief, the person who buys from the thief will be liable to re-imburse the true owner, either by returning the goods or paying compensation.

The law has long recognised however, that the innocent purchaser who buys in good faith needs some protection, and so there are various exceptions to the nemo dat rule.

16.3.1   Owner's conduct

If the owner has led the buyer to believe that the person has the right to sell, then the buyer will acquire a good title (s 21(1)). An agent might, for example, have obtained goods by fraud from his or her principal, and the principal might, before discovering the fraud, tell the buyer that the agent has the right to sell. The mere fact that the owner has allowed the seller to be in possession of the goods, however, is not enough to bring this exception into operation. A person who is in possession under a hire purchase agreement will not generally, therefore, be able to pass on a good title. Note, however, that there is special protection for the private purchasers of motor cars which are subject to hire purchase agreements, under Hire Purchase Act 1965, ss 27-29.

16.3.2   Sale by factor

Section 2 of the Factors Act 1889 provides an exception to the rule where a mercantile agent is in possession of goods, or documents of title, and is acting in the ordinary course of business. This is recognised by s 21(2)(a) of the 1979 Act.

This exception, which appears in s 21(2)(b) covers sales of goods which have been pledged, or which are the subject of a court order.

There are currently proposals to remove this rather antiquated exception, which is contained in s 22. It applies to sales at any 'open public and legally constituted market' - eg markets established by Royal Charter. It also covers sales by any shop in the City of London which deals in goods of the kind in question.

The exception of a sale under a voidable title, which is contained in s 23, deals with the situation where the original owner has sold goods under a contract which is voidable. This might be because of misrepresentation on the part of the buyer. If the goods are sold on before the contract is avoided, the new buyer will acquire a good title. The original seller thus needs to move quickly as soon as any fraud is discovered. In *Car & Universal Finance Co Ltd v Caldwell* (1964) the owner had sold a car to N in return for a cheque, which was dishonoured. The owner at once informed the police and the Automobile Association. It was held that this was sufficient to avoid the contract, in the circumstances. Since the owner had acted before N had managed to resell the car, the innocent third party who had bought it had acquired no title, and could not rely on s 23. The owner could therefore recover the car.

Where the seller has retained possession of the goods after property has passed to the buyer, the seller may 'resell' the goods to another. If the second buyer is an innocent purchaser in good faith, and without notice of the previous sale, he or she will obtain a good title: s 24. There must, however, be actual delivery of the goods, or documents of title, in order for this exception to apply.

This is the converse situation to the previous one, and is dealt with by s 25, that is, the buyer has been allowed by the seller to take possession of the goods or documents of title before property has passed, and then resells. Provided again that there is actual delivery, the new purchaser who takes in good faith and without notice will obtain a good title. In *National Employers Mutual General Assurance v Jones* (1987) the Court of Appeal confirmed that the references to the 'seller' in s 25 were to be taken to refer to the true owner. Where the 'buyer in possession' had obtained the goods from someone other than the true owner, s 25 did not apply.

16.3.3   Statutory or common law power

16.3.4   Market overt

16.3.5   Sale under a voidable title

16.3.6   Seller left in possession

16.3.7   Buyer in possession

16.4	**Retention of title**	A seller who is concerned that the buyer may become insolvent before paying for goods, may try to protect his or her position by inserting a clause into the contract whereby the property is not to pass until the seller has been paid. This is recognised by s 19, which refers to the reservation of the right of disposal. If effective, this will allow the seller to reclaim the goods themselves, rather than having to stand in line with the insolvent buyer's other creditors. Despite attempts to develop complicated 'Romalpa' clauses (named after the case of *Aluminium Industrie Vaasen BV v Romalpa Aluminium Ltd* (1976)), the device really only works if the goods are still in the buyer's possession. If they have been mixed with other goods, or sold to a third party, the original owner will be unlikely to establish any proprietary claim over the mixed goods, or the proceeds of any resale, unless a charge has been registered. The third party will of course be protected by s 25 (above, para 16.3.7).

16.5   Implied terms

Various terms are implied into all sale of goods contracts by virtue of ss 12-15 of the Act. We saw in Chapter 12, para 12.4.3, that these are labelled as 'conditions' or 'warranties'. The consequences of that labelling in terms of remedies is not discussed further here.

16.5.1   Title

Section 12 is concerned with 'title' in the sense of the 'right to sell'. There is an implied condition in every sale of goods contract that the seller has this right 'at the time when property is to pass'. The condition will be broken if the goods belong to someone else, or if they cannot be sold without infringing another's rights, eg in a trade mark: *Niblett v Confectioners' Materials* (1921). Note also the effects of a breach of this condition as regards a 'total failure of consideration'. This issue, and the decision in *Rowland v Divall* (1923) has been discussed in Chapter 14, para 14.2.1.

Section 12 also contains an implied warranty of quiet possession, and freedom from encumbrances.

16.5.2   Description

Section 13 says that where goods are sold by description there is an implied condition that they will match the description. The description may come from the seller or the buyer, and can apply to specific, as well as generic goods: *Varley v Whipp* (1900). Section 13(3) makes it clear that selection by the buyer, as in a self-service shop, does not prevent the sale being by description. Virtually all sales will, as a result, be sales by description, unless the buyer indicates a particular article which he or she wishes to buy, without describing it in any way, where the article itself has no label or packaging containing a description. There must, however, be some reliance on the description by the buyer in order for s 13 to apply. *Harlingdon & Leinster Enterprises v Christopher Hull Fine Art Ltd* (1990) concerned the sale of a painting which turned out not to be by the artist to whom it was attributed in the catalogue. It was found as a matter of fact that the buyer had not relied on this attribution, and therefore this was not a sale by description.

It is important to distinguish statements as to *quality* from statements of *description*. To describe a car as 'new' is description; to say that it has 'good acceleration' is a statement of quality, and not within s 13. Statements in advertisements can, however, be regarded as part of the description, even if the goods have subsequently been inspected. In *Beale v Taylor* (1967) a car was advertised as a 1961 model. In fact it was made of two halves welded together, only one of the halves dating from 1961. It was held that there was a breach of s 13.

Note that s 13 applies to private sales, as well as those in the course of a business.

Where a sale goods contract is made in the course of business, s 14(2) implies a term of 'merchantable quality'. This means, according to s 14(6), that the goods must be:

> 'as fit for the purpose or purposes for which goods of that kind are commonly used as it is reasonable to expect, having regard to any description applied to them, the price (if relevant) and all the other relevant circumstances.'

16.5.3   Merchantable quality

The emphasis is thus on the use to which goods of that type are normally put, looked at in the context of all the surrounding circumstances. The test will cover containers in which the goods are supplied, and may also include instructions for use. If the goods are supplied in bulk, extraneous items which are concealed within them may render the goods unmerchantable. In *Wilson v Rickett Cockerell Co* (1954) the presence of detonators in a bag of coal was held to make the coal unmerchantable.

Defects which have been brought to the buyer's attention prior to the contract, or which should have been revealed by any inspection actually undertaken by the buyer, will not make the goods unmerchantable: s 14(2).

The test does not relate to the particular use that the buyer has in mind (for which see s 14(3), below para 16.5.4) but to the general standard of the goods. Indeed, it has been held in *Aswan Engineering Establishment Co v Lupdine Ltd* (1986) that as long as the goods are fit for just *one* of the purposes for which they are commonly used they will be merchantable.

Three cases in recent years have considered the test of merchantability in the context of motor cars. In *Bernstein v Pamsons Motors (Golders Green) Ltd* (1987) the judge listed a number of factors which would be relevant. These were

(a) the safety of the car;

(b) the ease of repair;

(c) the effectiveness of repair (would the car be 'good as new');

(d) the cumulative effect of minor defects; and

(e) possibly, cosmetic factors.

In *Rogers v Parish (Scarborough) Ltd* (1987) the Court of Appeal held that a purchaser of a supposedly 'top range' car had a right to expect that it would not only be 'fit for its purpose' in the sense of being capable of being driven from place to place, but that it should have the appropriate degree of comfort, ease of handling, and outward appearance. Finally, and perhaps most controversially, in *Shine v General Guarantee Corp* (1987) the Court of Appeal, applying the equivalent merchantability test in a hire purchase contract, held that the past history of a car could affect its merchantability. The fact that it had at one time been a write-off meant that it was not of merchantable quality (taking into account the price at which it was sold), irrespective of the fact that there now appeared to be very little wrong with it.

All of this shows that the concept is a complex one, and that it may be difficult to predict exactly how it will be dealt with by a court.

16.5.4 Fitness for a particular purpose

If the buyer wants the goods for a particular purpose, and the seller is aware of this, there will be an implied term in all sales in the course of a business, that the goods will be reasonably fit for that purpose (s 14(3)), unless:

'... the circumstances show that the buyer does not rely, or that it is unreasonable for him to rely on the skill and judgment of the seller.'

The section can apply even though the goods only have one purpose, in which case the seller will be taken to have notice of it (*Priest v Last* (1903)), but it will usually be more appropriate to use s 14(2) in such circumstances. Section 14(3) may need to be relied on, however, if there is something special about the circumstances in which the goods are to be used. In *Griffiths v Peter Conway* (1939) the plaintiff contracted dermatitis from wearing a Harris Tweed coat. This was brought about by the fact that the plaintiff had an unusually sensitive skin. On the facts, this was not something which the seller knew, and so the claim under s 14(3) failed. If the seller had been aware, however, then the action under this section would have been the appropriate one, despite the fact that the coat only had one 'purpose', ie to be worn.

A claim will not succeed under s 14(3) where the problems arise from the buyer's misunderstanding of instructions supplied with the goods: *Wormell v RHM Agriculture (East) Ltd* (1987). This decision appears to accept, however, that defective instructions could lead to goods being found to be not fit for a particular purpose.

Once it is clear that the seller knew of the particular purpose, the burden is on the seller to show that there was no, or unreasonable, reliance. This is a hard test to satisfy, since the courts tend to favour the buyer, and have made it clear that partial reliance is sufficient to found an action: *Ashington Piggeries v Christopher Hill* (1972).

Where there is a sale by sample there is an implied condition, by virtue of s 15:

16.5.5   Sale by sample

'(a) that the bulk will correspond with the sample in quality;

(b) that the buyer will have a reasonable opportunity of comparing the bulk with the sample;

(c) that the goods will be free from any defect, rendering them unmerchantable, which would not be apparent on reasonable examination of the sample.'

This section does not seem to have given rise to any serious difficulties in application.

Exclusion of the implied terms under the 1979 Act is governed by s 6 of the Unfair Contract Terms Act 1977. Liability for breach of s 12 (title) may never be excluded. Similarly there can be no exclusion of liability under s 13 (description), s 14 (merchantable quality, fitness for particular purpose) or s 15 (sample) in relation to a consumer contract. Where the buyer contracts other than as a consumer, however, liability for breach of these sections may be excluded, provided the clause satisfies the 'requirement of reasonableness' under s 11 (for discussion of which see Chapter 7, para 7.8).

16.6   Exclusion of the implied terms

A person contracts 'as a consumer' when he or she does not contract 'in the course of a business'. The narrow definition of 'course of a business' adopted in *R & B Customs Brokers v UDT* (1988) should be noted (the case is discussed in Chapter 7, para 7.5.2). This significantly reduces the situations in which exclusion of the implied terms will be permissible.

16.7	**Delivery**	Payment and delivery are concurrent conditions, unless otherwise agreed: s 28. Delivery can include handing over the means of control, as well as physical transfer. In *Four Point Garage v Carter* (1985) it was held that delivery by the original seller (S) to a person who had bought from the original buyer (B) constituted delivery from S to B.
16.7.1	Place of delivery	Subject to anything contrary in the agreement, the buyer is obliged to collect the goods from the seller's premises, or wherever the goods are at the time of the contract: s 29(2). In practice this will often be varied by the contract, so that the seller arranges delivery to the buyer's premises.
16.7.2	Delivery of the wrong quantity	The rules relating to delivery of the wrong quantity are set out in s 30, and impose strict obligations on the seller. If less than the contract amount is delivered the buyer may refuse delivery, or may accept what is offered, and pay for it at the contract rate. Somewhat more surprisingly, if *more* than the contract quantity is delivered the buyer may again reject the whole consignment. The buyer may also, however, accept the whole amount, and pay for the excess at the contract rate, or accept the contract quantity, and reject the rest. If the goods delivered are mixed with goods which do not meet the contract description the buyer may reject the whole consignment, or accept the goods which do meet the contract, and reject the rest.
16.7.3	Instalments	The rules relating to instalments are set out in s 31. They follow the more general rules in this area discussed in Chapter 12, para 12.5.1, and so are not discussed again here.
16.8	**Acceptance**	It is important to identify whether or not the buyer has accepted the goods, because this will determine whether the buyer can reject for breach of condition, or simply sue for damages: s 11(4). Section 34 states that the buyer shall not be deemed to have accepted the goods until he or she has had a reasonable opportunity of examining them for the purpose of ascertaining whether they are in conformity with the contract. Section 35, on the other hand, sets out certain circumstances in which the buyer will be deemed to have accepted. This will be the case where the buyer intimates to the seller that the goods are being accepted, or (subject to s 34) where the buyer does some act which is inconsistent with the seller's ownership, such as the resale, or consumption of the goods. Furthermore, the goods will be deemed to have been accepted, and the right to reject for breach of condition lost, after the lapse of a 'reasonable time'. This was applied very strictly in *Bernstein v Pamsons Motors (Golders Green) Ltd* (1987). The buyer had

purchased a car, which he had had for three weeks, and driven for 140 miles, when, without warning, it broke down, owing to a serious defect in the engine. The judge held that there was a breach of s 14(2), in that the car was not of merchantable quality, but that the right to reject had been lost for lapse of time. This first instance decision has been regarded as very harsh, and is also not easy to reconcile with the Court of Appeal decision in *Rogers v Parish* (1987) in which the buyer of a car which had suffered from a series of defects from the point when it was purchased was allowed to reject it after it had been used for about six months, and driven for 5,500 miles. The point of distinction may be that the buyer in *Rogers v Parish* had from the start made it clear that the car would not be 'accepted' until all defects had been remedied.

The basic rules for the award of damages for breach of a sale of goods contract are the same as for any contract, as have been discussed in Chapter 13. The rule of remoteness, and the rules for recovery of consequential losses, apply in exactly the same way. The Act, however, sets out particular rules relating to non-acceptance, or non-delivery, based on the 'available market' test.

16.9   Damages

If the buyer wrongfully refuses to accept and pay for goods, the seller's damages may be based on the 'available market' test (s 50(3)). This means that if there is an available market, then damages will be based on the difference between the contract price and the market price at the time of breach. If the market price is lower, then the seller will receive this difference as damages. If the market price is higher, however, then the seller will only be able to recover nominal damages.

16.9.1   Non-acceptance

If there is no available market then the damages will be based on the lost profit on the particular transaction. But note that if the goods have been resold, there may be no lost profit. In *Lazenby Garages v Wright* (1976) the buyer refused delivery of a second-hand car. It was held that there was no 'available market' because each second-hand car is unique. But the seller had not lost anything on this transaction, because the car had been resold at a higher price, and it could not be shown that overall a sale had been lost by the buyer's rejection.

Where the seller wrongfully fails to deliver, the available market test will again be used to assess the buyer's damages (s 51(3)). Here, of course, substantial damages will only be recoverable if the market price is higher than the contract price. The courts will, in applying the available market test, generally ignore any resale that has in fact been arranged. In

16.9.2   Non-delivery

Williams Bros v Agius (1914) the contract price was 16 shillings per ton, and the buyer's had arranged a resale at 19 shillings. The market price at the time of the seller's default was 23 shillings. The buyer was allowed to recover the full seven shillings per ton in damages.

The court may decide that if the contract was for one particular load, or cargo, that the available market test should not be applied, even though similar goods are available. In *Re Hall (R&H) and WH Pim's Arbitration* (1928) the contract price for a cargo of wheat was 51 shillings per quarter. The buyer had arranged a resale at 56 shillings. When the seller defaulted, similar goods were available at 53 shillings. Nevertheless, the court held that the resale of this particular cargo had been in the contemplation of the parties at the time of the contract, so the available market test should not be applied, and the buyer was awarded five shillings per quarter damages.

16.9.3 Action for the price	An alternative action for the seller when the buyer refuses to pay for goods is the action for the price, under s 49. This will be available where either property, or the date fixed for payment in the contract, has passed. If the seller has not delivered the goods, he or she must be able and prepared to do so.

16.10 Unpaid sellers property rights

Sections 38 to 48 of the Act provide the unpaid seller with certain rights over the goods. These are available even where the property in the goods has passed to the buyer. There are three rights, namely lien, stoppage in transit, and resale.

16.10.1 Lien

Lien arises, under s 41, when the seller remains in possession of the goods. He or she is entitled to retain them until paid where:

(a) no credit has been given to the buyer; or

(b) the credit term has expired; or

(c) the buyer has become in insolvent.

16.10.2 Stoppage in transit

This right enables the seller to recover the goods from a carrier, and retain them pending payment of the price (s 44). It arises only where the buyer has become insolvent. It is exercised by taking possession of the goods, or by giving notice to the carrier (s 46).

The right seems to be of little practical importance in modern law. Increasingly sophisticated banking arrangements have probably rendered it largely unnecessary in relation to export sales, and as regards domestic sales the period of transit will generally be too short to enable the right to be exercised.

As we have seen (s 24, para 16.3.6) the seller who remains in possession can resell the goods and pass a good title to the second purchaser, whether or not property has passed. The seller will also pass a good title if he or she resells after exercising the rights of lien, or stoppage in transit (s 48(2)). But the seller will in all these cases almost certainly still be in breach of the contract with the original buyer, unless the following provisions of s 48 apply.

Where the goods are perishable, or the unpaid seller gives notice of an intention to resell and the buyer does not within a reasonable time pay or tender the price, the seller is entitled to resell the goods, and claim damages from the original buyer (s 48(3)).

Furthermore, if the seller has expressly reserved the right of resale in the event of the buyer's default, a resale by the unpaid seller will rescind the original contract. The seller may then also sue the original buyer for damages.

16.10.3   Resale

Sale of Goods

The definition of sale of goods is contained in s 2(1). It excludes exchanges, hp contracts, and contracts for work and materials. Note the distinction between 'sale' and 'agreement to sell': s 2(5).

Definition

Property passes according to the intentions of the parties (s 17), provided the goods are ascertained (s 16) (but note *Dennant v Skinner* (1948)). If no intention is expressed, the rules in s 18 apply. Re specific goods in a deliverable state, property passes on contract (rule 1). Re specific goods, which are not deliverable, or which need weighing etc to determine the price, property passes when the seller has done what is necessary, and has told the buyer (rules 2 and 3). Re sales on approval or sale or return, property passes the buyer's accepting by words or conduct, or by the lapse of time (rule 4). Re unascertained or future goods, property passes when goods are unconditionally appropriated to the contract (rule 5 - note also *Healey v Howlett* (1917)). Risk will normally pass with property (s 20).

Passing of property (ss 16-18)

The basic rule of transfer of title is *nemo dat* (s 21(1)). Exceptions exist in relation to indications from the conduct of the owner (s 21(1)); sale by a factor (s 21(2)(a)); sale under a statutory or common law power (s 21(2)(b)); market overt (s 22); sale under a voidable title (s 23); seller left in possession (s 24); buyer in possession (s 25).

Transfer of title

The possibility of the seller retaining a right of disposal pending payment is acknowledged by s 19, but *Romalpa* clauses have had limited effect in protecting the seller once the buyer no longer possesses the goods in their original state.

Retention of title

The Act implies various terms into all sale of goods contracts:

Implied terms

- Title (s 12)

  Implied condition of 'right to sell' at the time when property is to pass. There is also an implied warranty of quiet possession and freedom from encumbrances.

- Description (s 13)

  Most sales will be 'by description'. There is an implied condition of compliance with the description. Note the distinction between description and quality, and that there must be reliance on the description by the buyer: *Harlingdon & Leinster Enterprises v Christopher Hull Fine Art Ltd* (1990).

- Merchantable quality (s 14(2))

  Where the sale is made in the course of a business there is an implied condition of merchantable quality (s 14(6)). It covers everything supplied (*Wilson v Rickett Cockerell Co* (1954)), but not defects revealed, or which should have been discovered, by the buyer's inspection (s 14(2)). The goods must be fit for at least one of their common uses: *Aswan Engineering Establishment Co v Lupdine Ltd* (1986). Merchantability can relate not only to functionality, but also appearance (*Rogers v Parish (Scarborough) Ltd* (1987)), and past history (*Shine v General Guarantee Corp* (1987)).

- Fitness for a particular purpose (s 14(3))

  This implied condition can apply where the goods have only one purpose (*Priest v Last* (1903)). Otherwise, the particular purpose must be made known to the seller (*Griffiths v Peter Conway* (1939)), and there must have been reasonable reliance on the seller's skill and judgment.

- Sale by sample (s 15)

  There is a an implied condition of correspondence with the sample in quality.

Exclusion of implied terms

The exclusion of implied terms is governed by UCTA 1977, s 6. There can be no exclusion of s 12. Sections 13, 14, and 15 cannot be excluded from a consumer contract. In business contracts these can be excluded, provided the term meets the requirement of reasonableness.

Delivery

Delivery and payment are concurrent conditions: s 28. There are strict rules about delivery of the wrong quantity: s 30. Instalment deliveries are dealt with by s 31.

Acceptance

Acceptance of the goods will deprive the buyer of the right to reject. The buyer should have a chance to examine the goods (s 34). The buyer will be deemed to have accepted where this is intimated to the seller, or the buyer does some act inconsistent with the seller's ownership (s 35). Acceptance will also arise from lapse of time - a strict test was applied in *Bernstein v Pamsons Motors (Golders Green) Ltd* (1987).

Damages

The normal contractual rules apply to damages, but in relation to non-delivery, and non-acceptance, the starting point is the 'available market' test (ss 50 and 51). The seller may also bring an action for the price: s 49.

Unpaid seller's property rights

The unpaid seller's property rights are the right of lien (s 41); stoppage in transit (s 44); and resale (s 48).

Index

CARDIFF UWCC LIBRARY